The Collected Works of Paddy Chayefsky
THE SCREENPLAYS

VOLUME I

The Collected Works of Paddy Chayefsky
THE SCREENPLAYS

VOLUME I

Marty
The Goddess
The Americanization of Emily

APPLAUSE
BOOKS
NEW YORK • LONDON

An Applause Original
The Screenplays Volume I

Library of Congress Cataloging-in-Publication Data

Chayefsky, Paddy, 1923-1981.
    The screenplays / Paddy Chayefsky.
        p.   cm. -- (The collected works of Paddy Chayefsky ; 3-4)
      Contents: v. 1. Marty, The Goddess, The Americanization of Emily -- v. 2. The Hospital, Network, and Altered states.
     ISBN 1-55783-193-9 (v. 1) : $16.95. -- ISBN 1-55783-194-7 (v. 2) : $16.95
     1. Motion picture plays. I. Title. II. Series: Chayefsky, Paddy, 1923-1981. Works. 1994 ; 3-4.
    PS3505.H632A19   1994 vol. 3-4
    812'.54--dc20
                                                 94-24706
                                                 CIP

British Library Cataloging-in-Publication Data

A catalogue record for this book is available from the British Library.

Applause Books
211 West 71st Street
New York, NY 10023
Phone (212) 496-7511
Fax: (212) 721-2856

406 Vale Road
Tonbridge Kent TN9 1XR
Phone 073 235-7755
Fax 073 207-7219

First Applause Printing 1995

Printed in Canada

This collection is dedicated to the memory of its author, Paddy Chayefsky, and to the enormous gift of his talent and insight which fills these pages.

—Susan Chayefsky

An enormous debt of gratitude is owed to Karen Jaehne, who provided invaluable help on this publication. With care and uncommon dedication, she edited the screenplays and contributed greatly to compiling this work. She has our great thanks.

The following people were of special assistance in the preparation of these volumes, and their help is gratefully acknowledged: Susan Brown, Dan Chayefsky, David Cleaver, Barbara Cramer, Herb Gardner, Howard Gottfried, Arthur Hiller, Andrew Pontious, Arthur Schlesinger, Jr., J. Stephen Sheppard, Paul Sugarman, Ken Swezey, and all the staff at Applause.

Contents

The Collected Works of Paddy Chayefsky

The Stage Plays

•

The Television Plays

•

The Screenplays Volume I
Marty, The Goddess, The Americanization of Emily

•

The Screenplays Volume II
The Hospital, Network, Altered States

MARTY

1955

Story and Screenplay
by PADDY CHAYEFSKY
based on his television play

Produced by HAROLD HECHT

Directed by DELBERT MANN

CAST CREDITS

MARTY PILLETTI	Ernest Borgnine
CLARA SNYDER	Betsy Blair
MRS. PILLETTI	Esther Minciotti
CATHERINE	Augusta Ciolli
ANGIE	Joe Mantell
VIRGINIA	Karen Steele
THOMAS	Jerry Paris
RALPH	Frank Sutton
THE KID	Walter Kelley
JOE	Robin Morse

FADE IN:

NEW YORK CITY, 187TH STREET. A SUMMER DAY.

Just east of Webster Avenue in the North Bronx, 187th Street is a predominantly Italian community and the commercial avenue of the neighborhood. Fruit and vegetable stands, pizzerias, butcher shops, bakeries, cleaners and dyers and bars flourish. It is Saturday morning around eleven o'clock—a market day.

WOMEN, dark, gesticulative, with bulging cloth shopping bags, baby carriages. MERCHANTS at their improvised street stands, hawking their wares, disputing with their CUSTOMERS, roaring salutations to PASSERSBY.

In the midst of all this, CAMERA HOMES IN on a typical neighborhood...

BUTCHER SHOP.

Delicatessens hang on the walls, wreathed with garlands of garlic. PATSY, the boss, a swarthy man of sixty, is flopping a chunk of beef onto the scale for the benefit of a forty-year-old MATRON. There are three or four other WOMEN in the shop, all talking to one another. A four-year-old BOY lazily chases a cat.

The white refrigerator room door opens, and a second butcher, MARTY PILLETTI, comes out carrying a large leg of lamb. Marty is a mild-mannered, short, stout, balding man of thirty-four. His charm lies in an almost indestructible good humor. He drops the leg of lamb onto the chopping block, reaches up for the cleaver hanging with the other utensils over the block and makes quick incisive cuts into the leg of lamb. He sets the cleaver aside, picks up the saw to finish the cuts as he chats with his customer, MRS. FUSARI.

MRS. FUSARI Your kid brother got married last Sunday, eh, Marty?

MARTY *(sawing away)* That's right, Missus Fusari. It was a very nice affair.

MRS. FUSARI That's the big tall one, the fellow with the moustache.

MARTY *(still sawing)* No, that's my other brother, Freddie. My other brother Freddie, he's been married four years already. He lives down on Webb Avenue. The one who got married Sunday, that was my little brother, Nickie.

MRS. FUSARI I thought he was a big tall fat fellow. Didn't I meet him here one time? Big tall, fat fellow, he tried to sell me life insurance?

Marty sets the five chops on the scale, watches its weight register.

MARTY No, that's my sister Margaret's husband, Frank. My sister Margaret, she's married to the insurance salesman, and my sister Rose, she married a contractor. They moved to Detroit last year. And my other sister Frances, she got married about two and a half years ago in Saint John's Church on Kingsbridge Avenue. Oh, that was a big affair. Well, let's see now, that'll be about a dollar-seventy-nine. How's that with you?

MRS. FUSARI Well...

Mrs. Fusari produces an old leather change purse from her pocketbook and painfully extracts one single dollar bill and seventy-nine cents to the penny and lays the money piece by piece on the counter. From the rear of the shop a woman's VOICE rings out.

WOMAN'S VOICE *(off-screen)* Hey, Marty, I'm inna hurry.

MARTY You're next right now, Missus Canduso.

MRS. FUSARI When you gonna get married, Marty? You should be ashamed of yourself. All your brothers and sisters, they all younger than you, they married and they got children. I just saw your mother inna fruit shop, and she says to me, "Hey, you know a nice girl for my boy Marty?" Watsa matter with you? That's no way. Now you get married.

MARTY *(amiably)* Missus Fusari, Missus Canduso over there, she's inna big hurry, and...

Mrs. Fusari takes her parcel of meat, but apparently she feels she still hasn't quite made her point.

MRS. FUSARI My son Frank, he was married when he was nineteen years old. Watsa matter with you?

MARTY That's swell, Missus Fusari.

MRS. FUSARI You should be ashamed of yourself.

She takes her package of meat. Marty gathers up the money on the counter, turns to the cash register behind him to ring up the sale. Mrs. Canduso sidles up to the counter.

MRS. CANDUSO Marty, I want a nice, big fat pullet, about four pounds. I hear your kid brother got married last Sunday.

MARTY Yeah, it was a very nice affair.

MRS. CANDUSO Marty, you oughta be ashamed. All your kid brothers and sisters married and have children. When you gonna get married?

NEIGHBORHOOD BAR. LATE AFTERNOON.

A TV set on the wall. Mel Allen, smoking a White Owl cigar, is recapping the baseball game that has just finished as Marty comes in.

MARTY *(to two YOUNG MEN leaving)* What happened?

YOUNG MAN The Yanks took two.

MARTY Any homers?

The Young Men exit without answering. Marty moves further into the bar, which is crowded with locals, smoky, noisy. ACROSS GROUP at bar with

*Marty in the background approaching, we see a group consisting of RALPH,
who wears a suit and tie, the only man in the room who isn't in shirtsleeves
or a Basque shirt; JOE, thirty-two, hunched over a girlie magazine; a KID,
twenty-two, studying the magazine over Joe's shoulder.*

MARTY   *(to the Kid)* Angie come in yet?

*The Kid indicates a booth where a small wasp of a man, mid-thirties, is sit-
ting, bent over the sports pages of the* Daily News.

RALPH   So these two girls come over to the bar...

MARTY   Hey, Ang'...

RALPH   ...and they sit down right next to me...

MARTY   You want a beer, Ang'?

RALPH   I look over at this one nexta me, not bad, about thirty-five—
Hiya, Marty....

MARTY   Hiya, Ralph...

RALPH   ...I been talking about two nurses Leo and me picked up in a bar
on Seventy-First Street.

MARTY   *(to Bartender)* Hey, Lou, gimme two bottles-a beer...

RALPH   So, Marty, lemme tell you about these nurses, Marty...

MARTY   *(to Joe studying his magazine)* Waddaya read there, Joe?

AD LIB VOICE   *(off-screen)* Hey, Lou, turn the television off!

RALPH   Turns out these two girls are nurses in some hospital on
a Hundred and Fourth Street...

JOE   They shouldn't sell magazines like this on a public newsstand...

MARTY That's the truth.

JOE *(turning a page)* Can you imagine the effect this has on adolescents?

RALPH So, Marty, let me tell you about these nurses...

MARTY *(reaching for two bottles of beer proffered by the Bartender)* What nurses?

RALPH The nurses Leo and me picked up last night. We got a date with them tonight.

MARTY *(moving off to Angie's booth)* You still owe me ten bucks from last week, if that's what you're working up to.

Joe turns another page in the girlie magazine.

JOE Now that's something, eh?

RALPH I used to go out with a girl like that...

THE KID You should live so long.

THE BOOTH.

Marty joins his friend Angie and pushes a bottle of beer at him, pulling one of the pages loose from the paper Angie is reading. For a moment, the two men sit quietly, each poring over his separate piece of newspaper.

ANGIE *(without looking up)* So waddaya feel like doing tonight?

MARTY I don't know, Ang'. Wadda you feel like doing?

ANGIE Well, we oughta do something. It's Saturday night. I don't wanna go bowling like last Saturday. How about calling up that big girl we picked up inna movies about a month ago in the RKO Chester?

MARTY *(not very interested)* Which one was that?

ANGIE That big girl that was sitting in front of us with the skinny friend.

MARTY Oh, yeah.

ANGIE We took them home alla way out in Brooklyn. Her name was Mary Feeney. What do you say? You think I oughta give her a ring? I'll take the skinny one.

MARTY She probably got a date by now, Angie.

ANGIE Well, let's call her up. What can we lose?

MARTY I didn't like her, Angie. I don't feel like calling her up.

ANGIE Well, what do you feel like doing tonight?

MARTY I don't know. What do you feel like doing?

ANGIE Well, we're back to that, huh? I say to you, "What do you feel like doing tonight?" And you say to me, "I don't know, what do you feel like doing?" And then we wind up sitting around your house with a coupla cansa beer, watching Sid Caesar on television. Well, I tell you what I feel like doing. I feel like calling up this Mary Feeney. She likes you.

MARTY What makes you say that?

ANGIE I could see she likes you.

MARTY Yeah, sure.

ANGIE *(half-rising in his seat)* I'll call her up.

MARTY You call her up for yourself, Angie. I don't feel like calling her up.

Angie sits down again. They both return to their papers for a moment. Then Angie looks up again.

ANGIE How about going downa Seventy-Second Street, see what we can find? Ralph says you have to beat them off with clubs.

Marty makes a wry face at the suggestion.

ANGIE Boy, you're getting to be a real drag, you know that?

MARTY Angie, I'm thirty-four years old. I been looking for a girl every Saturday night of my life. I'm tired of looking. Everybody's always telling me to get married. Get married. Get married. Don't you think I wanna get married? I wanna get married. They drive me crazy. Now, I don't wanna wreck your Saturday night for you, Angie. You wanna go somewhere, you go ahead. I don't wanna go.

ANGIE My old lady, every word outta her mouth, when you gonna get married?

MARTY My mother, boy, she drives me crazy.

Angie leans back in his seat, scowls at the paper napkin container on the booth table. Marty returns to the sports page. For a moment, a silence hangs between them.

ANGIE So what do you feel like doing tonight?

MARTY *(without looking up)* I don't know. What do you feel like doing?

BARTENDER *(from phone booth in background)* Marty, your mother wants you onna phone.

MARTY *(rising in response; to Angie)* Come on over about half past seven, we'll think of something. *(settles into the phone booth, picks up the receiver)* Hello, Ma, what's the matter?

PILLETTI HOME, LIVING ROOM.

It's a typical lower-middle-class Italian home, and MRS. PILLETTI is on the phone, a round, dark woman. Beyond her, in the dining room, we can see a young couple—THOMAS, Marty's cousin, and his wife VIRGINIA, seated at the dining room table.

MRS. PILLETTI *(voice lowered)* Hello, Marty, when you coming home? Where you now? Because your cousin Thomas and his wife Virginia, they're here. They had another fight with your Aunt Catherine...I don't know...

THE BAR.

MARTY *(in the phone booth)* I'm coming home right now, Ma. I'll be home in about two minutes. Tell Thomas stick around, I wanna see him about something.

PILLETTI HOME, LIVING ROOM.

Mrs. Pilletti is on the phone.

MRS. PILLETTI Okay, you come on home, okay.

She hangs up, braces herself, turns and starts back to Thomas and Virginia in the dining room.

MRS. PILLETTI He coming home right now.

VIRGINIA So what happened, Aunt Theresa, about the milk bottle was my mother-in-law, she comes inna kitchen, Aunt Theresa, and she begins poking her head over my shoulder here and poking her head over my shoulder there, so then she begins telling me how I waste money and how I can't cook, and how I'm raising my baby all wrong, so she got me so nervous, I spilled some milk I was making for the baby...

MRS. PILLETTI She was here, you know, Wednesday, and I said, "Catherine, my sister..."

VIRGINIA So she say, "You're spilling the milk." So she kept talking about these coupla drops of milk I spilled, so she got me so mad, so I said, "Mama, you wanna see me really spill some milk?" So I took the bottle, and I threw it against the door. I didn't throw it at her. That's just something she made up. She goes around telling everybody I threw the bottla milk at her. I didn't throw it anywheres near her. Well, I was sorry right away, you know, but she ran outta the house.

MRS. PILLETTI Well, I don't know what you want me to do, Virginia. If you want me, I'll go talk to her tonight.

Thomas and Virginia suddenly frown and look down at their hands as if of one mind.

THOMAS Well, I'll tell you, Aunt Theresa...

VIRGINIA Lemme tell it, Tommy.

THOMAS Okay.

VIRGINIA We want you to do a very big favor for us, Aunt Theresa.

MRS. PILLETTI Sure.

VIRGINIA Aunt Theresa, you got this big house here. I mean, you got this big house just for you and Marty. And I thought maybe Tommy's mother could come here and live with you and Marty.

MRS. PILLETTI Well...

VIRGINIA Because I called up Tommy's brother Joe, and I said, "Joe, she's driving me crazy. Why don't you take her for a couple of years?" And he said, "Oh no!" I know I sound like a terrible woman...

MRS. PILLETTI No, Virginia, I know how you feel.

VIRGINIA   (*on the verge of tears*)   I just can't stand it any more!   Every
minute of the day!   Do this!   Do that!   I don't have ten minutes privacy with my husband!   We can't even have a fight!   We don't have no
privacy!   Everybody's miserable in our house!

THOMAS   All right, Ginnie, don't get so excited.

MRS. PILLETTI   She's right.   She's right.   Young husband and wife, they
should have their own home.   And my sister Catherine, she's my sister, but I gotta admit, she's an old goat.   And plenty-a times in my life,
I feel like throwing the milk bottle at her myself.   And I tell you now,
as far as I'm concerned, if Catherine wantsa come live here with me
and Marty, it's all right with me.

Virginia promptly bursts into tears.

THOMAS   (*not far from tears himself, lowers his face*)   That's very nice-a you,
Aunt Theresa.

MRS. PILLETTI   We gotta ask Marty, of course.

THOMAS   Sure.

MRS. PILLETTI   (*rises*)   You just sit here, I gotta turn the fire on under the
cooking.   (*exits into the kitchen*)

VIRGINIA   (*having mastered her tears*)   That's very nice-a you, Aunt
Theresa.

THOMAS   (*calling to his aunt in the kitchen*)   How's Marty been lately, Aunt
Theresa?

MRS. PILLETTI   (*off-screen*)   Oh, he's fine.   You know a nice girl he can
marry?

She comes back into the dining room, wiping her hands on a kitchen towel.

THOMAS   Oh, he'll get married, don't worry, Aunt Theresa.

MRS. PILLETTI (*sitting down again*) Well, I don't know. He sits arounna house alla time. You know a place he can go where he can find a bride?

THOMAS Well, there's the Stardust Ballroom. That's a kind of a big dance hall. Every Saturday night, it's just loaded with girls. It's a nice place to go. You pay seventy-seven cents. It used to be seventy-seven cents. It must be about a buck and half now. And you go in and you ask some girl to dance. That's how I met Virginia. Nice, respectable place to meet girls. You tell Marty, Aunt Theresa, you tell him, "Go to the Stardust Ballroom. It's loaded with tomatoes."

MRS. PILLETTI (*committing the line to memory*) The Stardust Ballroom. It's loaded with tomatoes.

THOMAS Right.

VIRGINIA This is very nice-a you, Aunt Theresa, what you're doing for us, and don't think we don't appreciate...

The SOUND of the DOOR BEING UNLATCHED in the kitchen can be heard. Mrs. Pilletti promptly rises.

MRS. PILLETTI He's here.

She hurries into...

THE KITCHEN.

Marty comes into the kitchen from the rear porch.

MARTY Hello, Ma.

MRS. PILLETTI (*whispers*) Marty, Thomas and Virginia are here. They had another fight with your Aunt Catherine. So they ask me, would it be all right if Catherine come to live with us. So I said, all right with me, but we have to ask you. Marty, she's a lonely old lady. Nobody wants her. Everybody's throwing her outta their house...

MARTY Sure, Ma, it's okay with me.

MRS. PILLETTI You gotta good heart.

She turns and leads the way back into the dining room. Marty follows.

DINING ROOM.

Thomas has risen. Mrs. Pilletti and Marty come in.

MRS. PILLETTI He says okay, it's all right Catherine comes here.

THOMAS Oh, Marty, thanks a lot. That really takes a load offa my mind.

MARTY Oh, we got plenny-a room here.

MRS. PILLETTI Sure! Sure! It's gonna be nice! It's gonna be nice! I'll come over tonight to your house, and I talk with Catherine, and you see, everything is gonna work out all right.

THOMAS I just wanna thank you people again, because the situation was just becoming impossible.

MRS. PILLETTI Siddown, Thomas, siddown.

She exits into the kitchen. Virginia follows her to the kitchen door, where the two women ad-lib the following lines over the ensuing scene between Marty and Thomas.

VIRGINIA I'm sorry we gotta rush like this....

MRS. PILLETTI That's all right, that's all right...

VIRGINIA On accounta...

MRS. PILLETTI I'm gonna see you tonight...

Over this, Thomas talks to Marty.

THOMAS Marty, I don't know how to tell you how much I appreciate what you and your mother are doing, because the kinda thing was happening in our house was Virginia was in the kitchen making some milk for the baby. So my mother comes in...

VIRGINIA Tommy, I promised the babysitter six o'clock.

MARTY Tommy, before you go, I wonder if you gimme a little advice.

THOMAS Sure, what?

MARTY You're the accountant inna family, and I figure you might know about these things. My boss wantsa sell his shop to me. His kids are all married, you know, and he and his wife live alone, and they wanna move out to California where his daughter lives, so he wantsa sell his shop. He wants five thousand dollars down, although I think I can knock him downa four...

VIRGINIA (off-screen, from deep in the kitchen) Tommy!

THOMAS (rises) I'll see you at mass tomorrow. We'll sit down and we'll discuss the whole thing.

MARTY All right, I'll see you, Thomas, because he wants an answer by Monday.

THOMAS Sure. Thanks a lot about my mother. We'll work out some arrangement, because naturally I want to pay...

MARTY Don't worry about it.

THOMAS No, listen, that's my mother, I'm gonna pay for her...

VIRGINIA (off-screen) Goodby, Marty!

MARTY Goodby, Virginia! See you soon!

Thomas has moved off to join his wife in the kitchen where we can hear them exchanging final protestations and goodbys with Mrs. Pilletti. Marty sits at the table, hands folded in front of him, stolid, pensive.

THE KITCHEN. DUSK.

Mrs. Pilletti bends over her steaming kettles. Through the window we see evening is gathering.

MARTY'S BEDROOM.

It's a small room with bed, chest of drawers, religious pictures, etc. Marty sits squatly on the edge of the bed, absorbed in thought. He stands, moves out into...

THE GROUND FLOOR CORRIDOR.

...and down that into...

THE DINING ROOM.

...now lit by the overhead neo-Tiffany lampshade and the beaded old-fashioned lamps. He crosses to the kitchen door, looks in on his mother, cooking away, turns, crosses back to...

THE LIVING ROOM.

He closes the sliding doors that separate the living and dining rooms. He extracts a small black address book from his hip pocket, flips through it, finds the page he wants, studies it intently.

He sits on the chair by the phone, dials.

MARTY   *(with a vague pretense at good diction)*   Hello, is this Mary Feeney?...Could I speak to Miss Mary Feeney?...Just tell her an old friend...*(He waits again. With his free hand he wipes the gathering sweat on his brow.)*...Oh, hello there, is this Mary Feeney? Hello there, this is Marty Pilletti. I wonder if you recall me...Well, I'm kind of a stocky guy. The last time we met was in a movie, the RKO Chester. You was with another girl, and I was with a friend of mine named Angie. This was about a month ago...(*The girl apparently doesn't remember him. A sort of panic begins to seize Marty. His voice rises a little.*) The RKO Chester in Westchester Square. You was sitting in front of us, and we was annoying you, and you got mad, and...I'm the fellow who works in a butcher shop...Come on, you know who I am!...That's right, we went to Howard Johnson's and we had hamburgers. You hadda milkshake....Yeah, that's right. I'm the stocky one, the heavy-set feller...Well, I'm glad you recall me, because I hadda swell time that night, and I was just wondering how everything was with you. How's everything?...That's swell....Yeah, well, I'll tell you why I called...I was figuring on taking in a movie tonight, and I was wondering if you and your friend would care to see a movie tonight with me and my friend...(*His eyes are closed now.*) Yeah, tonight. I know it's pretty late to call for a date, but I didn't know myself, till...Yeah, I know, well how about...Yeah, I know, well maybe next Saturday night. You free next Saturday night?...Well, how about the Saturday after that?...Yeah, I know....Yeah...Yeah...Oh, I understand, I mean...

He hangs up, sits for a moment, then rises, opens the sliding doors, enters...

THE DINING ROOM.

He sits at the heavy, wooden table with its white-on-white table cloth.

THE KITCHEN.

Mrs. Pilletti ladles portions of food from the steaming kettles onto a plate that she brings into...

THE DINING ROOM.

...and sets it down before her son. Without a word, he picks up his fork and spoon and plunges into the mountain of spaghetti, adds cheese, eats away. Mrs. Pilletti takes her seat, folds her hands on the table, and sits watching Marty eat.

MRS. PILLETTI So what are you gonna do tonight, Marty?

MARTY I don't know, Ma. I'm all knocked out. I may just hang arounna house.

Mrs. Pilletti nods a couple of times. A moment of silence.

MRS. PILLETTI Why don't you go to the Stardust Ballroom?

This gives Marty pause. He looks up.

MARTY What?

MRS. PILLETTI I say, why don't you go to the Stardust Ballroom? It's loaded with tomatoes.

Marty regards his mother for a moment.

MARTY It's loaded with what?

MRS. PILLETTI Tomatoes.

MARTY Ha! Who told you about the Stardust Ballroom?

MRS. PILLETTI Thomas. He told me it was a very nice place.

MARTY Oh, Thomas. Ma, it's just a big dance hall, and that's all it is. I been there a hundred times. Loaded with tomatoes. Boy, you're funny, Ma.

MRS. PILLETTI Marty, I don't want you hang arounna house tonight. I want you to go take a shave and go out and dance.

MARTY Ma, when are you gonna give up? You gotta bachelor on your hands. I ain't never gonna get married.

MRS. PILLETTI You gonna get married.

MARTY Sooner or later, there comes a point in a man's life when he gotta face some facts, and one fact I gotta face is that whatever it is that women like, I ain't got it. I chased enough girls in my life. I went to enough dances. I got hurt enough. I don't wanna get hurt no more. I just called a girl just now, and I got a real brush-off, boy. I figured I was past the point of being hurt, but that hurt. Some stupid woman who I didn't even wanna call up. She gave me the brush. I don't wanna go to the Stardust Ballroom because all that ever happened to me there was girls made me feel like I was a bug. I got feelings, you know. I had enough pain. No, thank you.

MRS. PILLETTI Marty...

MARTY Ma, I'm gonna stay home and watch Jackie Gleason.

MRS. PILLETTI You gonna die without a son.

MARTY So I'll die without a son.

MRS. PILLETTI Put on your blue suit...

MARTY Blue suit, gray suit, I'm still a fat man. A fat ugly man.

MRS. PILLETTI You not ugly.

MARTY *(his voice rising)* I'm ugly...I'm ugly! I'm UGLY!

MRS. PILLETTI Marty...

MARTY Ma! Leave me alone!

He stands abruptly, his face pained and drawn. He makes half-formed gestures to his mother, but he can't find words at the moment. He turns and marches a few paces away, turns to his mother again.

MARTY Ma, waddaya want from me?! Waddaya want from me?! I'm miserable enough as it is! Leave me alone! I'll go to the Stardust Ballroom! I'll put onna blue suit and I'll go! And you know what I'm gonna get for my trouble? Heartache! A big night of heartache!

Sullenly, he marches back to his seat, sits down, picks up his fork, plunges it into the spaghetti, stuffs a mouthful into his mouth, and chews vigorously for a moment. It is impossible for him to remain angry long. After a while, he is shaking his head.

MARTY   Loaded with tomatoes...boy, that's rich.

He plunges his fork in again, starts to eat. Mrs. Pilletti watches Marty anxiously as we...

                                                                    FADE OUT.

FADE IN:

NEW YORK CITY, WEST FARMS SQUARE. NIGHT.

West Farms Square is a big street in the Bronx, filled with stores, bowling alleys and bars. Cars push along between the pillars of the elevated subway structure. The NOISE of the subway trains ROARS by overhead every few moments.

CAMERA FINDS and ESTABLISHES the Stardust Ballroom. It occupies the second floor of a large, dirty gray three-story building. It is a hot June night, and the windows are open for ventilation purposes. MUSIC manufactured by Dave Greenglass and His Band blends with the NOISES of the street.

STARDUST BALLROOM. ENTRANCE VESTIBULE/STAIRS.

MUSIC plays in the background. CAMERA views CLARA, a plain girl in her late twenties; her younger sister, MILLIE, prettier; Millie's fiancé ANDY, 30; and a second young man DR. KEEGAN, also 30, who is a resident at Fordham Hospital. They are all huddled over a cigarette machine near the street door.

ANDY   *(in a low voice)* I told you she wasn't especially attractive, but that she had a good deal of charm, and she's really a real nice girl...

DR. KEEGAN *(extracting cigarettes from the machine)* She's all right, Andy. It's just that I get one Saturday night off every three weeks, and I was expecting something better, that's all.

ANDY I told you she wasn't attractive...

DR. KEEGAN You told me that she was a little tall, but that she wasn't bad-looking at all.

ANDY Millie's been after me to fix her up with a date, so I...

DR. KEEGAN All right, I'm having a fair time. It's just that I get one Saturday night off in three weeks, and I wanted to wind up with something tonight.

They join the two girls waiting for them and start up the broad stairway to the second floor. They are halfway up, when two GIRLS come in at the top of the stairs and start down. Dr. Keegan, who is holding Clara's arm, looks up, nods.

STARDUST BALLROOM, ANTEROOM.

This is a small, carpeted lobby with TICKET TAKER in booth, a cloak room and rest rooms. Painted posters on the walls announce coming events and caution against smoking. There are also large blow-ups of musicians who had played this ballroom at one time and went on to bigger things. About six or seven PEOPLE congregate in the lobby, engaged in various indifferent activities.

CAMERA ANGLES include the swinging doors, as Clara, Andy, Millie and Dr. Keegan come in. As they enter, the doors to the ballroom proper are pushed out, and a GIRL in a black dress, quite pretty, comes in. She starts across the anteroom toward the cloak room, when Dr. Keegan calls out suddenly to her.

DR. KEEGAN Hey!

The girl turns. Recognition floods her face.

GIRL   Herbie! Wadda you doing here?!

DR. KEEGAN   I came up to dance, wadda you think?   You here with
somebody?

GIRL   I'm just here with another girl.

DR. KEEGAN   Where you going now?

GIRL   I'm just gonna get my cigarettes. I left them in my coat.

DR. KEEGAN   I'll see you around.

GIRL   I'll see you.

She turns and continues on to the cloak room. Dr. Keegan turns to Clara.

DR. KEEGAN   That's a girl I used to know.

BALLROOM, LOUNGE.

*A fairly long room, lined on one side by a bar and on the other by cheap
leatherette booths. It is brightly lit and crowded. There is a constant movement in and out of the lounge. At the far end of the lounge, there are two
large iron fire doors open to allow the heat to flow out. Dance MUSIC from
dance floor.*

*Clara, Dr. Keegan, Millie and Andy come into the lounge and form a little
group in the midst of moving PASSERSBY around them. A kind of strange
excitement has begun to enter Dr. Keegan. He stands with the others, but
his attention is devoted to ogling the passing GIRLS, occasionally looking
back to the doors leading to the anteroom.*

ANDY   Boy, it's packed in here.

MILLIE   *(to Clara)* Some of these kids are awful young. Aren't you afraid
you'll bump into one of your students?

CLARA *(nervously looking at Dr. Keegan)* I wouldn't think so. I teach out in Brooklyn.

ANDY You been up here before, Clara?

CLARA Yeah, twice.

MILLIE Shall we try to get a table and get something to drink or shall we just go in and start dancing?

ANDY Hey, Herbie...

Dr. Keegan doesn't seem to hear.

ANDY *(continues)* Hey, Herbie...

DR. KEEGAN What?

ANDY You wanna have a drink before we start dancing?

DR. KEEGAN Listen. You people go grab a table. I'll be back inna minute. I'll be right back.

He turns and moves quickly through the crowded lounge, back to the swinging doors leading into the anteroom. CAMERA STAYS with Clara, Millie and Andy staring after him.

ANDY So what do you say, Clara? Wanna see if we can get a table?

CLARA All right.

They turn and move toward the booths.

BALLROOM.

The dance floor is fairly dark. A romantic effect is achieved by papier-mâché over the chandeliers. Around the walls are the stag lines—the MEN and waiting GIRLS. They stand singly or in small uneasy groups. There is constant flux and movement.

CAMERA DOLLIES slowly past the stag line, moving past faces, short, fat, tall, thin stags. Some pretend indifference. Some exhibit patent hunger.

CAMERA HOLDS ANGLING to include Marty, Angie near the end of the stag line. They are freshly shaved and groomed.

MARTY AND ANGIE.

They are leaning against the wall smoking, watching their more fortunate brethren on the floor in the background.

ANGIE Not a bad crowd tonight, you know?

MARTY There was one nice-looking one there inna black dress and beads, but she's dancing now.

ANGIE *(looking off-screen)* There's a nice-looking little short one for you right now.

MARTY *(following his gaze)* Where?

ANGIE Down there. That little one there.

REVERSE ANGLE PAST Marty and Angie across the dance floor toward the wall opposite, where three GIRLS are standing. Two are leaning against the wall. The third is facing them with her back to the dance floor. This last girl is the one Angie has in mind. She is a cute little kid about twenty and wears a bright smile.

MARTY AND ANGIE.

They stare off toward the three girls across the room.

MARTY Yeah, she looks all right from here.

ANGIE   Well, waddaya say, you wanna ask them? I'll take the one inna green dress.

MARTY   I think this number is a little fast. Wait a minute.

He tries a few tentative steps, testing for tempo.

MARTY   It's all right, I think. They still there?

The two cavaliers turn their heads and look off-screen in the direction of the three girls. Apparently, the girls are still there. Marty and Angie relinquish their lounging positions against the wall and slouch along past the line of stags with a show of determined unconcern. They edge through the crush of people on the non-dancing margin of the dance floor and slowly push their way toward the...

THREE GIRLS.

Marty and Angie come in and start to approach the three girls. The girls, aware of the boys' presence, stiffen and their chatter comes to a halt. Angie advances to one of the girls.

ANGIE   Waddaya say, you wanna dance?

The girl looks surprised, as if this were an extraordinary invitation to receive in a dance hall, looks confounded at her two friends, shrugs, detaches herself from the wall, moves to the outer fringe of the pack of dancers, raises her hand languidly to dancing position and awaits Angie with ineffable boredom. Marty, smiling tentatively, addresses the SHORT GIRL.

MARTY   Excuse me, would you care for this dance?

The Short Girl gives Marty a quick glance of appraisal, then looks quickly at her remaining friend.

SHORT GIRL   *(but not unpleasantly)*   I don't feel like dancing just yet.

MARTY Sure.

He turns and heads sluggishly in the direction of the stag line.

THE STAG LINE.

A TRAVEL SHOT follows Marty, as he moves past the line of stags, all of whom are watching him. CAMERA HOLDS as he finds his old niche by the wall, leans there. A moment later, he glances guardedly down to where the short girl and her friend are.

MARTY'S P.O.V.: The Short Girl is approached by a dapper young BOY who asks her to dance. She smiles, excuses herself to her friend and follows the boy out onto the dance floor.

Marty stares at the Short Girl. He shrugs, he's used to this kind of thing, then turns his attention bleakly back to watching...

THE DANCE FLOOR.

The band starts up again and the MUSIC blares. It's a Lindy Hop number. Couples swirl past; the MUSIC comes up BIG.

THE BALLROOM.

Marty leans against the wall, smoking and watching the dancers swirl past. Dr. Keegan's VOICE is heard.

DR. KEEGAN *(off-screen)* You here stag or with a girl?

Marty's attention is on the passing couples, so he doesn't seem to hear. ANGLE WIDENS to include the Doctor standing on Marty's right. Suddenly aware of the Doctor, Marty turns his head.

MARTY You say something?

DR. KEEGAN Yeah. I was just asking you if you was here stag or with a girl.

MARTY I'm stag.

DR. KEEGAN Well, I'll tell you. I got stuck on a blind date with a dog, and I just met an old girl I used to know, and I was wondering how I'm gonna get rid of the girl I'm with. Somebody to take her home, you know what I mean? I'd be glad to pay you five bucks if you take her home for me.

MARTY *(confused)* What?

DR. KEEGAN I'll take you over, and I'll introduce you as an old army buddy of mine, and then I'll cut out. Because I got this other girl waiting for me out by the hatcheck, and I'll pay you five bucks.

MARTY *(stares at the man)* Are you kidding?

DR. KEEGAN No, I'm not kidding.

MARTY You can't just walk off onna girl like that.

Dr. Keegan shrugs, moves down the line of stag guys. Marty turns to watch him, still a little shocked at the proposition. The Doctor approaches THREE STAGS and obviously broaches the subject with one of them. This STAG seems more receptive to the idea. Dr. Keegan takes out a wallet and gives the Stag a five dollar bill. The Stag detaches himself from the wall and, a little ill-at-ease, follows the Doctor.

Marty stands against the wall, watching the Doctor and the Stag, who come in and move past him. Concerned and curious, Marty stares after them, then moves out of his leaning position, following in their general direction.

Marty moves through the crush of young men and women in the area around the dance floor.

ALCOVE NEAR ARCHWAY.

As Marty reaches the alcove that separates the dance floor proper from the lounge, he pauses and looks off toward the booths.

LOUNGE.

Clara sits about halfway down the length of the booths. Dr. Keegan and the Stag stand over her, talking to her. She is looking up at them, her hands nervously gripping a Coca Cola glass. Dr. Keegan is obviously introducing the Stag to Clara and is going through some story about being called away on an emergency. The Stag is presented as her escort-to-be, who will see to it that she gets home safely.

Clara is not taken in by any of this, although she is trying hard not to seem affected. She politely rejects the Stag's company and will go home by herself, thanks for asking anyway. Dr. Keegan makes a few mild protestations, and then he and the Stag leave the booth and start back toward the archway.

ARCHWAY.

From where Marty stands, he can watch Clara, as well as Dr. Keegan and the Stag. The Doctor and the Stag start past Marty, and he catches their conversation.

DR. KEEGAN ...in that case, as long as she's going home alone, give me the five bucks back...

STAG Look, Mac, you paid me the five bucks. I was willing. It's my five bucks...

They move past and away and Marty stares after them before he turns his attention toward Clara off-screen.

Clara is sitting as she was, gripping and ungripping the glass of Coca Cola in front of her. Her eyes are closed. Then, with a little nervous shake of her head she gets out of the booth and stands momentarily at a loss for what next to do. As she glances around, CAMERA ANGLES to include a sign over an exit that reads "Fire Escape." Clara starts moving toward that door.

Marty is staring off-screen toward Clara. He slowly works his way down the length of the lounge in the general direction of the fire escape.

LOUNGE.

Near the entrance to the fire escape, Clara comes into view. Background sounds continue steadily.

Marty is walking the length of the lounge and suddenly stops and stares off-screen.

Clara disappears through the exit onto the fire escape outside.

Marty watches. Then he continues on, crossing the threshold of the...

FIRE ESCAPE.

It is sizeable, almost a small balcony. It looks out onto the backs of innumerable five-story apartment houses. Clara is standing by the railing, her back toward the camera, her head sunk down. She is crying. Marty watches her for a moment before moving a step or two forward.

Clara doesn't turn. Marty tries to think of something to say.

MARTY *(finally)* Excuse me, Miss, would you care to dance?

Clara slowly turns to Marty, her face streaked with tears, her lips trembling. Then, in one of those moments of simultaneous impulse, she lurches to Marty with a sob, and Marty takes her to him.

They stand in an awkward embrace, Marty a little embarrassed, looking back through the fire escape doors to the lounge, wondering if anybody is seeing them. He reaches back with one hand, and contrives, with some effort, to push one of the heavy iron doors shut. He returns his hand around the girl's shoulders. He stands stiffly, allowing her to cry on his chest, as we...

                                                              FADE OUT.

FADE IN:

BRONX APARTMENT HOUSE, STAIRWAY. NIGHT.

Mrs. Pilletti, in her hat and coat and carrying a purse, is making her heavy way up the last few steps toward the landing. She pauses to catch her breath on the landing. Then she moves down the hallway to...

ENTRANCE TO APARTMENT 4-B.

Mrs. Pilletti rings the bell. The SOUND can be heard as she waits. The door is opened by Virginia.

VIRGINIA Hello, Aunt Theresa. Come in.

Mrs. Pilletti enters the apartment.

APARTMENT.

Virginia closes the door after Mrs. Pilletti enters, and they stand in a small narrow hallway, brightly lit. At the far end to the right is the living room in the background.

MRS. PILLETTI *(in a low voice as she pulls off her coat)* Is Catherine here?

Virginia helps her with her coat.

VIRGINIA *(nods, keeping her voice low)* We didn't tell her anything yet. We thought that we'd leave it to you. We thought you'd put it like how you were lonely, and why don't she come to live with you. Because that way it looks like she's doing you a favor, insteada we're throwing her out, and it won't be so cruel on her. Do you want Tommy and me to stay here with you?

MRS. PILLETTI I think it be a better idea if you and Thomas go out, because otherwise she's gonna start a fight with you, and everybody's gonna be yelling.

Thomas appears at the living room end of the foyer with an anxious smile on his face.

THOMAS Hello, Aunt Theresa.

MRS. PILLETTI Hello, Thomas.

THOMAS I just this minute got the baby to sleep.

He comes down to Mrs. Pilletti and Virginia, lowers his voice to a conspiratorial whisper.

THOMAS Aunt Theresa, we figure the best way to ask her is you say that you're very lonely, see? And wouldn't she come and keep you company, because that way, you see...

MRS. PILLETTI Don't worry. I'm gonna take care-a the whole thing.

A shrill, imperious woman's voice breaks into the whispered conference in the hallway.

CATHERINE'S VOICE *(off-screen)* Who's there?! Who's there?!

Mrs. Pilletti heads up the foyer to the living room, followed by Virginia and Thomas.

MRS. PILLETTI *(calling back)* It's me, Catherine! How you feel?

CATHERINE comes in at the end of the foyer. She is a gaunt woman with a face carved out of granite. She is tough, embittered, with a history of pain and mirthless hard work engrained into her features.

CATHERINE Hey! What are you doing here?

MRS. PILLETTI I came to see you. How you feel?

The two sisters quickly embrace and release each other.

CATHERINE I gotta pain in my left side, and my leg throbs like a drum.

MRS. PILLETTI I been getting a pain in my shoulder.

CATHERINE   I gotta pains in my shoulder too. I have a pain in my hip, and my right arm aches so much I can't sleep. It's a curse to be old. How you feel?

MRS. PILLETTI   I feel fine.

CATHERINE   That's nice.

Now that the standard greetings are over, Aunt Catherine abruptly turns and goes back into the living room. Mrs. Pilletti follows. Virginia and Thomas remain in the doorway.

LIVING ROOM.

Catherine and Mrs. Pilletti enter and Catherine heads straight to a chair— obviously her chair. It is an old heavy oaken chair with thick armrests. The rest of the apartment is furnished in what is known as "modern." A piece from House Beautiful *here, a piece from* American Homes and Gardens *there. Aunt Catherine sits erect and forbidding in her chair. Mrs. Pilletti seats herself with a sigh in a neighboring chair. Thomas and Virginia remain off-screen in the hallway for a moment to hang up Mrs. Pilletti's coat. The two old sisters sit for a moment.*

MRS. PILLETTI   Well, how's everything with you?

Aunt Catherine grimaces to describe how everything is with her.

MRS. PILLETTI   My son Marty's fine. Everybody's fine...

Thomas comes in from the hallway, stands in the back of the room, somewhat apprehensively.

MRS. PILLETTI   We gotta postcard from my son Nickie and his bride. They're inna big hotel in Florida on their honeymoon. Everything is very nice.

CATHERINE   That's nice. I gotta letter from my husband's cousin in Abruzzi. His mother died.

MRS. PILLETTI Oh.

CATHERINE Do you remember Emilio DiGiorgio, owned the tavern in Abruzzi?

MRS. PILLETTI I don't think I remember him.

CATHERINE Well, he died. You know who else died?

MRS. PILLETTI Who?

CATHERINE You know the old man upstairs in this house. Old Irishman, always drunk. He got pleurisy. He was inna hospital two weeks. He died yesterday.

MRS. PILLETTI Well, I always like to visit you, Catherine, because you always got such cheerful news.

Virginia comes into the living room with Thomas. They remain in the background.

THOMAS *(suddenly)* Ma, you want something to eat, some tuna fish?

MRS. PILLETTI Hey, why don't you go to the movie? Your mother and me, we're gonna be baby-sitter.

Thomas looks indecisively at his wife.

VIRGINIA Listen, let's go downa Kaplans' apartment. They told us to come down.

MRS. PILLETTI Sure, sure.

Thomas ponders a moment.

THOMAS All right, Ma, we're going downstairs to the Kaplans, if you want us for anything.

They exit. The two old sisters sit rigidly until they hear the SOUND of the door closing. Catherine cocks an eyebrow and promptly launches into her statement.

CATHERINE   I wake up this morning, I hear the baby crying. So I wake up. I come in their room. That girl is shaking her hand atta baby. I said, "You brute! Don't you strike that baby! That's my son's baby!"

MRS. PILLETTI   It's her baby too, you know.

CATHERINE   That's my son Thomas's baby.

MRS. PILLETTI   Well, it ain't your baby.

CATHERINE   Did I tell you she threw the bottle-a milk at me?

MRS. PILLETTI   You told me.

CATHERINE   She's a witch, that one. I tell you what happen yesterday?

MRS. PILLETTI   What happen?

CATHERINE   She gave me the evil eye. *(She demonstrates this by pulling the lower lid of one eye down and staring grotesquely at the ceiling.)*

MRS. PILLETTI   *(scoffing)* Ufa!

CATHERINE   I keep one eye open when I sleep, because she's gonna come in, stab me in my bed.

MRS. PILLETTI   Catherine, I want you come live in my house with Marty and me.

Her sister turns, genuinely surprised at this request.

CATHERINE   Ah?

MRS. PILLETTI   You son Thomas and Virginia, they come to my house this afternoon...

CATHERINE   *(sharply)* Who?

MRS. PILLETTI   Your son Thomas and his wife Virginia...

CATHERINE   When was this?

MRS. PILLETTI   This afternoon, about four, five o'clock.

CATHERINE   What they say?

MRS. PILLETTI   You know what they say. They say things are no good in this house. Catherine, your son is married. Leave him in peace. He wantsa be alone with his wife. They don't want no old lady sitting inna balcony. Now I tell you what I think. I want you come live with me in my house with Marty and me. In my house, you have your own room. You don't have to sleep onna couch inna living room like here. We will cook inna kitchen and talk like when we were girls. You are dear to me, and you are dear to Marty. We are pleased for you to come.

Catherine surveys her sister coldly.

CATHERINE   My son Thomas came to see you this afternoon, and he said to you he wants to cast his mother from his house?

MRS. PILLETTI   Catherine, don't make an opera outta this. The three-a you anna baby live in three skinny rooms. You are an old goat, and she has an Italian temper. She is a good girl, but you drive her crazy. Catherine, you are no fool. You know this is no good, an old woman living with a husband and wife. Two women inna same kitchen, anna house burns down.

Catherine stands abruptly. She is deeply hurt.

CATHERINE   So I am an old garbage bag, put inna street.

MRS. PILLETTI   Oh, Catherine, please! Don't make a tragedy. You come
to my house where you know you be happier yourself.

CATHERINE   It pains that they should do this.

MRS. PILLETTI   I know it pains.

*Catherine turns and meanders a few steps. The stiff edge of mordant humor
that has been her one defense against life has deserted her, and she is just a
hurt old lady now.*

CATHERINE   These are the worst years, I tell you.

*She seats herself on an Eames chair. On her right, a Modern-Age lamp tow-
ers slimly. On her left is a Modern-Age endtable with a Modern-Age ashtray on it. The hardened muscles in her face suddenly slacken.*

MRS. PILLETTI   *(with deep compassion)* Catherine, you are very dear to me.
We have cried many times together. When my husband died, I would
have gone insane if it were not for you. I ask you to come to my
house, because I can make you happy. Please come to my house.

CATHERINE   These are the worst years. I tell you. It's gonna happen
to you. I'm afraida look inna mirror. I'm afraid I'm gonna see an old
lady with white hair, like the old ladies inna park, little bundles inna
black shawl, waiting for the coffin. I'm fifty-six years old. What am I
to do with myself? I have strength in my hands. I wanna cook. I
wanna clean. I wanna make dinner for my children. Am I an old dog
to lie in fronta the fire til my eyes close? These are the terrible years,
Theresa! Terrible years!

MRS. PILLETTI   Catherine, my sister...

Catherine stares distraught at Mrs. Pilletti.

CATHERINE   It's gonna happen to you! It's gonna happen to you! What will you do if Marty gets married?! What will you cook? What happen to alla children playing in alla rooms? Where is the noise?! It is a curse to be a widow! A curse. What will you do if Marty gets married?! What will you do?

She stares at Mrs. Pilletti, her deep eyes haggard and pained. Mrs. Pilletti stares back for a moment, then her own eyes close. Catherine has hit home. Catherine sinks back onto her chair, sitting stiffly, her arms on the thick armrests. Mrs. Pilletti sits hunched a little forward, her hands folded nervously in her lap.

CATHERINE *(continuing quietly)* I will put my clothes inna bag, and I will come to you tomorrow.

The two sisters, somber and silent, continue to just stare at one another.

THE STARDUST BALLROOM. NIGHT.

CAMERA PANS the crowd, picking up Marty and Clara dancing cheek-to-cheek on the crowded, darkened dance floor. The MUSIC rides over the top of the scene.

MARTY You come up here often?

CLARA I was up here twice before. Once with a friend of mine and once I came up alone. The last time...do you see that girl in the gray dress sitting over there?

MARTY Yeah.

CLARA Well, the last time I was up here, that's where I sat. I sat there for an hour and a half, without moving a muscle. Now and then, some fellow would sort of walk up to me and then change his mind. I'll never forget just sitting there for an hour and a half with my hands in my lap. Then I began to cry, and I had to get up and go home.

MARTY I cry a lot too. I'm a big cryer.

CLARA   This is something recent with me, this bursting into tears at the least thing.

MARTY   Oh, I cry all the time, any little thing. My brothers, my brother-in-laws, they're always telling me what a goodhearted guy I am. Well, you don't get goodhearted by accident. You get kicked around long enough, you get to be a real professor of pain. I know exactly how you feel. And I also want you to know I'm having a very good time with you now and really enjoying myself. So you see, you're not such a dog as you think you are.

CLARA   I'm having a very good time, too.

MARTY   So there you are. So I guess I'm not such a dog as I think I am.

CLARA   You're a very nice guy, and I don't know why some girl hasn't grabbed you off long ago.

MARTY   I don't know either. I think I'm a very nice guy. I also think I'm a pretty smart guy in my own way. *(Clara smiles briefly at this.)* Now I figure, two people get married, and they gonna live together forty, fifty years. So it's just gotta be more than whether they're good looking or not. You tell me you think you're not very good-looking. My father was a really ugly man, but my mother adored him. She told me that she used to get so miserable sometimes, like everybody, you know? And she says my father always tried to understand. I used to see them sometimes when I was a kid, sitting in the living room, talking and talking, and I used to adore my old man, because he was so kind. That's one of the most beautiful things I have in my life, the way my father and mother were. And my father was a real ugly man. So it doesn't matter if you look like a gorilla. So you see, dogs like us, we ain't such dogs as we think we are.

They dance silently for a moment, cheeks pressed against each other.

CLARA   I'm twenty-nine years old. How old are you?

MARTY   I'm thirty-four.

BALLROOM, STAIRWAY.

Marty and Clara are about halfway down the steps leading to the street entrance to the ballroom. Clara has on a light summer coat. Marty is about two steps ahead of her and has to keep turning his head to talk to her. He is in an elevated mood, intoxicated—on a talking jag.

MARTY   ...you teach chemistry? That's funny. Where? What school?

CLARA   Benjamin Franklin High School.

MARTY   Benjamin Franklin, where's that? Brooklyn? I went to Theodore Roosevelt right up here on Fordham Road. It's right arounna corner from my house. I have a cousin who's a teacher. He teaches Latin. He lives in Chicago. He was studying to be a Jesuit, but he gave it up after his first vows.

He has reached the street landing and waits for Clara to catch up with him. They stand in front of the glass doors leading to the street.

BALLROOM VESTIBULE. GLASS DOORS.

MARTY   *(prattling on)* I was pretty good in high school. I sound like a jerk now, but I was pretty good. I graduated with an eighty-two average. That ain't bad. I was accepted at City College. I filled out the application and everything, but my old man died, so I hadda go to work. My best class was German. That was my first language. Der, die, das—des, der, des. There you are, I still remember...

He pushes the glass door open to...

THE STREET OUTSIDE THE STARDUST BALLROOM.

As Marty and Clara emerge onto the sidewalk of West Farms Square, they pause again.

It is about nine o'clock, and the busy street is brightly lit from the stores.

*PASSERSBY hurry on their way. The elevated subway RUMBLES over-
head intermittently.*

MARTY   *(chattering on)* You know what I was good at in high school?
I was good in Math. You know how long ago I graduated high school?
June, nineteen-thirty-seven. Holy cow! June, nineteen-thirty-seven!
What is that? Fifteen, seventeen years ago! Holy cow! Seventeen
years ago! Is that right? Seventeen, that's right. Where did it all go?
I'm getting old. I'm gonna be thirty-five November eighth. Thirty-
five. Wow. Time goes on, boy.

He takes her arm, and they start walking.

MARTY   Nineteen-thirty-seven...that's right. My old man died December,
nineteen-thirty-seven.

SIDEWALK.

*MOVING SHOT as they stroll toward the corner of Jerome and Burnside
Avenues.*

MARTY   Two o'clock in the morning he died. The doorbell rings, and
I knew something was wrong right away. Because my room is onna
ground floor inna front, you see, and I got outta bed, and I answered
the door...

*CAMERA HOLDS as Marty, caught in his story, stops and continues
intently.*

MARTY   There was Mr. Stern. He had a house down about a block from
us. He moved out though. My old man, he used to play cards with
him and some other old guys. He's a Jewish feller. So he said, "Is your
mother home?" So I knew right away there was something wrong. I
was only eighteen, exactly eighteen years old, just the month before.
So I said, "Is something wrong, Mr. Stern?" I was in my pajamas, you
know? So he said, "Marty, your father died." My father died right
inna middle of playing cards, right at the table. He had a heart attack.
He had low blood pressure, my old man. He used to faint a lot.

(Suddenly he looks at Clara, rather startled.) Boy, am I talking, I never talked so much in my life. Usually, everybody comes to me and tells me all their troubles. Well, I'm gonna shut up now, and I'm gonna let you get a word in... *(He takes her arm again, and they continue strolling toward the corner intersection in silence.)* Seventeen years ago. What I been doing with myself all that time?... Well, I'm talking again. I must be driving you crazy. Mosta the time I'm with a girl, I can't find a word to say. Well, I'm gonna shut up now. Because I'm not like this usually. Usually, I...well, here I go again.

They reach the corner intersection. CAMERA HOLDS on Marty as he pauses again. He stares at Clara, confused at his strange loquacity.

MARTY   I can't shut my mouth...I'm on a jag, for Pete's sake. You'd think I was loaded...

Marty stares at Clara, absolutely aghast at his inability to stop talking.

MARTY   I can't stop talking! Isn't this stupid?!

He stands there in the middle of the sidewalk with PEOPLE moving past, back and forth. Marty continues to stare at Clara, his broad face widened by a foolish, confused smile. Clara regards him affectionately.

MARTY   *(with sudden sincerity)*   You gotta real nice face, you know? It's really a nice face.

CLARA   Thank you.

They stroll along farther up the noisy, jangled, trafficked Saturday night avenue.

GRAND CONCOURSE LUNCHEONETTE. NIGHT.

Once a candy store, now a soda fountain where booths have been installed in the rear. One wall of the luncheonette in front is covered with magazines from floor to ceiling. It is a nice clean joint, brightly lit. Several CUSTOMERS are occupying three of the four booths.

BOOTH.

They sit opposite each other in the booth. Each has a cup of coffee. Marty is still talking, but now he is apparently telling a story so funny that he can hardly get the words out. The hilarity has communicated itself to Clara. Her eyes are burning with suppressed laughter. Every now and then she has to gasp to control the bubbly giggling inside of her.

MARTY   ...so I'm inna kneeling position, and if you ever try shooting a BAR inna kneeling position, you know what I mean. I can't holda steady position. I'm wavering back and forth...*(He has to interrupt the narrative to control a seizure of giggles. Clara wipes her eyes and catches her breath.)* ...so the guy next to me, he's shooting from the prone position, and he's cross-eyed like I told you...*(He can't go on. He has to stop and cover his face with one hand.)* So just then... *(stops to control himself again)*...so just then I hear five shots go off from the guy next to me... *(It's too much for him. He lets out a sudden guffaw and instantly smothers it under shaking shoulders. Clara hides her face in her hands and giggles desperately. Some of the other people turn to look at them.)* So my target goes down, and a minute later, the flag comes up. I got five bulls-eyes. This cross-eyed guy next to me, he shot five bulls-eyes into my target... *(He stares at the girl, spent from laughter.)* ...so I said to the sergeant who was checking my score, "Pretty good, eh, Sarge? Five bulls-eyes? So this sergeant, he don't know what happened, he says, "Say, that's all right, Pilletti"...*(He closes his eyes, shakes his head.)* Oh, man. So that's what happened. That's how I got the reputation-a being the best shot inna whole battalion...oh, man....

For a moment they seem to have controlled their laughter. They sit, shaking their heads, studying their fingers on the table in front of them. Then slowly, Marty begins to giggle again. It communicates itself to Clara. In a moment they are hiding their faces in their hands, their shoulders shivering with laughter.

STARDUST BALLROOM.

CLOSE ON Angie. His eyes look slowly in every direction. CAMERA

PULLS BACK disclosing Angie standing on the fringe of the dance floor, head arched high, looking at the crowded dance floor. He starts back to the archway toward the lounge, looking over his shoulder.

ARCHWAY.

Angie comes into the archway, throws one more glance over his shoulder at the dance floor, then turns and enters the...

LOUNGE.

Angie walks down the length of the lounge, looking into the booths and simultaneously at the PEOPLE moving back and forth in the lounge. At the far end of the lounge, he turns and comes back along the bar side, checking each face at the bar.

ANTEROOM.

There are three young BUCKOES laying out their money for admission. One of them calls to Angie.

BUCKO   Anything good in there, Mac?

ANGIE   A buncha dogs.

He crosses to the Men's Room.

MEN'S ROOM.

Angie comes into a momentarily empty room. Angie goes the full length of the white tiled room, past the wash bowls, the long mirror, bending to look under the doors of the stalls. Suddenly he calls out.

ANGIE   Hey, Marty! Hey, Marty, you in here?!

He waits for an answer...

GRAND CONCOURSE LUNCHEONETTE.

CLOSE ON Marty and Clara still in the booth, but two more cups of coffee have been set down in front of each of them. There are also two pie-plates. Clara has left half of her pie. Also an empty pack of cigarettes, and another pack half-gone. They are both smoking. Marty is still talking, but the mood is no longer laughter. A pensive, speculative hush has fallen over them. They have been talking for hours, and they have reached the stage where you start tearing designs in the paper napkins.

MARTY   ...When I got outta the army, Clara, I was lost. I didn't know what I wanted to do. I was twenny-five years old, what was I gonna do, go back to my old job, forty cents an hour. I thought maybe I go to college under the G.I. Biller Rights, you know? But I wouldn't graduate till I was twenny-eight, twenny-nine years old, even if I made it in three years. And my brother Freddie wanted to get married, and I had three unmarried sisters—in an Italian home, that's a terrible thing. And my kid brother Nickie, he's a one got married last week. So I just went to pieces. I used to walk inna streets till three, four o'clock inna mornings. My mother used to be so worried about me. My uncle Mario come over one time. He offered me a job driving his hack onna night shift. He got his own cab, you know. And God forgive me for what I'm gonna say now, but I used to thinka doing away with myself. I used to stand sometimes in the subway, and God forgive me what I'm going to say, I used to feel the tracks sucking me down under the wheels.

CLARA   *(deeply sympathetic)* Yes, I know.

MARTY   I'm a Catholic, you know, and even to think about suicide is a terrible sin.

CLARA   Yes, I know.

MARTY   So then Mr. Gazzara—he was a frienda my father—he offered me this job in his butcher shop, and everybody pleaded with me to take it. So that's what happened. I didn't wanna be a butcher.

CLARA   There's nothing wrong with being a butcher.

MARTY   Well, I wouldn't call it an elegant profession. It's in a lower social scale. People look down on butchers.

CLARA   I don't.

Marty looks quickly up at her, then back down.

MARTY   Well, the point is Mr. Gazzara wantsa sell his shop now, because he and his wife are lonely, and they wanna move out to California in Los Angeles and live near their married daughter. Because she's always writing them to come out there. So it's a nice little shop. I handle his books for him, so I know he has a thirty-five percent mark-up which is not unreasonable, and he takes home net maybe a hundred, hundred and fifty bucks a week. The point is, of course, you gotta worry about the supermarkets. There's two inna neighborhood now, and there's an A&P coming in, at least that's the rumor. Of course, mosta his trade is strictly Italian, but the younger Italian girls, they get married, and they don't stick to the old Italian dishes so much. I mean, you gotta take that into account too.

CLARA   It's my feeling that you really want to buy this shop, Marty.

MARTY   That's true. I do. But I'm gonna have to take outta loan inna bank eight thousand dollars. That's a big note to carry, because I have to give Mr. Gazzara a mortgage, and what I have to weigh is: will it pay off in the end more than I can make onna salary?

Clara looks down at her fingers, her face alive and sensitive. She carefully assembles her words in her mind. Then she looks at the squat butcher across the table from her.

CLARA   Marty, I know you for three hours, but I know you're a good butcher. You're an intelligent, sensitive, decent man. I have a feeling about you like sometimes a kid comes in to see me for one reason or another. And some of these kids, Marty, in my classes, they have so much warmth in them, so much capacity. And that's the feeling I get about you.

Marty shuts his eyes, then opens them quickly, bows his head.

CLARA   If you were one of my students, I would say, "Go ahead and buy the butcher shop. You're a good butcher."

Clara pauses.

MARTY   (*not quite trusting the timbre of his voice*) Well, there's a lotta things I could do with this shop. I could organize my own supermarket. Get a buncha neighborhood merchants together. That's what a lotta them are doing. (*He looks up at her now.*) Wadda you think?

CLARA   I think anything you want to do, you'll do well.

Tears begin to flood his eyes again. He quickly looks away. He licks his lips.

MARTY   (*still looking down*) I'm Catholic. Are you Catholic?

Clara looks down at her hands.

CLARA   (*also in a low voice*) Yes, I am.

Marty looks up at her.

MARTY   I only got about three bucks on me now, but I just live about eight blocks from here on the other side of Webster Avenue. Why don't we walk back to my house? I'll run in, pick up some dough, and let's step out somewhere.

CLARA   I really should get home...

She twists in her seat and looks toward the back of the luncheonette.

MARTY   It's only a quarter of twelve. The clock's right over there.

CLARA   I really should get home, I told my father....Well, I suppose a little while longer. I wonder if there's any place around here I could put some makeup on...

Marty considers this problem for a second, then leans out of the booth and calls out.

MARTY   Hey, Mac!

CAMERA ANGLES to include the PROPRIETOR of the luncheonette. He is sitting in one of the booths ahead reading the Sunday Mirror. *He looks up toward Marty.*

MARTY   You gotta Ladies' Room around here?

PROPRIETOR   Inna back.

MARTY   *(to Clara)* Inna back.

Clara smiles at this innocent gaucherie, then edges out of the booth, taking her purse with her.

187TH STREET. NIGHT.

HIGH ANGLE SHOT of Angie meandering down the street on which the neighborhood bar is located. It is near midnight, and the street is empty except for Angie and the CLACKING of his leather heels on the pavement. He comes to the bar, opens the door, enters...

THE BAR. NIGHT.

The SOUNDS of Saturday night revelry are loud, coming mostly from the Irish contingent of the neighborhood. They are grouped along practically the whole bar. Three or four WOMEN and a number of shirtsleeved MEN, mostly in their late forties, early fifties. We know they're Irish, because one of the younger men is chanting an auld country ballad.

CAMERA ANGLES disclose the entrance to the bar in the background, showing Angie coming in, looking here and there. He starts toward the bar.

NEAR BAR.

TWO IRISH WOMEN, middle-aged, squat heavily on bar stools over their schooners of beer, gassing away at each other.

FIRST IRISH WOMAN ...so she told me that the doctor told her that if she had any more babies, she would do so at the risk of her life...

Angie shuffles in, pausing near the bar and standing behind the two Irish women.

SECOND IRISH WOMAN She was always a bit thin in the hips...

FIRST IRISH WOMAN Well, at the time she told me this, she already had six. Every time I saw the woman, she was either...

ANGIE Hey, Lou!

FIRST IRISH WOMAN ...going to the hospital or coming from it. She was hatching them out like eggs.

SECOND IRISH WOMAN And that husband of hers is a skinny bit of a fellow, isn't he?

FIRST IRISH WOMAN Well, I bumped into her on the street, and she was as big as a barrel.

ANGIE *(loudly)* Hey, Lou!

CAMERA ANGLES to include Lou, the Bartender.

BARTENDER *(looking up from opening a batch of beer bottles)* What?

FIRST IRISH WOMAN ...so I said to her, "Mary...

ANGIE *(calling to the Bartender)* Marty been in here the last coupla hours or so?

FIRST IRISH WOMAN "...Mary, for heaven's sakes, didn't you tell me that another one'll kill you?"

BARTENDER I ain't seen Marty all night...

SECOND IRISH WOMAN And her husband is a little bit of a man, isn't he?

ANGIE *(calling to the Bartender, but even more to himself)* Where is everybody? I been walking around, I can't find anybody...

FIRST IRISH WOMAN Well, last week Tuesday, she gave birth to the baby in Saint Elizabeth's hospital...a big healthy boy of nine pounds...

SECOND IRISH WOMAN Oh, that's nice. So the doctor was wrong, wasn't he?

FIRST IRISH WOMAN Oh, no! She died right in the hospital...

SECOND IRISH WOMAN Oh, that's a sad story. And her husband is that little fellow, works in Peter Reeves.

FIRST IRISH WOMAN That's the one.

SECOND IRISH WOMAN Oh, that's a sad story.

Angie has nothing better to do than give his attention to the last lines of the story. Perturbed, he turns and leaves.

NEAR ELEVATED SUBWAY. NIGHT.

With street NOISES over the scene, Marty and Clara walk along through the intricate understructure of the elevated subway toward Webster Avenue.

STREET.

*Marty and Clara walk slowly along a side street in Marty's neighborhood.
The streets are almost empty; perhaps an occasional PEDESTRIAN on the
other side of the street. The cars are parked bumper-to-bumper in lines along
the curb. The five-story apartment buildings are mostly dark, an occasional
window lit.*

*Marty suddenly stops and bends down; his shoe lace has become untied. Clara
sits back against the fender of the nearest car and continues talking.*

CLARA   ...It's really a fine opportunity for me. But I'm not sure I want
to be a department head. It's mostly executive and administrative
work. Well, anyway, I told you about my father, and he depends on
me a great deal, and...

MARTY   *(still concentrating on his shoelace)* Why don't you just move out
to Portchester?

CLARA   Well, that's what I was saying. My father is getting old. And we're
very close. He's a wonderful man, really...

She pauses as he straightens. He looks at her a moment.

MARTY   I think you're kidding yourself, Clara. I used to think about
moving out, you know? And that's what I used to say. "My mother
needs me." But when you really get down to it, that ain't it at all.
Actually, you need your father. You know what I mean? You're living
at home, and you got your father and mother there, and you can go
on like that—being a little girl all your life.

CLARA   I'm afraid of being lonely.

MARTY   Oh, you won't be so lonely. You'll make friends right away.

CLARA   Actually, I don't make friends easily.

MARTY   What're you talking about? You're a real likeable person. You'll make friends out there in Portchester one, two, three. You'll have people visiting you alla time. I'll come visit you. I'll borrow my brother Freddie's car, or you can call me up when you feel blue, or I'll call you up. And it's gonna be nice. Don't be so afraid.

They have only gone a few paces farther when Marty's shoelace comes loose again. He fidgets self-consciously, bends down and begins to retie it. The VOICE of Ralph, the well-dressed man, established previously, is heard.

RALPH'S VOICE   *(off-screen)* Hey, Marty!

Marty and Clara both look off...

STREET. CAR WINDOW.

Ralph is leaning out the car window twisting to look back up the street.

RALPH   *(yelling)* Hey, Marty!

Marty and Clara look around to find the source of the voice.

RALPH   Marty! Over here!

Marty and Clara again look around trying to find Ralph. Marty spots him leaning out of the window of a '47 Chevy parked in the background.

MARTY   Hello, Ralph.

RALPH   *(yelling)* Hey, Marty, come over here a minute.

Marty and Clara start walking toward the Chevy.

INSIDE THE CHEVY.

Ralph and MABEL, a young woman in her early thirties, are seated in front. In the rear seat of the car, LEO is sandwiched in between a MISS LOUISE KELLY and a MISS ELAINE RITCHIE.

RALPH   *(explaining to girls)* You'll like this guy. This guy's a nice guy.

LEO   Who's this? Marty?

RALPH   Yeah.

LEO   *(confirming Ralph's statement)* Oh, this guy's a nice guy.

STREET.

Marty stops and excuses himself from Clara to walk slowly toward the Chevy. It's about five cars down from him. The camera pans with him.

OUTSIDE THE CHEVY.

Ralph is leaning out of the window again, watching Marty approach.

MARTY   *(approaching the car)* Hello, Ralph, what's new? *(looks through the back window, recognizes Leo)* Hiya, Leo.

LEO   Hiya, Marty.

RALPH   *(He indicates with his head that he wishes to hold a whispered conference with Marty.)* Hey, Marty, come here a minute.

Marty leans with his elbow on the open front window of the car, his head bowed, waiting for Ralph to speak his piece. He studiously avoids looking at the girls in the car.

RALPH   *(lowering his voice)* Hey, Marty, we got an odd squirrel here, you interested?

Marty allows his eyes to flicker quickly over the girl in the seat next to Ralph.

MARTY   Waddaya mean, Ralph?

RALPH   *(turning his head toward the rear of the car and raising his voice)* Hey,

Louise, I want you to meet Marty Pilletti. Marty, that's Louise Kelly, inna back seat there.

MARTY Hiya.

Louise, not an unattractive girl by any means, is a little surly at the moment. She merely nods at the introduction.

LOUISE What are we going to do, just sit around here all night?

RALPH *(addressing Marty's bowed head in a quick mutter)* Listen, Marty, these three squirrels are nurses. We're all going over Leo's house later because there's nobody there. These are the squirrels I told you about. Money inna bank, man. Wanna get inna car? She's a pretty nice-looking doll.

MARTY I'm with a girl, Ralph.

RALPH Get ridda her. This is money inna bank.

MARTY I can't do that, Ralph, because somebody already brushed her off once tonight.

RALPH This is a good deal here, Marty.

Marty straightens, looks surreptitiously back to the corner where Clara is standing.

Clara stands alone on the corner. She is an angular, awkward, plain girl. Marty brings his attention back around to Ralph who is leaning out of the car window.

MARTY *(bending down to Ralph)* I can't do it, Ralph. Thanks anyway. *(looks toward back seat)* Very nice to have met you all.

LOUISE Come on, let's get outta here.

LEO Hey, Ralph, we might as well get going.

Ralph bends forward and starts the car.

MARTY   I'll see you, Leo.

LEO   I'll see you, Marty.

Marty takes a step or two back from the car, and Ralph begins the business of wheeling the car from out of its parking place. The car backs and fills once or twice and eventually clears and whisks into the street.

Marty stands looking after the departing car, then slowly turns and goes back up the sidewalk. He joins Clara and we...

DISSOLVE TO:

PILLETTI HOME, KITCHEN. NIGHT.

Marty and Clara come into the dark house. Nobody is home. Marty and Clara's silhouettes block the doorway momentarily.

MARTY   Wait a minute. Lemme find the light.

He finds the lights. The kitchen is suddenly brightly lit. The two of them stand squinting to adjust to the sudden glare.

MARTY   I guess my mother ain't home yet. I figure my cousin Thomas and Virginia musta gone to the movies, so they won't get back till one o'clock at least.

Clara advances into the kitchen, a little ill at ease, and looks around. Marty closes the porch door.

MARTY   This is the kitchen.

CLARA   Yes, I know.

MARTY   Come on inna dining room.

He turns the light on as he enters.   Clara follows him into the...

DINING ROOM.

MARTY   Siddown, take off your coat. You want something to eat? We gotta whole half-chicken in the icebox.

CLARA   *(alighting tentatively on the edge of a chair)* No, thank you. I don't think I should stay very long.

MARTY   Sure. Just take off your coat a minute.

He helps her off with her coat. He remains behind her, looking down at her. Conscious of his scrutiny, she sits uncomfortably, breathing unevenly. Marty takes her coat into the dark living room. Clara is patient but nervous. Marty comes back, sits on another chair, and there is an awkward silence.

MARTY   So I was telling you, my kid brother Nickie got married last Sunday. That was a very nice affair. And they had this statue of some woman, and they had whiskey spouting outta her mouth. I never saw anything so grand in my life. *(The silence again falls between them.)* And watta meal. I'm a butcher, so I know a good hunka steak when I see one. That was choice filet, right off the toppa the chuck. A buck eighty a pound. Of course, if you wanna cheaper cut, get rib steak. That gotta lotta waste on it, but it comes to about a buck and a quarter a pound, if it's trimmed. Listen, Clara, make yourself comfortable. You're all tense.

CLARA   Oh, I'm fine.

MARTY   You want me to take you home, I'll take you home.

CLARA   Maybe that would be a good idea.

She stands. He stands. He's a little angry. He turns and sullenly goes back to the living room for her coat. Wordlessly, he begins to help her into the coat.

Standing behind her, he puts his hands on her shoulders, then suddenly seizes her, and begins kissing her on the neck. As Marty holds Clara, kissing the back of her neck, the dialogue drops to quick, hushed whispers.

CLARA   No, Marty, please...

MARTY   I like you. I like you. I been telling you all night, I like you...

CLARA   Marty...

MARTY   I just wanna kiss, that's all.

He attempts to turn her face toward him. She resists.

CLARA   No...

MARTY   Please...

CLARA   No....

MARTY   Please...

CLARA   Marty...

He releases her and turns away violently.

MARTY   All right! I'll take you home! All right!

He marches a few paces away, deeply disturbed. He turns back to her.

MARTY   All I wanted was a lousy kiss! What do you think, I was gonna try something serious with my mother coming home any minute!? What am I, a leper or something?!

He turns and goes into the living room to hide the flush of hot tears threatening to fill his eyes. Clara is also on the verge of tears.

CLARA   *(more to herself than to him)* I just didn't feel like it, that's all.

Slowly, she moves to the archway leading to the living room. CAMERA ANGLES to include the living room where Marty sits on the couch with his hands in his lap, staring straight ahead. The room is dark except for the slanted light coming from the dining room.

Clara goes to the couch and sits on the edge beside him. He doesn't look at her.

LIVING ROOM.

MARTY   I'm old enough to know better. Comes New Year's Eve, everybody starts arranging parties, I'm the guy they gotta dig up a date for. Let me getta packa cigarettes, and I'll take you home.

He starts to rise but instead sinks back onto the couch, looking straight ahead. Clara looks at him, her face peculiarly soft and compassionate.

CLARA   I'd like to see you again. Very much. The reason I didn't let you kiss me was because I just didn't know how to handle the situation. You're the kindest man I ever met. The reason I tell you this is because I want to see you again very much. I know that when you take me home, I'm going to just lie on my bed and think about you. I want very much to see you again.

Marty stares down at his hands.

MARTY   *(without looking over at her)* Waddaya doing tomorrow night?

CLARA   Nothing.

MARTY   I'll call you up tomorrow morning. Maybe, we'll go see a movie.

CLARA   I'd like that very much.

MARTY   The reason I can't be definite about it now is my Aunt Catherine is probably coming over tomorrow, and I may have to help out.

CLARA   I'll wait for your call.

MARTY We better get started to your house, because the buses only run about one an hour now.

CLARA All right. *(She stands.)*

MARTY I'll just get a packa cigarettes.

He rises and goes into his bedroom. CAMERA ANGLES to include door to bedroom. Marty opens his bureau drawer and extracts a pack of cigarettes. He comes back out and looks at Clara for the first time. They start to walk to the dining room. In the archway, Marty pauses and turns to her.

MARTY Waddaya doing New Year's Eve?

CLARA Nothing.

They quietly slip into each other's arms and kiss. Slowly their faces part, and Marty's head sinks down upon her shoulder. He is crying, detectable from the slight shake of his shoulders. The girl presses her cheek against the back of his head. They stand. The SOUND of the kitchen door opening splits them out of their embrace. A moment later Mrs. Pilletti's voice is heard.

MRS. PILLETTI'S VOICE *(off-screen)* Hallo! Hallo! Marty?!

She comes into the dining room, stops at the sight of Marty and Clara.

MRS. PILLETTI Hello, Marty, when you come home?

MARTY We just got here about fifteen minutes ago. Ma, I want you to meet Miss Clara Snyder. She's a graduate of New York University. She teaches chemistry in Benjamin Franklin High School.

This seems to impress Mrs. Pilletti.

MRS. PILLETTI Siddown, siddown. You want some chicken? We got some chicken in the ice box.

CLARA No, Mrs. Pilletti. We were just going home. Thank you very much anyway.

MRS. PILLETTI Well, siddown a minute. I just come inna house. I'll take off my coat. Siddown a minute.

Mrs. Pilletti pulls her coat off.

MARTY How'd you come home, Ma? Thomas give you a ride?

MRS. PILLETTI *(nodding)* Oh, it's a sad business. *(turning to Clara)* My sister, Catherine, she don't get along with her daughter-in-law, so she's gonna come live with us.

MARTY Oh, she's coming, eh, Ma?

MRS. PILLETTI Oh, sure. *(to Clara)* Siddown, siddown. Marty, tell her siddown.

MARTY Might as well siddown a minute, Clara.

Clara smiles and sits. Mrs. Pilletti likewise seats herself, holding her coat in her lap.

MRS. PILLETTI *(to Marty)* Did you offer the young lady some fruit?

MARTY I offered her, Ma, she don't want nothing.

CLARA No, thank you, really, Mrs. Pilletti.

MRS. PILLETTI *(to Clara with a sigh)* It's a very sad business, I tell you. A woman, fifty-six years old, all her life, she had her own home. Now she's just an old lady, sleeping on her daughter-in-law's couch. It's a curse to be a mother, I tell you. Your children grow up and then what is left for you to do? What is a mother's life but her children? It is a very cruel thing when your son has no place for you in his home.

CLARA   Couldn't she find some sort of hobby to fill out her time?

MRS. PILLETTI   Hobby! What can she do? She cooks and she cleans. You gotta have a house to clean. You gotta have children to cook for. These are the terrible years for a woman, the terrible years.

CLARA   You mustn't feel too harshly against her daughter-in-law. She also wants to have a house to clean and a family to cook for.

Mrs. Pilletti darts a quick, sharp look at Clara. Then she looks back to her own hands, which are beginning to twist nervously.

MRS. PILLETTI   You don't think my sister Catherine should live in her daughter-in-law's house?

CLARA   Well, I don't know the people, of course, but as a rule, I don't think a mother-in-law should live with a young couple.

MRS. PILLETTI   Where do you think a mother-in-law should go?

CLARA   I don't think a mother should depend so much upon her children for her rewards in life.

MRS. PILLETTI   Well, maybe that's what they teach you in New York University. In real life, it don't work out that way. You wait till you are a mother.

CLARA   It's silly of me to argue about it. I don't know the people involved.

MARTY   Ma, I'm gonna take her home now. It's getting late, and the buses only run about one an hour.

MRS. PILLETTI   *(standing)* Sure.

CLARA   *(standing)* It was very nice meeting you, Mrs. Pilletti. I hope I'll see you again.

MRS. PILLETTI   Sure.

Marty and Clara move toward the kitchen.

MARTY   All right, Ma. I'll be back in about an hour, an hour anna half.

MRS. PILLETTI   Sure.

CLARA   Goodnight, Mrs. Pilletti.

MRS. PILLETTI   Goodnight.

Marty and Clara go out through the kitchen. CAMERA STAYS on Mrs. Pilletti, who stands expressionlessly by her chair, staring after them. She remains there rigid even after the kitchen door has OPENED and SHUT.

FORDHAM ROAD. NIGHT.

The biggest intersection in the Bronx is near the Grand Concourse at Fordham Road, which is the biggest boulevard. Despite the hour, the sidewalks are crowded with PEOPLE. The TRAFFIC is heavy with buses.

We PICK UP Angie walking up Fordham Road just about to the Grand Concourse. As he reaches the northeast corner of the intersection and stands, waiting for the light to change, he looks off-screen. Something captures his attention, and he calls out.

ANGIE   Hey!!

STREET OUTSIDE A DEPARTMENT STORE.

In front of Alexander's Department Store, the street is crowded, and a bus queue waits for the downtown Concourse bus. Marty and Clara are part of the queue.

ANGIE   *(starting toward Marty and Clara, shouting)* Hey!

Angie starts into the street without waiting for the lights to change. Impatiently, he has to wait until traffic stops for the light.

ANGIE   *(shouting as he goes)* Hey, Marty! Hey!

Marty and Clara still stand, seeming not to hear Angie.

ANGIE'S VOICE   *(off-screen)* Hey, Marty! Marty!

Marty and Clara turn and stare off-screen.

Angie pushes his way through the CROWD on the sidewalk and manages to join Marty and Clara.

ANGIE   Where you been, for Pete sakes?! I been looking all over for you.

MARTY   I looked for you, Angie, before I cut out, but I couldn't find you.

ANGIE   I been looking all over for you!

Angie is absolutely unaware of, or simply refuses to acknowledge the presence of the girl. He has pushed himself in between Marty and Clara, and addresses himself entirely to Marty.

MARTY   What happened, Angie, was that we thought we were just gonna go for a short walk, and then we thought we were gonna come right back, but we got to talking. Listen, Angie, I want you to meet Clara...*(He tries to turn the sullen Angie toward Clara.)* Clara, this is my best friend, Angie. I told you about him.

CLARA   How do you do?

Angie acknowledges the introduction with a surly nod.

ANGIE   *(completely ignoring Clara now)* Waddaya gonna do now?

MARTY   I'm gonna take Clara home. It's close to one.

ANGIE   You want me to ride down with you?

MARTY   What for?

ANGIE   It's early.

MARTY   It must be one o'clock.

ANGIE   It's Saturday night! There's still plenty-a action around!

MARTY   Angie, by the time I get Clara home, it's gonna be one, one-thirty. By the time I get home, it's gonna be two o'clock. I gotta get up for ten o'clock mass tomorrow.

Angie stares with thick, sullen jealousy at his best friend. He turns sharply and starts away from Marty and Clara.

ANGIE   *(as he goes)* All right, I'll see you!

MARTY   *(calling after him)* Where you going?

Angie, feeling rejected and jealous, moves swiftly out into the other PEDES-TRIANS on Fordham Road.

MARTY   *(calling more loudly after him)* I'll see you tomorrow after mass!

He stares for a moment at the departing form of his friend, then turns to Clara with a shrug and a smile, as if to say, "I don't know what's the matter with him." The long-awaited downtown bus ROARS up to the corner, blocking our view of Marty and Clara.

LOWER-MIDDLE-CLASS BRONX STREET. NIGHT.

Marty and Clara stroll along the walk toward the front doors of an apartment house.

APARTMENT HOUSE LOBBY. NIGHT.

Marty and Clara enter and cross the lobby toward the stairway. They move slowly.

MARTY   You got an elevator in this house?

CLARA   We just live one flight up.

MARTY   So I'll call you tomorrow.

CLARA   Okay.

Clara leans against the iron banister of the stairway.

CLARA   Call me about two-thirty, because I won't be home from my aunt's till about then.

The doors of the ELEVATOR slide open, and a middle-aged COUPLE comes out. They have obviously been having a heated exchange; but at the sight of Marty and the girl at the stairway, they become silent. They march across the lobby and out to the street in repressed silence. The door CLANGS behind them.

Marty and Clara have waited stiffly through this interruption, and now they look at each other and smile.

MARTY   Okay, so I'll see you tomorrow night then.

CLARA   Okay.

Marty turns and moves across the lobby toward the street door.

OUTSIDE THE APARTMENT HOUSE.

Marty stands a moment in the clear black night air, expressionless, but within him, a strange exhilaration is beginning to stir. He mosies away from the building along the sidewalk, CAMERA panning with him.

He strikes out suddenly with a spirited stride, as if he knew where he was going.

176TH STREET.

CLOSER SHOT of Marty marching along 176th Street. He quickly reaches the Grand Concourse. Here he pauses a moment, a little at a loss for what direction to take—then remembers he needs the uptown bus.

He moves across the wide street to get to the other side of the boulevard. Again, he seems to lose track of which direction is homeward.

He walks uptown a ways with a strange jerky stride, pausing every once in a while to see whether there's a bus coming.

Suddenly Marty breaks into a dog-trot, then drops back into the stiff stride as he approaches...

THE INTERSECTION OF THE GRAND CONCOURSE.

The corner near the bus stop is deserted. Marty stops, leans against the pole of the bus stop sign.

Abruptly, he turns and walks uptown a little further.

SERIES OF INTERCUTS: Marty strides, walks, stops short, goes to the curb desultorily, a few paces into the street, moves back. The traffic moves by him. He stands in the wide street, then with a gesture of magnificent expansiveness, he raises his arm and calls out.

MARTY Taxi! Taxi! Hey, taxi! Taxi! Taxi!

CLOSE-UP of Marty standing in the street, crying...

MARTY Taxi!...Taxi!...

FADE OUT.

PILLETTI HOME, MARTY'S BEDROOM. DAY.

Marty is in his trousers and T-shirt. He whistles as he assembles his toilet articles for a shave. He starts out toward the living room, still whistling. Bright sunlight pours through the curtains on his window.

SECOND FLOOR.

Marty's whistling accompanies him to the second floor where he turns into the bathroom. CAMERA ANGLES to include Mrs. Pilletti's bedroom, disclosing her wearing an old faded batiste kimona, puttering around her room and cleaning. As Marty's toneless tune reaches her, Mrs. Pilletti turns her head and stares off, listening.

THOMAS AND VIRGINIA'S APARTMENT. DAY.

Catherine, in the living room, is packing her meager but neatly folded belongings into an old European carpet bag. She has regained her stiff, mordant crustiness. The mild WAIL of a baby can be heard.

BEDROOM.

The crowded bedroom is furnished in white modern. It is cluttered by a baby's bassinet and other baby items. Virginia sits on the edge of the bed, holding the baby, quieting it. She is half-dressed, wearing her pajama top, a half-slip, no stockings; her hair is still uncombed. Thomas slouches against a chest of drawers, in morning semi-deshabille. He is obviously sick with guilt. Virginia looks anxiously at her husband then to the baby in her arms.

VIRGINIA *(heavy whisper)* Don't you think I feel lousy about this too?

THOMAS All right, Ginnie. I don't wanna talk anymore about it. *(sits on a wooden chair, unrolls a fresh pair of socks he's been holding)* I don't think I got one hour's sleep the whole night. *(raises one leg to put a sock on, pauses with his heel on the edge of his chair)* Last night was the first time in my life I ever heard my mother cry, you know that?

VIRGINIA Tommy...

THOMAS *(snapping)* I don't wanna talk about it!

He pulls his sock on angrily, then lets his leg fall back to the floor and just sits, one sock on, one sock in his hand. He looks sullenly in the direction of his wife.

THOMAS *(continuing, huffy)* I know what you're gonna say. A man's gotta stop being his mother's baby sooner or later. How many times you gonna say it? She's my mother, you know. I oughta have some feelings about her, don't you think?

VIRGINIA Why do you always put me inna position of being the louse?

THOMAS *(in a furious whisper)* Virginia, I don't wanna hear no more about it!

He stands, then becomes aware he has to put on his other sock. He sits down again and pulls the second sock on. Virginia has had a hot reply in her mouth, but she forces it back. She rocks the baby a little.

VIRGINIA Tommy, I love you, and I know you feel lousy right now, but we're never gonna be happy unless we have a chance to work out our own lives. We can't keep talking in whispers like this the resta our lives. We gotta have some privacy. We...

Thomas has risen, a slim, dark, unsettled young man in undershirt and trousers, holding his shoes in one hand. He starts toward the...

FOYER.

Thomas strides down the little foyer. He turns and looks into the living room. He watches his mother packing strange brown parcels into her bag.

THOMAS *(scowling)* Can't you wait five minutes? I'll drive you over inna car. I just gotta put my shirt on, that's all.

The old lady nods brusquely.

LIVING ROOM.

Thomas stands with his head bowed to hide the tears he feels sweeping into his hot eyes. Then he returns to his bedroom in his stocking-feet, carrying his shoes.

BEDROOM.

Thomas comes in just as Virginia bends over the bassinet, having gotten the baby back to sleep. Thomas cries to her in a furious whisper.

THOMAS   All right, get dressed, because we're gonna drive my mother over. Why couldn't you get along with her?! Why couldn't you make just a little effort?! She's a little hard to get along with! All right! All I asked you was try a little.

He turns from her, sits down on the bed miserably angry with the world, his wife, his mother, himself. The baby begins to whimper again. Virginia turns wearily to her husband.

VIRGINIA   Tommy...

THOMAS   *(roaring out)* I don't wanna hear anymore about it, you hear me?

MARTY'S HOME, FRONT PORCH. DAY.

A small procession consisting of Thomas carrying his mother's carpet bag, his mother carrying small paper-wrapped bundles, and Virginia holding the baby comes across the front hedge. Thomas leads the parade with a muffled sorrow. They turn up the porch to the front door. Virginia remains in the small front yard. She is miserable.

PILLETTI HOME, DINING ROOM. DAY.

Mrs. Pilletti is dressed in hat and coat and all set to go to mass. She is bent over the dining room table piling the breakfast dishes and crumbing the table. She looks up as Thomas comes in carrying his mother's bag. Aunt Catherine is right behind him. Beyond the porch, we can see Virginia walking the baby around outside.

THOMAS Hello, Aunt Theresa.

MRS. PILLETTI Hello, Thomas, how do you feel?

THOMAS *(setting the bag down)* Ah, my mother, she drives me crazy. I hadda beg her to let me drive her over here. The martyr. She always gotta be the big martyr.

CATHERINE Hey, will you go to mass, please. This one, he woke up this morning with salt in his nose. Do this! Do that! Will you leave me in peace, ah?

A burst of spirited song soars from upstairs. Mrs. Pilletti, Aunt Catherine and even Thomas pause to look up in the direction of the voice.

HALLWAY/STAIRWAY.

Marty descends the stairs whistling. He carries his jacket over his arm. He makes some final adjustments to his tie.

DINING ROOM.

Alert to Marty's mood, Mrs. Pilletti, Aunt Catherine and Thomas stand, waiting for him to join them downstairs.

MARTY *(ebulliently)* Hello, Aunt Catherine! How are you? Hello, Thomas. You going to mass with us?

CATHERINE I was at mass two hours ago.

MARTY Well, make yourself at home. The refrigerator is loaded with food. Go upstairs, take any room you want. Thomas, you going to mass with us?

THOMAS *(nods)* Yeah, yeah, sure.

He abruptly goes out into the living room and onto the front porch.

MRS. PILLETTI   *(to Catherine)* You wanna cuppa coffee?

Marty has followed Thomas out into the living room.

MARTY   Boy, beautiful day, hey, Thomas?

THOMAS   Sure, great if you ain't married.

Thomas goes out the door onto the porch. Marty stands in the open doorway. He looks out into the warm sunshine in the front yard.

MARTY   Hi, Virginia.

He goes out into the yard to Virginia. He is as gay as a bird. He takes the baby from Virginia's arms, holds it high up above him.

MARTY   *(to baby)* Hey, little boy, you sure getting fat. You weigh more than a side-a beef now. *(beams at the baby)* Hey, Thomas, so I was telling you yesterday you was over my house—Mr. Gazzara, my boss, so he wantsa sell his shop, go out to California because his kids are all married, and he...

Thomas hasn't been listening to Marty and crosses quickly to Virginia.

THOMAS   Wadda *you* so sore about?

VIRGINIA   Oh shaddup, will you do me a favor?

Marty comes up to them, holding the baby.

MARTY   So Thomas, he does about twelve, thirteen hundred gross. Rent's a hundred and two. The problem, of course, is the supermarkets. That's what I wanna ask you. If I get together with a coupla other merchants, make our own supermarket...

Thomas has been trying to listen to Marty, but his thoughts are all with his own problem. He whirls on Virginia.

THOMAS   What about the time she wanted to make an old-fashioned Italian dinner for my brother, but you wouldn't let her!?

VIRGINIA   *(with her own temper)* Waddaya talking about?!!

THOMAS   Once a month you couldn't let her use the kitchen!

VIRGINIA   I told her she could use the kitchen any time she wanted...

THOMAS   ...You hadda be the boss inna kitchen alla time!

VIRGINIA   She don't wanna use my pots and pans!

MARTY   So Tommy...

VIRGINIA   Waddaya want me to do, go out and buy a whole new setta pots and pans?!

The baby in Marty's arms has started to cry a little.

MARTY   Tommy, gimme a coupla minutes, because I promised Mr. Gazzara I'd let him know tomorrow. See, what I wanna know, Tom, if a buncha individual retail merchants get together, how does it operate? On individual mark-ups? You know what I mean? Say I'm the butcher and Aldo Capelli, he's the dairyman and grocer, so suppose I mark up thirty-five percent, but he works on forty, so...

THOMAS   Waddaya talking about, do you know what you're talking about?

MARTY   No, I don't know. That's why I'm asking you.

The baby starts to cry again. Thomas turns to his wife.

THOMAS   Take the baby, will you?!

Virginia hurries over and takes the crying baby from Marty's arms, walks around comforting the child. Thomas turns back to Marty.

THOMAS   Wadda you wanna buy a shop for, will you tell me? You gotta good job, you got no wife, you got no responsibilities. Boy, I wish I was you, boy. Waddaya wanna tie yourself down with a shop? What's he want? Five thousand down? You're gonna have to carry a mortgage sixty, seventy bucks a month. A mortgage anna note from the bank. For Pete's sake, you're a single man with no responsibilities. Stay that way, boy. Take my advice.

MARTY   Well, you see, Thomas I figure the big problem is the supermarkets. But Patsy's shop, that's a specialized trade. The supermarkets don't carry Italian meat.

THOMAS   Who buys Italian meat anymore? You think my wife buys Italian meat? *(throws a baleful glance at his wife)* She goes to the A&P, picks up some lamb chops wrapped in cellophane, opens up a canna peas, and that's dinner, boy.

VIRGINIA   Sure, all you wanna eat is that greasy stuff your mother makes.

Marty is a little taken aback by Thomas's frontal assault.

MARTY   Well, I understand the problem about the supermarkets, but I was talking to this girl last night, and she made the point that a likeable personality is a valuable business asset.

THOMAS   Marty, see that my mother is nice and comfortable, eh?

MARTY   Sure. This girl said...

THOMAS   What girl, what does she know? *(He whirls on his wife again.)* Why don't you let her hold the baby once in a while?! Your mother, boy, she wantsa take the kid for a day, that's fine!

VIRGINIA *(her temper flaring again)* Your mother handles the kid like he was a yoyo!

Marty stands, watching the young couple yakking at each other. The little baby starts to cry again.

KITCHEN.

The two old sisters sit at the kitchen table, two untouched cups of coffee in front of them.

MRS. PILLETTI Hey, I come home from your house last night, Marty was here with a girl.

CATHERINE Who?

MRS. PILLETTI Marty.

CATHERINE Your son Marty?

MRS. PILLETTI Well, what Marty you think is gonna be here in this house with a girl?

CATHERINE Were the lights on?

MRS. PILLETTI Oh sure. *(frowns at her sister)* This girl is a college graduate.

CATHERINE They're the worst. College girls are one step from the streets. They smoke like men inna saloon. My son Joseph, his wife, you know, she types onna typewriter. One step from the streets, I tell you.

Mrs. Pilletti ponders this philosophy for a moment.

MRS. PILLETTI That's the first time Marty ever brought a girl to this house. She seems like a nice girl. I think he has a feeling for this girl. You heard him sing. He been singing like that all morning.

Catherine nods bleakly.

CATHERINE   Well, that's all. You will see. Today, tomorrow, inna week, he's gonna say to you, "Hey, Ma, it's no good being a single man. I'm tired-a running around." Then he's gonna say, "Hey, Ma, wadda we need this old house? Why don't we sell this old house, move into a nicer parta town? A nice little apartment?"

MRS. PILLETTI   I don't sell this house, I tell you that. This is my husband's house. I had six children in this house.

CATHERINE   You will see. A coupla months, you gonna be an old lady, sleeping onna couch in her daughter-in-law's house.

MRS. PILLETTI   Catherine, you are a blanket of gloom. Wherever you are, the rain follows. Someday, you gonna smile, and we gonna declare a holiday.

Marty comes in from the living room, a little down after his session with Thomas and Virginia.

MARTY   Hello, Ma, waddaya say, it's getting a little late.

MRS. PILLETTI   Sure.

Marty goes to the sink to get himself a glass of water. He examines a piece of plaster that has fallen from the ceiling.

MARTY   Boy, this place is really coming to pieces. *(turning to his mother)* You know, Ma, I think we oughta sell this place. The whole joint's going to pieces. The plumbing is rusty. Everything. I'm gonna have to replaster the whole ceiling now. You know what we oughta do? We oughta get one of those new apartments they're building down on Southern Boulevard. A nicer parta town, you know?...You all set, Ma?

Mrs. Pilletti exchanges a brief frightened glance with her sister.

MRS. PILLETTI   I'm all set.

She sends another frightened look at her sister and follows Marty out into the living room.

MARTY'S PORCH.

Marty, his mother, Thomas and Virginia with the baby file down the porch to the street on their way to church. Marty and his mother are both troubled. The anger has left both Thomas and Virginia, but they are both silent. At the far end of the alleyway, as they reach the street, Virginia puts her free arm through her husband's elbow. Thomas looks briefly at her and they exchange a look of commiseration. Everyone turns and disappears off into the street.

CHURCH.

A HIGH, WIDE ANGLE SHOT of the church establishes that stage of Sunday morning between the nine and ten o'clock masses. People flock around the doors of the church.

INSIDE THE CHURCH.

The parishioners are making their ways to the door. A few silent penitents still kneel here and there in the long empty rows of pews. The large, almost empty church is filled now with organ MUSIC.

Both Marty and his mother seem a little depressed as they stand at the doorway just inside the church, as the nine o'clock mass people flow out, and the first of the ten o'clock mass people file in.

MRS. PILLETTI   That was a nice girl last night, Marty. *(Marty nods.)* She wasn't a very good-looking girl, but she looks like a nice girl. *(She pauses, Marty makes no reply.)* I said, she wasn't a very good-looking girl...not very pretty...

MARTY   *(still amiable)* I heard you, Ma.

MRS. PILLETTI   She looks a little old for you. About thirty-five, forty
years old?

MARTY   She's twenty-nine, Ma.

*A nearby kneeling penitent looks disapprovingly at Mrs. Pilletti and shushes
her. The mother nods briefly.*

MRS. PILLETTI   She's more than twenty-nine years old, Marty. That's
what she tells you.

MARTY   What, Ma?

MRS. PILLETTI   She looks thirty-five, forty. She didn't look Italian to me.

Marty frowns but remains silent.

MRS. PILLETTI   I said, is she Italian girl?

MARTY   I don't know. I don't think so.

It's Mrs. Pilletti's turn to frown. A silence. She turns back to Marty.

MRS. PILLETTI   She don't look Italian to me. What kinda family she come
from? There was something about her I didn't like. It seems funny,
the first time you meet her, she comes to your empty house alone.
These college girls, they all one step fromma streets.

Marty turns, on the verge of anger with his mother.

MARTY   What are you talking about? She's a nice girl.

MRS. PILLETTI   She didn't look Italian to me.

A silence hangs between them.

MRS. PILLETTI   I don't like her.

MARTY   You don't like her. You only met her for two minutes.

MRS. PILLETTI   Don't bring her to the house no more.

MARTY   What didn't you like about her?

MRS. PILLETTI   I don't know! She don't look like Italian to me. Plenny a nice Italian girls around.

MARTY   Well, let's not get inna fight about it, Ma.

The kneeling woman shushes them again. By now the nine o'clock worshipers have filed out, and Marty joins the flow of ten o'clock people moving in. His mother turns back to him again.

MARTY   *(stopping her before she gets started)* What are you getting so worked up about? I just met the girl last night. I'm probably not gonna see her again.

They continue down the aisle of the church.

BAR. DAY.

An hour later, the after-mass CROWD is there. It's a little more crowded than weekdays. A WOMAN with a glass of beer in one hand, rocks a baby carriage with the other.

Marty enters the bar, moves along, ad-libbing "Hello" to someone at the bar, gets the attention of Lou, the bartender.

MARTY   Hello, Lou, Angie come in yet?

BARTENDER   He was here last night till about two o'clock. I hear you really got stuck with a dog last night.

MARTY   *(glancing quickly at him)* Who told you that?

BARTENDER   Angie. He says she was a real scrawny-looking thing.

MARTY   She wasn't so bad.

He turns away from the bar annoyed, notes Ralph, sitting alone in one of the booths, reading the Sunday comics. Marty ambles over to him.

MARTY   Hello, Ralph. How'd you make out with those nurses last night, Ralph?

RALPH   *(looking up)* Oh man, you shoulda come with us last night, Marty. That one for you was a real lunatic. How'd you make out?

The abruptness of the question rather startles Marty. It is not an expression he would normally associate with an evening with Clara.

MARTY   Oh, I hadda nice time...I didn't try nothing. She's a nice girl. I just met her last night, you know. I just talked with her. I didn't even try nothing...

He feels very ill at ease and a little guilty for defending himself.

MARTY   Listen, you see Angie, tell him I went home, I'll meet him after lunch.

He moves back down the bar and goes out into the street.

DISSOLVE TO:

MARTY'S HOUSE, DINING ROOM. AFTERNOON.

Marty is seated at the dining room table. He has removed his jacket, tie and shirt, even his shoes, and is making himself comfortable over a late Sunday lunch. With him are Angie and Joe, the Critic. Lounging in a chair but not at the table is Leo.

JOE   ...so the whole book winds up, Mike Hammer, he's inna room there with this doll. So he says, "You rat, you are the murderer." So she begins to con him, you know? She tells him how she loves him. And then Bam! He shoots her in the stomach. So she's laying there, gasping for breath, and she says, "How could you do that?" And he says, "It was easy."

LEO *(without looking up from his magazine)* Boy, that Mickey Spillane, boy he can write.

Angie reaches over to Marty's plate and filches a piece of rissole, evidently annoying Marty.

MARTY   We gotta whole pot inna kitchen. We give you a plate-a your own.

ANGIE   Oh, I couldn't eat nothing. My mother just stuffed me right up to the jaws.

This doesn't prevent him from filching a second piece of rissole.

JOE   What I like about Mickey Spillane is he knows how to handle women. In one book, he picks up a tomato who gets hit with a car, and she throws a pass at him. And then he meets two beautiful twins, and they throw passes at him. And then he meets some beautiful society leader, and she throws a pass at him, and...

LEO   Boy, that Mickey Spillane, he sure can write.

ANGIE   Listen, somebody turn onna ballgame. It must be after one o'clock by now.

Marty looks down at his watch, then stands and starts for the phone, sitting on a chest of drawers at the other end of the room.

ANGIE   Who you gonna call?

MARTY   I was gonna call that girl from last night. Take her to a movie tonight.

ANGIE   Are you kidding?

MARTY   Listen, Angie, I wanna tell you, you were very impolite last night. I introduced you to the girl, you just turned and walked off. Now, why did you do that?

ANGIE   You got me mad, that's why. Hey, Joe, show Marty that picture.

Joe, having finished his dissertation on Mickey Spillane, is now studying another girlie magazine. He proffers an opened page to Marty, who stands over by the phone.

MARTY   Put that away, for Pete's sake. My mother's right out onna porch.

JOE   I wonder where they find those girls that pose for them pictures.

LEO   Those are Hollywood starlets.

MARTY   Put it away, Joe. My mother'll come walking in.

Joe closes the magazine.

ANGIE   Marty, let's go downna Seventy-Second Street area tonight.

MARTY   I don't feel like going, Angie. I thought I'd take this girl to a movie.

ANGIE   Boy, you really musta made out good last night.

MARTY   We just talked.

ANGIE   Boy, she musta been some talker. She musta been about fifty years old.

JOE   I always figure a guy oughta marry a girl who's twenny years younger than he is so that when he's forty, his wife is a real nice-looking doll.

LEO   That means he'd have to marry the girl when she was one year old.

JOE   I never thoughta that.

MARTY   I didn't think she was so bad-looking.

ANGIE   She musta kept you inna shadows all night.

RALPH   Marty, you don't wanna hang around with dogs. It gives you a bad reputation.

ANGIE   Let's go downa Seventy-Second Street.

MARTY   I told this dog I was gonna call her today about two-thirty.

ANGIE   *(angry)* Brush her. Listen, you wanna come with me tonight, or you wanna go with this dog?

MARTY   Waddaya getting so sore about?

ANGIE   I looked all over for you last night, you know that?

He turns away sulking. Marty doesn't pick up the phone but returns to his seat, upset.

JOE   Another book that I read by Mickey Spillane, I can't remember the name of it, but it was about this red-headed tramp he finds inna street, and he gives her some dough, because he's sorry for her...Wait a minute, I think that's the same book I was telling you about before...

MARTY   *(to Angie)* You didn't like her at all?

ANGIE   A nothing. A real nothing.

Marty lowers his head. Over this, Joe's VOICE DRONES on.

JOE'S VOICE *(off-screen)* You know something...?

CAMERA ANGLE HOLDS on Marty looking down, as Joe's VOICE continues.

JOE'S VOICE *(off-screen)* ...I can't tell one-a those Mickey Spillane books from the other, but he's a real good writer, though...

SLOW DISSOLVE TO:

SNYDER APARTMENT. NIGHT.

CLOSE ON television screen. Ed Sullivan is on, indicating the time is a little after half past seven. CAMERA PULLS BACK, disclosing Clara, Mr. and Mrs. Snyder in their living room. Apparently the Sullivan show is very funny at the moment, for the television audience roars with laughter. CAMERA MOVES IN CLOSE ON Clara. Another ROAR of LAUGHTER from the television that Clara watches, although her eyes are flooded with tears, several of which have already traced wet paths down her cheeks. Another ROAR of laughter.

DISSOLVE TO:

PILLETTI HOME, DINING ROOM. NIGHT.

Marty, Mrs. Pilletti and Catherine are eating silently at the table. Catherine reads an Italian newspaper as she eats.

MRS. PILLETTI So what are you gonna do tonight, Marty?

MARTY I don't know, Ma. I'm all knocked out. I think I'll just hang arounna house and watch...

Suddenly he pauses, sharply aware of the repetition in his life. Mrs. Pilletti is also aware of it.

MARTY Maybe, I'll go out and see what Angie and the boys are doing...

They eat silently a moment.

187TH STREET. BAR. NIGHT.

CLOSE-UP of Marty leaning against the wall in front of the bar. A group of young men lounge about, killing time.

Angie, Leo and Joe are among them. There are perhaps four or five other young MEN, loosely divided into two groups. The group that concerns us has Marty and the others mentioned and GEORGE, a young man in a sport jacket.

LEO What time is it?

JOE About eight o'clock.

ANGIE *(to George)* You don't feel like going downna Seventy-Second Street?

GEORGE It'll take an hour anna hour back, and the whole evening's gone.

JOE What's playing on Fordham Road? I think there's a good picture in the Loew's Paradise.

GEORGE You guys feel like working up a game-a cards?

ANGIE Come on, let's go down Seventy-Second Street, walk around. We're sure to wind up with something.

CLOSE-UP of Marty, his head down, his eyes closed. The group continues their dialogue back and forth. Their VOICES can be heard as Marty's head slowly comes up.

JOE'S VOICE *(off-screen)* I'll never forgive LaGuardia for cutting out burlesque outta New York City...

GEORGE'S VOICE (*off-screen*) There's a burlesque in Union City. Let's go over to Union City...

ANGIE'S VOICE (*off-screen*) Yeah, you're the one who don't even wanna take a ride onna subway for half an hour. Now, you wanna go alla way over to Union City...

GEORGE'S VOICE (*off-screen*) I feel like playing cards. I saw Richie Rizzo, that's what he said he felt like doing...

JOE'S VOICE (*off-screen*) I don't feel like playing cards. Waddaya feel like doing tonight, Angie?

ANGIE'S VOICE (*off-screen*) I don't know. Wadda you feel like doing?

JOE'S VOICE (*off-screen*) I don't know, Angie. Wadda you feel like doing?

A fury rises in Marty's face. He cries out at them.

MARTY   "What are you doing tonight?"..."I don't know, what are you doing?!"...

CAMERA ANGLES over to the others who, at this outburst, stare at Marty astounded.

MARTY (*continuing*) The burlesque! Loew's Paradise! Miserable and lonely! Miserable and lonely and stupid! What am I, crazy or something?! I got something good here! What am I hanging around with you guys for?!

He has said this in tones so loud that it attracts the attention of the few PEO-PLE on the street. A little embarrassed by the attention he's getting, he turns, opens the door to the bar, and goes into it.

After a stunned moment, Angie hurries after him.

INSIDE THE BAR.

Marty marches the length of the room toward the phone booths in the rear. CAMERA ANGLES to disclose Angie right behind him.

Marty is about to enter one of the phone booths, but he stops as Angie hurries up to him.

ANGIE   Watsa matter with you?

Marty pauses, one foot in the booth.

MARTY   You don't like her. My mother don't like her. She's a dog, and I'm a fat, ugly little man. All I know is I hadda good time last night. I'm gonna have a good time tonight. If we have enough good times together, I'm gonna go down on my knees and beg that girl to marry me. If we make a party again this New Year's, I gotta date for the party. You don't like her, that's too bad.

Marty has been fishing in his pocket for his address book. He opens it to its proper page and steps decisively into the phone booth.

Nearby, Angie prowls around outside the booth. The booth door is open. Marty starts to dial. A hush fills the room except for the CLICKING of the telephone dial.

INSIDE THE PHONE BOOTH.

The look of fury has drained from Marty's face. He holds the receiver to his ear, glances out toward Angie. CAMERA ANGLES to include Angie.

MARTY   *(his old amiable self)* When you gonna get married, Angie? Aren't you ashamed of yourself? You're thirty-three years old. All your kid brothers are married. You oughta be ashamed of yourself.

Still smiling at his very private joke, Marty returns to the phone, and after a fraction of a second...

MARTY Hello...Clara?...

As Angie looks miserable, and Marty slowly reaches out and pushes the phone booth door shut, and continues to talk into the phone, we very slowly...

FADE OUT.

THE END

THE GODDESS

1958

Original Story and Screenplay
by PADDY CHAYEFSKY

Produced by MILTON PERLMAN

Directed by JOHN CROMWELL

FOR SUE

CAST CREDITS

EMILY ANN FAULKNER & RITA SHAWN	Kim Stanley
DUTCH SEYMOUR	Lloyd Bridges
EMILY ANN FAULKNER (age 4)	Chris Flanagan
THE MOTHER (LORRAINE)	Betty Lou Holland
THE AUNT (ALICE MARIE)	Joan Copeland
THE UNCLE (GEORGE)	Gerald Hiken
EMILY ANN FAULKNER (age 8)	Patty Duke
THE BOY (LEWIS)	Burt Brinckerhoff
THE FIRST G.I.	Roy Shuman
THE SECOND G.I.	John Lawrence
JOHN TOWER	Steve Hill
THE MINISTER	Gerald Petrarca
BRIDESMAID	Linda Soma
THE WRITER	Curt Conway
JOANNA	Joanna Linville
HILLARY	Joyce Van Patten
BURT HARRES	David White
FIRST MAN	Mike O'Dowd
SECOND MAN	Sid Raymond
LESTER BRACKMAN	Bert Freed
R.M. LUCAS	Donald McKee
MRS. WOOLSY	Margaret Brayton
MR. WOOLSY	Werner Klemperer
THE COOK	Louise Beavers
THE ELDER	Fred Herrick
THE SECRETARY	Elizabeth Wilson
THE DAUGHTER	Gail Haworth

FADE IN:

UNDER THE CREDITS: A Greyhound bus, vintage 1930, rolls along on a highway. It is a bright summer day. This is tobacco and farm country, long, flat fields, farmhouses.

The following legend appears:

PART ONE
Portrait of a Girl

After this has faded, this legend:

BEACON CITY, MARYLAND
1930

THE GODDESS

FADE IN on interior of the bus.

CLOSE TWO SHOT of a young MOTHER, aged 26, and her four-year-old daughter. The mother is somber, staring out of the window. The little GIRL is sleeping in her seat. The bus is half-filled with people whose faces are grim.

CLOSE UP of the mother looking expressionlessly out the window.

MOTHER'S P.O.V.: A desolate farm, a broken-down deserted barn, a rusted plow or barrow projecting forlornly out of a wild tobacco field.

MOTHER'S P.O.V.: A deserted "loose-floor" or tobacco warehouse, windows broken or boarded up, the large front door gaping open and hanging loose on broken hinges. We see a large, crude, hand-printed sign as we rumble by. It reads: "CLOSED FOR DEPRESSION."

EXTERIOR. Main street. Dusk. The bus rumbles into the main street of a fair-to-middling-sized town.

MEDIUM SHOT: The bus as the mother and the little girl disembark. They stand a moment, looking at the strange town. The bus pulls away.

MOTHER'S P.O.V.: A row of stores, boarded up or with broken windows. A feed shop with a large sign slashed across its window: "NO CREDIT!" Camera pans slowly. Four or five gloomy men stand morosely, incommunicatively, in front of the courthouse. Two old 1930 and older trucks, two cars, dusty and beaten, stagger down the almost empty street. A greasy hamburger joint where two men lounge silently in front of it, watching to see who gets off the bus. The Hotel Montgomery silent and grimy. A dry-cleaning shop, and then a series of indistinguishable shops, gray and listless in the gathering dusk. The stores eventually trail off into small two-story brick buildings and small white clapboard houses. In short, the main street of a Southern town of 10,000 population in 1930.

The mother checks an address on a piece of paper that she has taken out of her purse, studies the numbers on the stores in front of her, and starts off down the street toward the private houses in the distance. The little girl tags after her.

THE UNCLE'S HOME.

A pleasant-looking woman in her early thirties wearing a house dress admires the little girl and beams at her. The little girl is the center of a circle consisting of the woman holding her who is her AUNT, a smiling but harried-looking man in his late thirties who is her UNCLE, and her mother. When they begin talking, we will realize that all three are Southerners.

The parlor is typically lower-middle-class Southern. It has a cluttered feeling, owing more to the sobriety of the furnishings than to an excess of bric-a-brac. There is a long table on which sits a series of family portraits, and a small fireplace over which sits a modest mantel. The end tables all have doilies, and there is a candy dish on each one. There is the inevitable overstuffed chair and the platform rocker, a heavy standing lamp with fringed shade and a heavy table lamp with fringed shade. The somberness is hardly relieved by a calendar with a Protestant-type religious picture on it and two or three other pictures in the temper of "Jesus in the Garden." There are a number of maga-

zines and catalogues piled neatly on the mantel, mostly Good Housekeeping, *Sears, Roebuck catalogues, and* The Progressive Farmer.

THE AUNT *(bursting with enthusiasm at the little girl she holds)* Oh, she's just adorable!

THE MOTHER Emily Ann, what do you say to your Aunt Alice when she says how pretty you are?

The mother seems abruptly to have forsaken the stony melancholia that hung over her in the preceding scenes. She is all pretty Southern belle now, eyes flashing, gay almost to the point of lightheadedness, comfortable in the flurry of formalities of visiting and being welcomed.

THE UNCLE She is the spitting image of you, Lorraine!

THE MOTHER I can't believe you never saw her before! Has it been that long? Wasn't you down in Mama's, George, when we was...No, you wasn't there. Betty Flo said you was sick. That's right, you was sick. Oh, my, you have a lovely home here. I sold my house, George. It broke my heart, but the creditors were hovering around us like vultures, and the mortgages—I don't know how many there was. Papa came down and handled all the details. We got four thousand dollars for it from a man who lived in Knoxville, but all that was left when we paid Herbert's debts was seven hundred dollars. Well, wasn't that just like Herbert, committing suicide and leaving me with so many debts—I don't have a house any more! Oh, for heaven's sakes, George, don't look so alarmed. I haven't come up here to stay with you more than a four- or five-day visit.

THE UNCLE Well, Lorraine, we fixed you up a nice room here and you can stay as long as you want.

He darts a quick look at his wife, who points out things through the window for the little girl.

THE AUNT *(from the window)* Lorraine, I'm sure you would like something to eat or drink or something.

THE MOTHER   Well, I been riding six hours in that bus, and I'll tell you
what I would like. I'd like a good drink of whisky. That's what I would
like.

THE UNCLE   *(going to the sideboard)* Sure.

THE MOTHER   *(sinking into a soft chair, exhausted)* Mama's fine, George,
and sends you her love.

THE AUNT   *(carrying the little girl to the kitchen)* I'm going to get this little
girl some milk and cake.

THE MOTHER   Well, she certainly takes to you, Alice Marie. She don't
readily let people hold her like that.

*The aunt exits. The mother sends a quick, probing look over to her brother,
who is pouring a drink for her at the sideboard.*

THE MOTHER   Well, she certainly does take to Alice Marie, George. It's a
pity you all never had children. I know how much Alice Marie has
wanted a child. They are a joy and a mainstay in times of distress. The
night that Herbert shot himself in the head I cried and I cried. And
then I went upstairs and I went into Emily Ann's room, and I looked
down at her sweet, sleeping face, and I was able to face the terrible
burdens that were ahead of me.

THE UNCLE   *(bringing the drink to her)* We meant to come down to
Herbert's funeral, but I had my jaundice, and...

THE MOTHER   *(takes the drink and sips it a little nervously)* I can't tell you
what the five years of my marriage was like. Mama said I shouldn't
have married him. I could have had any number of boys. You know
that, George. I thought he was going to be such a successful man.
Everybody said he was a live wire. He was going to have a chain of
drycleaning stores all through Tennessee. Oh, he was a big talker, he
was. Well, he was a failure, and I told him so. He was common, and I
married beneath me, and I got my proper due. Left alone with a four-

year-old child, without even a nigger to help me, and a hundred and seventy-one dollars in the bank. What am I supposed to do now?

She swallows the rest of her whisky and hands the glass back for more.

THE UNCLE *(pouring the second drink)* I could let you have a little bit of money, but there's a depression on, you know, and...

The mother stands, takes the second drink and smiles, the brittle facade of the lighthearted Southern belle promptly restored to her face.

THE MOTHER Now, let's not talk about these things! My goodness, I haven't seen my own brother in five years, and this should be a joyous occasion!

UNCLE'S HOUSE, GUESTROOM.

Emily Ann now lies in a bed but not asleep. Her eyes are wide open. The room is dark and hushed. The only light is a thin shaft coming sharply in from the second-story landing outside. A silhouette and then a second silhouette pass across the slightly open doorway, momentarily blocking out the light. The little girl's head turns to see what it was.

LANDING OUTSIDE THE BEDROOM.

The uncle and the aunt are at the top of the stairs leading down to the first floor. The uncle has already started down the stairs but is being kept from going any farther by his wife's desire for a whispered conference. The uncle has the air of having gone through this particular conference a thousand times.

THE UNCLE *(heavy whisper, containing his irritation)* I don't know what she wants, Ellie. She says she don't want any money. She says she don't want to live with us. I don't know what she wants.

They stand a moment, at the head of the stairs, silent, frowning, anxious, and then the uncle starts down the stairs. A moment later, the aunt follows

*him. Three quarters of the way down the narrow staircase there is a closed
door which the uncle opens.*

THE AUNT   Might as well leave the door open, George. Let the heat up.

*They continue out of sight past the door. CAMERA PULLS BACK so as to
see the bedroom door open and the little girl cautiously pad barefoot onto the
upper landing. She stands at the head of the dark, narrow stairs trying to
look down. She wears a cotton nightie.*

THE PARLOR. NIGHT.

*The mother, wearing a flouncy Southern-belle-type dress, is at the mantel
looking at a pile of magazines on a table. The uncle is seated warily, still
glum, in his soft chair. The aunt perches watchfully on the edge of the mohair
davenport. Through the chintz-curtained window, we see it is a dark night
out.*

THE MOTHER   Don't you have no movie magazines, Alice Marie? Is all you
   got, *The Progressive Farmer?*

THE AUNT   I tucked your little girl in and...

THE MOTHER   *(straightening)* Well, she certainly takes to you, Alice Marie.
   She is absolutely crazy about you. I never did see her take to anybody
   like she takes to you.

*She moves restlessly around the room, noting the pictures of Jesus on the wall,
the radio with its gaping speaker, the endless Georgian moldings on the wall,
all the while the bright toothy smile fixed on her face.*

THE MOTHER   Well, I must say that was a wonderful dinner. George, Alice
   Marie has made a wonderful home for you.

THE AUNT   Oh, come on in the kitchen. What we sitting out here in the
   parlor for?

THE MOTHER I always envied girls who can cook because I am dreadful in the kitchen. I am sort of gay and giddy, but that's my nature, smiling in the face of adversity. Can I turn the radio on?

The question is rhetorical; she has already done so.

THE AUNT Go right ahead, Lorraine.

THE MOTHER I can't remember the last time I went dancing. I can't remember the last time I did anything.

A razz-ma-tazz orchestra suddenly bursts out from the radio, playing "Exactly Like You," and the mother hurriedly bends to lower the volume.

THE MOTHER I do think I kept my figure, don't you think so, Alice Marie?

THE AUNT You don't look more than nineteen years old, Lorraine.

The mother dances a step or two of a fox trot. She is nervous, restless, fidgety.

THE MOTHER If I have a fault, it's I'm a little vain. I was anxious about my figure after Emily Ann was born, but I assiduously did exercises every morning, and I think everything is where it should be. I still catch an eye when I walk down a street. There was a man in the seat in front of me in the bus coming over to here that like to broke his neck trying to strike up an acquaintance. I do think I would like to get married again. What do you think a proper period of grace should be—about Herbert, I mean—before I go out seriously with a man? There is a man who I know is interested in me back in Clarksville. I don't know what else I can do except get married. I can't stand being alone! Can I please turn off the radio? It's driving me crazy!

She flicks the radio off.

THE UNCLE Well, now, Lorraine, you just sit down and take it easy and don't be so excited.

The mother shuts her eyes, sighs and makes a visible effort to get hold of herself.

THE AUNT   Sit down, Lorraine. You have been living through a terrible ordeal.

THE MOTHER   *(distraught)* Mama said I could come live with them in Knoxville, but she and Papa are living in that little dirty two-room apartment right on Main Street, right over the five-and-dime store. I would think they would die of shame living there! I couldn't live there! And this man says he's been in love with me for years! He's a very attractive man. A little elderly, but attractive! I mean, five days after we had buried Herbert, he was asking me to marry him! I said I would think about it. He has a very nice home. He lives there all by himself with his sister. But he doesn't like children. *(She stares at her sister-in-law and then at her brother.)* He says he don't want no four-year-old little girl hanging around his neck.

Again she stares at the two other people, wondering if they get the point. Then, taking the bit in her mouth, she says it.

THE MOTHER   I was wondering, since she's absolutely crazy about you, Alice Marie—I never saw her take to anyone like she took to you this afternoon—so I wonder if I could just leave her here just for a year or so, just till I manage matters better with this man.

THE AUNT   Lorraine, she's your own little girl!

THE MOTHER   You always said you wanted children, but...

THE AUNT   You can't just drop her on somebody's door-step like that, Lorraine.

THE UNCLE   Lorraine...

The mother fights back tears of fury and guilt, shame and confusion.

THE MOTHER (*crying out*) I'm only twenty-six years old! I still got my figure. I want to have a little fun. I can't support her. I haven't got any money!

THE UNCLE Maybe I could help you get a job.

THE MOTHER (*whirling on him*) I don't want no job! I don't want no dirty job!

THE AUNT Lorraine, honey, she's your baby.

THE MOTHER (*whirling on the aunt, a tantrumy little girl herself*) I don't want her! I don't want her! I was seventeen hours in labor with her, and she's been trouble ever since! I didn't want her when she was born, and I don't want her now!

THE UNCLE (*sharply*) Lorraine!

She turns away dissolved in tears, her thin shoulders shaking.

THE UNCLE (*airier for a moment*) Well, how about his family?

THE MOTHER I can't go to them.

THE UNCLE (*didn't hear her*) What?

THE MOTHER I can't go to them.

THE UNCLE Well, it's his kid too, Lorraine.

The mother now sits on the edge of the straight-back chair, her head bowed, her eyes closed against her tears.

THE MOTHER (*in a low voice*) I don't rightly think it is. (*She swallows, beyond shame now.*) Well, we didn't get along almost from the beginning, and I had to do something.

She stands, in control of herself again, but unable to face the other two, who are staring down at the floor.

THE MOTHER   Well, I expect I'll have to go out and get a job or something.

She moves out of the parlor into the entrance foyer, which contains the iron hall furnace and a settee. She suddenly looks up, conscious of being watched.

MOTHER'S P.O.V.:   Looking up the dark narrow stairway leading to the second floor. Just beyond the opened door, which is about six steps up, we can make out little Emily Ann, half lighted by the upstairs landing light, hunched over peering down into the entrance foyer.

CLOSE-UP of Emily Ann. Her little face is expressionless, but she has heard just about everything. She turns and moves back up the stairs away from the camera. We watch her till she disappears at the head of the stairs.

                                                                FADE OUT.

FADE IN:

SCHOOL PLAYGROUND. DAY.

HIGH ANGLE SHOT looking down on a crowded playground of a public school on a bright June day. The place is filled with boys and girls of all ages up to fourteen, a few teachers, and the sounds of high childish laughter.

Emily Ann, now a pretty girl of eight, in a plain cotton dress, carries a thin textbook and a brown envelope. She wears high ankle-support shoes and her hair is cut in the straight pageboy style of those years. She comes out of one of the doors of the school into the playground. We can now distinguish some of the words the kids are shouting at each other and to their parents. Apparently, it is promotion day, and some of the kids are comparing report cards or showing them to their teachers. We hear the following ad libs as camera slowly pans Emily Ann walking alone through the exuberance of the playground.

"I got promoted today. You get promoted?"

"I got Miss Coyne next year. Who you got?"

"We're in the same class! Hurrah! Hurrah! Hey, Thelma Sue, Sara Anne and I, we're in the same class next year."

Emily Ann has made her way to the gate in the high wire fence leading to the street.

MAIN STREET.

HIGH ANGLE SHOT looking down the length of Main Street, somewhat more thriving than the last time we saw it. The signs of the depression are gone, and the people seem more cheerful.

Men in their shirt sleeves, women shopping, stores open. Way down at the far end of the street we see the little form of Emily Ann walking toward us, carrying her textbook and her brown envelope.

THE FIVE-AND-DIME SHOP. DAY.

Emily Ann enters and looks around. The store consists of five counters running the length of the store. There is a sixth counter in the back. All of these counters are jammed with every conceivable form of notion, knickknack and odds and ends. Each wall is piled to the ceiling with boxes and cartons. Dresses and coats hang from the ceiling, obscuring the overhead light fixtures. It is a jumbled, crowded store, yet there are only one or two customers.

There are three salesladies; two of them stand leaning against one of the counters, gassing about this and that. One of these salesladies is Emily Ann's mother. She is thirty now, and hard lines have settled on her face. She uses too much rouge.

Emily Ann comes up the aisle toward them. The saleslady calls the mother's attention to her daughter's presence. She turns to the girl with a frown of annoyance.

THE MOTHER *(annoyed)* What do you want, what do you want, honey?

The little girl regards her mother for a moment.

EMILY ANN   I got promoted today.

THE MOTHER   That's fine. Now you go on home.

EMILY ANN   *(proffering the envelope)* Here's my report card.

THE MOTHER   I'll look at it later. Now go on home. I told you not to come around here when I'm working.

She turns back to her colleague and starts gassing away again. The little girl turns and goes back down the aisle to the open street door and out into the street.

RESIDENTIAL STREET. DAY.

Emily Ann stands in the driveway of a pretty, typically Southern shingle house and calls to a friend who apparently lives here.

EMILY ANN   *(calling to the second floor)* Sylvia! You home, Sylvia? *(no answer; pause)* Sylvia! I got promoted. I'm in Miss Cahill's class next year! *(She waits for some answer again; there is apparently nobody home.)* Missus Lyons, you home? Anybody home? *(Apparently not; she waits another moment, then turns and walks away.)*

STREET IN SLUM SECTION.

LONG SHOT ACROSS Emily Ann's thin back to an empty lot in which four or five black kids are playing. Camera pans a little bit around, just enough to see the wistful expression on Emily Ann's face as she watches them. Then she turns and walks a little farther down what seems to be a pretty ramshackle street and turns in at one of the ramshackle houses. This is one of those two-family houses in which the family on the second floor climbs an out-side stairway to get to its apartment.

Emily Ann gets to the top of the stairs, taking a key from the window sill, opening the door, and going into the apartment. In the background we see clothes hanging on lines and other indications of the slum quality of the area.

EMILY ANN'S HOME.

LONG SHOT looking from the kitchen through the living room to the front door of the apartment as Emily Ann enters. It is a cheerless, inadequately furnished place; bare walls, sparse furniture, several religious calendars on the wall, dark, even on this bright June afternoon. A large old white icebox with the paint chipping off stands in the living room by the kitchen door. The reason it isn't in the kitchen is because the wood-burning stove lets off so much heat it would melt all the ice.

The kitchen itself is dank and unappetizing. Worn, patchy linoleum covers the floor. There is a tall wall cupboard known as a "safe" but which, when opened, reveals itself to be a thinly stocked pantry containing a few dishes and some cans and cereal containers. An old porcelain-topped kitchen table covered by an old oilcloth sits in the middle of the kitchen, flanked on three sides by three different chairs—two cane-bottom chairs and a battered straight-back wooden relic of many another kitchen. There are dishes in the sink, empty milk bottles, and empty beer bottles.

THE KITCHEN.

Emily Ann comes into the kitchen. She places her book and report card on the table, goes to the icebox and opens it. Over her shoulder we see two bottles of milk, some bread, some butter, nine bottles of beer, and that's all. She takes the milk and bread out, goes back to the wall pantry in the kitchen, reaches on her tiptoes and gets out a glass, pours herself a glass of milk.

Then, taking a mouthful out of her slice of bread, she carries her glass of milk to the table and sits down. LONG SHOT of a forlorn eight-year-old sitting all alone in a drab little kitchen chewing a piece of bread and holding a glass of milk.

Suddenly a cat jumps into the room through the window. It is a tough, big, wild-looking alley cat. The girl sits up, startled, a little afraid. The cat prowls panther-like around the kitchen, its tail swishing, its eyes darting quick appraisals of the little girl who sits rigid in her chair watching it.

After a moment, a strangely calculating look comes over the little girl's face, and she carefully stands, wary not to frighten the cat, and moves back to the cupboard shelf where the bottle of milk still stands. The cat continues its restless patrolling of the room, on guard, muscles tensed.

The little girl slowly pours some milk into a soup plate and carefully sets it on the floor, and then stands unmoving, rigid, watching. For a long moment a thick silence fills the room, the cat moving around softly. Then, almost nonchalantly, it pads to the soup plate and dips its head in. For a moment the little girl watches. Then with a swoop she seizes the cat and presses it against her face.

CLOSE UP of Emily Ann, her face pressed against the torn, patchy skin of the alley cat, her eyes closed, hugging the startled, frenzied animal.

EMILY ANN *(to the cat)* I got promoted today.

The cat leaps out of the little girl's clutches and out of the window. Camera pulls back to a LONG SHOT so that we can see the sad little girl standing in the middle of the kitchen, staring off through the window through which the cat has just jumped.

MAIN STREET. 1942. DAY.

Emily Ann, now sixteen, a pretty, full-blown young girl, walks down Main Street. There is an air of wanton arrogance to her, as if she is well aware that the two men lounging in the door of the liquor shop are giving her a covertly approving eye. She wears a skirt and high heels. She holds two high-school textbooks. Her hair is swept up to the top of her head in the fashion of the day. She is too young to carry all this.

Camera pans with her until she turns in at the five-and-dime store. There are three high-school boys, around seventeen, wearing slacks and T-shirts or sports shirts out over their trousers, lounging at the five-and-dime entrance. They say hello to her as she sweeps past them. Then all three snicker.

ACROSS the three high-school boys into the interior of the five-and-dime store. One of the boys watches her. The second boy seems to be giving the third boy intense instructions. The third boy, a stoutish young fellow, seems a little nervous.

THE FIVE-AND-DIME STORE.

Emily Ann walks toward the rear of the shop—the same store her mother worked in. She throws a greeting to a middle-aged SALESLADY as she heads to the back of the shop.

EMILY ANN Good afternoon, Mrs. Kimbrough.

SALESLADY *(without looking up)* Good afternoon, honey.

Emily Ann puts her textbooks on top of a carton in the back, turns and ambles back down the aisle. There are about four customers in the shop. THE BOSS, a thin, middle-aged, not thoroughly shaven man, is selling two middle-aged women some men's socks. She gives her boss a greeting.

EMILY ANN Hiya, Mr. Rice.

Her boss nods. Emily Ann's attention is actually on the entrance of the shop where the three high-school boys are still in whispered conference.

HER P.O.V.: Looking down the aisle to the street door where two of the boys seem to be encouraging the short, stout boy to go in. They see Emily Ann watching them, and the first two boys duck out of sight, leaving the third boy in the doorway.

THE BOY *(mumbling; in the doorway)* Could I see you a minute, Emily Ann?

EMILY ANN *(moving down to him)* You say something to me, Lewis?

Behind them, the boss looks up, disapprovingly.

THE BOY *(mumbling)* You want to go to the movies tonight?

EMILY ANN   What's playing?

THE BOY   *A Woman's Face* with Joan Crawford and Melvyn Douglas.

EMILY ANN   I saw it.

This apparently dashes the boy, who is on the verge of turning and taking flight.

THE BOY   Well, I'll see you then.

EMILY ANN   I'm surprised at you, Lewis, hanging out with James Pinckney Miller and Frank Sutton out there. You're one of the nice boys in school, from one of the better families. I mean your daddy is a doctor. I don't know what James Pinckney Miller told you about me, but I wouldn't take anything he said to be very true. I went out with him just once, and he tried all sorts of things, but he didn't get very far, so I wouldn't believe anything he or Frank Sutton said. What did they say about me?

THE BOY   They didn't say anything.

EMILY ANN   I really want to know. What did they say about me?

THE BOY   We could drive over to Hagerstown. They got three movies there. There must be one there you didn't see.

EMILY ANN   Well, I would like to go out with you, Lewis, because you're from one of the better families, but I don't like you listening to any of those stories James Pinckney Miller might tell you.

Pause. The boy is afraid to push his luck. He just waits.

EMILY ANN   Well, you know where I live, and you can call for me at seven o'clock.

THE BOY   (*anxious to get out of the store*) All right, I'll see you.

EMILY ANN You have to call for me at my house like you'd call for any girl. And you have to wear a necktie and a jacket.

The boss turns from the two women he has been selling socks to and barks.

THE BOSS You going to buy something, boy, or you going to stand there blocking up the door?

THE BOY I'm going, Mr. Rice.

He turns and hurries out of the shop.

MAIN STREET.

The boy comes out of the five-and-dime. His two friends have been waiting a few store-fronts down. The three boys congregate in a little group for a moment. The boy, Lewis, is nodding his head to let them know he's made the date. The three boys start down the street, giggling to each other over some private little lechery of their own.

EMILY'S HOUSE. LANDING OUTSIDE THE DOOR.

Emily Ann stands on the upper landing of the two-story house, looking down to the street, waiting for her date to show up. It is dusk, near night, and lightning bugs flit about. She wears an inexpensive organdy dress, and, despite the rather gauche upswept hair-do, she looks extremely pretty.

Behind her, sitting on rockers, are her mother and Aunt Alice Marie. Her mother is now a thin ascetic-looking religionist. She wears steel-rimmed glasses, and her face is drawn into intense sobriety. The two older women are singing with quiet sternness: "I come to the garden alone while the dew is still on the roses..."

Emily Ann's P.O.V.: Looking down to the street as a 1942 Oldsmobile sedan pulls up to the house. Emily Ann starts for the stairs.

EMILY ANN I'll do the dishes when I get home.

THE TWO WOMEN *(singing)* "...And the words I hear falling on my ear, the voice of God discloses."

The two women watch from the balcony, as Emily Ann reaches the bottom of the stairs and hurries down the path to the waiting sedan at the curb.

THE TWO WOMEN *(off-screen)* "And He walks with me, and He talks with me ..."

Emily Ann gets quickly into the sedan, closes the door after her, and the car moves off.

INSIDE THE SEDAN, MOVING DOWN THE ROAD. NIGHT.

Emily Ann and the boy, now dressed in blue suit and tie, drive along through the night. Through the windows of the sedan we see the quiet lights of the towns residential district for a while, fading eventually into the black silence of the open road to Hagerstown. For a moment they ride in silence, the boy getting nervous, concentrating on his driving, and Emily Ann composed, even thoughtful.

EMILY ANN I sewed this I'm wearing myself, you know.

THE BOY Is that a fact?

EMILY ANN Oh, I sew most of my clothes. I'm very good at that. I sewed the dress I wore in the show last month when the Dramatic Club, we did *Stage Door* by George Kaufman and Edna Ferber. Was you there? It was a triumph. Everybody said that was the best show the Dramatic Club has ever done. Everybody said it was just wonderful. Thelma Doris's mother said to me she never laughed so much in her life as the way I said my lines. It was a triumph! *(She is quite excited now, turned in her seat toward him, her eyes glowing.)* That was the most wonderful evening of my life. Was you there?

THE BOY Sure, I mean I...

EMILY ANN   Everybody just came over to me and was so nice. Miss
Gillespie said I was the best girl she ever had in the Dramatic Club.
Well, I was so scared. I was just saying words. I didn't know I was
doing anything special. Everybody was so nice to me. I began to cry.
Just all of a sudden I began to cry. Miss Gillespie, she said, "What are
you crying about?" I said, "I don't know. Everybody's so nice to me."
She said, "You should be happy. Tonight was a triumph for you." Well,
I just couldn't stop bawling. My mother was there. She said, "What
are you crying about?" I said, "I don't know." Well, I'm going to tell
you, we went home, my mother and I—I just didn't want to go home
at all that night. I was up in the clouds. But we finally went home, and
my mother gave me a hug. And I began to cry all over again. My
mother, as you might know, is a Seventh-Day Adventist, and is very
pious and severe, and she didn't even want me to be in the play. And
we don't do much hugging in our house. I do believe that was the first
hug she gave me in I don't remember—since I was an infant, I believe.
She's a Seventh-Day Adventist, you know.   She won't work on
Saturday, not even in the defense plant down there where she's working now, in the Goodrich Rubber Company. All of a sudden in the last
few years my mother has become very religious. She was a very pretty girl when she was young. My Uncle George says she was the belle
of Clarksville, Tennessee. That's where I was born—that's near Fort
Donelson, where Grant won the first Northern victory in the Civil
War. Well, I couldn't stop crying all night long. And I woke up the
next morning, I no sooner opened my eyes, and I began bawling again.
I got tears in my eyes right now just talking about it.   Isn't that the
silliest thing you ever saw?

*She dries her eyes quickly with a finger, turns back and looks out the front
windshield at the road rolling underneath the wheels.*

EMILY ANN   That was the most wonderful night of my life.

*The boy smiles briefly, concentrates on his driving.   A silence falls between
them.*

EMILY ANN   *(after a moment)*   I hope you don't mind my rattling on like
this.   I'm well aware I have the reputation of being a real ear-bender.

THE BOY Oh, no. I'm always happy when the girl takes over the burden of the conversation.

EMILY ANN Well, I understand I have the reputation of carrying that burden very well.

She smiles quickly at the boy and he smiles nervously back. A sudden sweet air settles over the two kids. Emily Ann is painfully aware of the feeling.

EMILY ANN *(suddenly smiling)* I daydream sometimes about being a movie star. I guess every girl daydreams about that. I mean, I don't think I'm so terribly pretty and all that, but they have these cosmeticians in Hollywood who make the movie stars look a lot more beautiful than they are. I mean, you ought to read some of these magazines which tell you the inside stories on some of these movie stars. I mean, most of it is all cosmetics. I do believe, however, that Ann Sheridan is just beautiful, don't you think so? Lana Turner was only seventeen when they discovered her. I daydream sometimes about that. Do you daydream about that ever?

THE BOY *(horribly shy)* Well, no, I don't daydream about that.

A pause sits between them.

EMILY ANN What do you daydream about?

THE BOY *(embarrassed to blushing)* Oh, I wouldn't even tell you.

EMILY ANN There's nothing wrong with daydreaming.

THE BOY Well, I daydream about girls, I guess. I don't get along well with girls and... *(He is suffused with embarrassment.)*

EMILY ANN Well, I have to tell you, Lewis, your fault is that you are too shy. The girls all like you, they talk about you, and...

THE BOY They do?

EMILY ANN   Oh, sure. Saranne Searle had a case on you for months. You're a very attractive boy, Lewis. You mustn't be so shy.

If the boy weren't driving, he would close his eyes, he is so embarrassed. Emily Ann studies her fingers in her lap.

EMILY ANN   I didn't exactly have a case on you myself, but I was very pleased when you asked me to go out with you today. I'm well aware that your daddy is a doctor and that there are many people in this city who look upon my mother and myself as common. Well, before my daddy died, we lived in Clarksville, Tennessee, and my father had the drycleaning store, and we were well thought of. My mother had a nigger come in twice a week to help her with the washing and ironing. We were one of the better families. *(She has been getting angry, and her expressive young eyes begin to flash.)* There's lots of girls here wish they had my background. I know I don't get invited to the Cotillion and the Subdeb, and you don't know how that hurt me! I cried for weeks! I could have killed Thelma Doris and her mother. Supposed to be my friend. Didn't even invite me to her sweet-sixteen party. I begged my mother a hundred times—let's move out of niggertown. But she's crazy about money. She hoards it away. I don't even know where myself. She don't want to pay more than seven dollars a month for that tacky little old three rooms we got there. What do you think I work in Rice's five-and-dime after school for? She won't give me a penny to buy new clothes! I have to buy all my own clothes. I even saved up and bought my own public-school graduation dress, the material, and sewed it myself. Everybody thought it was beautiful. They thought I'd gone to Baltimore to get it! *(She is aware she is being very angry and she subsides a bit.)* Well, I certainly have a temper, don't I? I apologize, Lewis, for that outburst, but I feel these things very deeply. *(She sits, her turbulent thoughts still welling in her mind.)* I don't expect you can understand the shame and degradation that a girl feels when she isn't invited to a sweet-sixteen party.

THE BOY   *(essentially a very decent boy)*   I do understand, Emily Ann.

She looks quickly at him and then bows her head quickly not to show the sud-

den welling of tears his simple sympathy has generated. The car buckets along into the night.

EMILY ANN   I ask nothing except to be treated with the simple courtesy and respect that any other girl is treated.

THE BOY   I don't think that's asking too much, Emily.

She raises her head and looks at the chubby profile of the boy driving the car.

EMILY ANN   You're a very sweet boy, Lewis. I like you very much.

The sedan speeds along. Emily Ann leans back against the seat and kind of looks out the side window at the swiftly passing black landscape. A vague, drifting smile curls her lips. She seems a very pretty and nice girl at the moment.

A MOVIE THEATER.

Emily Ann is really enjoying the movie. She sits in the dark theater, her eyes rapt with attention and her well-formed mouth slightly open, ready to laugh. Indistinguishable words and sounds emanate from the screen, and Emily Ann's face contorts and follows each off-stage movement like a little girl at a puppet show. Something on the screen produces a laugh from the audience and a fit of giggles from Emily Ann. Then she suddenly erupts into a laugh she can no longer stifle. She is having a wonderful time.

Camera pans a little so that we get a better look at the boy. His interest is not with the picture. He has his arm balanced on the space between the two seats he and Emily Ann are occupying, and he is mustering his last shred of courage to force himself to slide his arm around the back of her chair. This decision is making him sweat. His eyes are not looking at the screen; they are covertly examining Emily Ann. Every now and then he pretends to look at the screen. He finally contrives to get his arm around the back of Emily Ann's chair, and his fingers fall vaguely on her neck and that part of her shoulder left exposed by the scalloped cut of the dress. Emily Ann doesn't even notice it, but the boy's face would indicate he had his hand in a flame. His chin trembles and his forehead is coated with sweat. He catches his breath as if he had run the twenty miles from their home town. Emily Ann and the audience suddenly burst into laughter again. The boy just sits.

THE SEDAN. NIGHT.

Emily Ann and the boy are driving home. Emily Ann is still bubbling over the show. The boy's face is set in rigid determination. Through the windows of the car we can perhaps tell that we are on open highway, and only an occasional gas station light interrupts the black flow of the wooded areas along the road.

EMILY ANN *(bubbling with good humor)* Her real name isn't Ginger Rogers, you know. Her real name is Virginia McMath, and you know how she got started? She used to dance in Charleston contests, and somebody saw her, and that's how she became a star. I was thinking of taking dancing lessons, tap dancing and things like that, but they don't even have any place there in Hagerstown where they teach that. Do you know of any? Lana Turner was discovered in a drugstore, and there was one star—I think it was Priscilla Lane or Carole Landis—was just an old secretary, and she was riding up in the elevator, and this producer saw her and that's how she got her start. But I was talking about Ginger Rogers. I mean, she ain't like some of them stars. She don't go out to night clubs much, although there was one time there everybody thought she was going to marry Howard Hughes—it was in all the magazines. Anyway, she lives in a lovely home in Beverly Hills with her mother. She keeps her mother right there with her. I think that's nice. Ginger Rogers's dressing room has mirrors on the ceiling and the walls, and she has fruitwood furniture, and she loves classical music, you know? She's very close with Deems Taylor. He's a well-known classical musician. She has his picture on her wall, but there's no romance there in the wind, I don't think—just good friends. *(She has suddenly become aware that the boy is turning the car into a side road.)* Where are we going, Lewis?

The boy says nothing, afraid actually to trust his voice. The road they are on now is not too well paved, and the sedan jostles and bumps. She abruptly and surely knows what the boy is up to and it stings her sharply. The bubbling enthusiasm flips off her face to be replaced by an eye-narrowed coldness.

EMILY ANN   I think, Lewis, you ought to just turn this car around and take me home.

The boy's only answer is to pull over to the side of the road, foliage and fallen branches crackling under the wheels.

EMILY ANN   Them stories that James Pinckney Miller and all the other boys may have told you are not true!

The car is stopped now, but the boy just sits staring at the steering wheel, mustering his courage again, a short, stout boy, brow beaded with sweat. For a moment they are both almost on the verge of tears, sitting stiffly, rigidly, the silence sick and tense between them.

Then abruptly the boy reaches for her, twisting his stout torso past the steering wheel, clumsily trying to get both arms around her, frantically trying to put his face next to hers. Emily Ann fends him off easily.

EMILY ANN   Leave me alone!

The boy, utterly shattered, twists back behind the steering wheel. It is all he can do to keep from crying. Emily Ann sits in numb fury.

THE BOY   *(sick with shame and guilt)* You do it for all the other boys. What's the matter with me?

EMILY ANN   *(head down)*   I just as soon be dead. I know what everybody thinks of me, all the boys whispering about me when I walk in the school. I'm afraid not to let them, that's all. I wouldn't get no dates at all if I didn't let them. Please take me home, Lewis. I just as soon be dead, and that's the truth.

The boy is actually deeply touched, but he doesn't know what to say. He starts the motor and shifts into first gear. The sedan pulls across the road, backing up in order to reverse direction and head back the way it came.

STREET OUTSIDE EMILY'S HOUSE. NIGHT.

The sedan comes down the street, wheeling to a halt in front of Emily Ann's house. It is around midnight, and the street is dark except for one lone light in some distant house. The shabby little homes are outlined vaguely against the murky sky.

INSIDE THE SEDAN.

Emily Ann and the boy just sit, he before the steering wheel, she against the door on her side. They have nothing to say but seem to feel something should be said. Emily Ann is too hurt to conceal the deep pain of her life from show-ing on her pretty, young, over-rouged face.

EMILY ANN *(mumbling)* I would love to see you again, Lewis. I don't suppose you would care to.

The boy says nothing, only because he wouldn't know how to say it. He just wants to get home and forget all about everything. Somehow Emily Ann is aware that the boy is perhaps as deeply shattered as she is. She darts a quick look at his tense face.

EMILY ANN *(utter desolation)* Oh, I don't care. If you still want to, it's all right with me.

The boy looks at her, not quite sure he knows what she means. She slides over to him, spiritlessly puts her arms around his neck and kisses him in a gesture of ultimate futility. The boy cannot adjust to this for a moment, but then he seizes her almost desperately and begins kissing her on the neck.

CLOSE-UP of Emily Ann looking over the boy's shoulder. Her eyes are wide, and there are tears in them. She seems absolutely unaware of the fact that she is being made love to.

EMILY ANN *(almost calmly)* I'm going to go to Hollywood some day, and I'm going to be a star. I'm going to be a star.

STREET OUTSIDE EMILY'S HOUSE. NIGHT.

MEDIUM SHOT of the closed, dark sedan. Through the front side window we catch a vague glimpse of the two lost young kids clutched in each other's embrace, a little movement of the white of his shirt, of the light pastel of her dress. Camera pans away from the car across the unpaved sidewalk along the wall of Emily Ann's building to the upper landing.

CLOSE SHOT of the mother, still sitting on her rocker on the balcony in her faded print dress. The aunt has gone. The mother sits alone, singing almost inaudibly to herself. "And He walks with me and He talks with me...."

FADE OUT.

MAIN STREET. 1944. NIGHT.

Several shots looking down on Main Street again. But a marked change. We have faded in with a sharp blare of military music, which indicates what has happened to the small city of Butler, Maryland. It is an Army town now.

From where we sit, the sidewalks look jammed with G.I.s, meandering, lounging, clogging up store doorways, looking into shop windows. They are lined up outside the movie house. There is a lot of weekend-pass high spirits. Underneath this, the martial music drums and fifes up a storm.

STREET OFF MAIN STREET. NIGHT.

From the corner we look down the street that joins Main Street at right angles. It is essentially a quiet street with a little cluster of stores where it joins Main Street. The stores are closed now, and the street is dark. Way down on Main Street, we can still see a few lights. It is drizzling.

A tall young G.I. is sprawled on the curb. His eyes are closed, but an occasional movement shows he is alive. His face and his uniform are drenched with rain and smeared with mud, and the drizzle beats lightly down on his face. A group of four people come hurrying around the corner from Main Street. They are two G.I.s and two girls. The G.I.s have their jacket collars up, and the two girls have found impromptu protection against the rain, a newspaper or magazine. They are walking quickly, a giggly, laughing, whispery little group. We may possibly recognize Emily Ann as one of the girls. She is now eighteen, full, sensual, wearing a light fall topcoat and high-heeled wedgies.

The four young people approach the body of the drunken G.I. sprawled on the street in the foreground. The boy with Emily Ann has his arm around her. The FIRST G.I. becomes aware of something in the street. A few steps later, he recognizes the form to be a G.I. He slows his walk as he approaches.

FIRST G.I.   Hey, look at that.

The others are also aware of the body in the street now. The girl with Emily Ann is frightened and hangs back, but Emily Ann is fascinated. She edges forward with the two G.I.s, who are now coming to make a closer examination of the body.

FIRST G.I.   Boy, he's loaded, huh?

SECOND G.I.   Maybe he's dead.

The body on the street moves slightly now, relieving everybody of this possibility. Behind the two G.I.s we can see Emily Ann, a few steps back, watching, fascinated, and the other girl even farther back. The two G.I.s stand regarding the form, a little at a loss for what to do.

FIRST G.I.   We ought to get him somewhere. He'll get pneumonia.

SECOND G.I.   Yeah.

He squats down beside the body, lifts the head.

SECOND G.I.   *(to the head)* Hey, Mac.

FIRST G.I.   *(squatting down; impressed)* You know who that is? That's Tower, "E" Company. John Tower. *(to Emily Ann)* You know who this is? This is John Tower, the son of the movie star. Oh, what a lunatic this guy is!

Emily Ann is quite impressed. She stares at the thin, gaunt, wet face; young Tower is being helped to his feet with great difficulty by the second G.I.

SECOND G.I. *(to first G.I.)*   Give me a hand with this, will you?

THE GIRL *(in background)*   Is he all right?

EMILY ANN *(turning to the girl ten steps or so back)*   Lucy, that's John Tower, the son of the movie star.

THE GIRL   Is he dead?

The movie star's son hangs limply between the two G.I.s. We see a tall, thin boy of twenty-five. Water streaks down the gaunt face. His eyes are closed; he is out cold. The first G.I. has been digging into Tower's pocket.

FIRST G.I.   He's got a hotel key here.

EMILY ANN   Lucy, that's the son of John Tower, the movie star.

THE HOTEL ROOM. NIGHT.

Through the open doorway come the two G.I.s, holding young Tower. Emily Ann follows. The other girl can possibly be seen in the corridor outside. The room is dark, and the only light for a moment is a diffused shaft pouring weakly in from the hallway. Everybody is in silhouette for a moment. Then somebody turns on the light and the room is filled with a vague, fitful sort of light coming from a naked and inadequate bulb hanging overhead.

The second G.I. has managed to get Tower over to the bed, where he lets him down. Tower slides back onto the bed, his feet dangling over the side. He is awake, but almost comatose. He is mumbling "Get out of here" over and over again, so that the words are indistinguishable and the effect is gibberish. His face and hair are matted with the filth of the street he was lying in, and the front of his uniform is drenched through in ugly wet splotches. Black rivulets run off onto the wildly rumpled white sheets.

The bed is in great disorder. It is an old-fashioned brass bed. The room itself is the inevitably dreary room of all small hotels, with faded wallpaper, a stained washbasin in the corner (the towel is lying in a heap on the floor), a cheap mahogany chest of drawers topped by a cracked mirror, and a worn soft chair with a hole in its slipcover.

The first G.I. is standing by the wall switch; it was he who turned on the light. Emily Ann stands framed in the open doorway, watching the proceedings with wide-eyed fascination. She has never seen anybody so drunk, and the son of a well-known movie star at that.

The second G.I. lifts Tower's feet onto the bed with no apparent concern for the fact that the sopping-wet G.I.'s shoes are smearing the disarrayed spread. Three empty fifths of whisky and a half-empty gallon jug of wine are on the floor in various locations.

FIRST G.I.   What are we going to do with him, because it's almost twelve o'clock? We got to get to the bus, boy. Why don't we tell the desk clerk to send up a doctor or something? *(turning to Emily Ann)* Listen, honey, I'm sorry, but we got to make the bus, so you girls will have to get home alone.

EMILY ANN   Oh, don't worry about me, honey.

SECOND G.I.   *(to the other girl, now in the doorway)*   You girls can get home alone, can't you?

EMILY ANN   Oh, you boys go run get your bus. I'll take care of this boy.

The second G.I. has already gone out into the corridor. The first G.I. follows him.

FIRST G.I.   I'll call you during the week, honey.

EMILY ANN   That's fine, honey.

He exits. Emily Ann goes to the doorway.

EMILY ANN   (to Lucy, who has moved off) Lucy, I'll stay here a couple of minutes, take care of this boy, take off his shoes—you know. You go on home, honey.

On the bed, young Tower lies limp and unmoving, his eyes open and staring without seeing up to the ceiling above him. Emily Ann closes the door and turns to him. She regards him for a moment, then moves quickly across the room to where the towel is lying on the floor, picks it up, and comes back to the bed where he is lying.

TOWER   (mumbling) Get out of here get out of here get out of here get out of here...

She regards him for a moment, and then bends down and begins drying his hair and face.

THE HOTEL ROOM. THE FOLLOWING DAWN.

DISSOLVE to a WIDE SHOT of the room, showing Emily Ann sitting in the soft chair uncomfortably asleep, and young Tower on the bed, sleeping fitfully. The sheets are twisted around him, and his thin arms and shoulders make sudden involuntary twists and jerks. He is wearing only a T-shirt and the trousers now.

The window by the bed shows a gray-black dawn hanging sullenly over the roofs of the town. The slight persistent drizzle continues. With a sudden start he is awake. He sits bolt upright, as if he has been startled awake by a nightmare.

CLOSE UP of young Tower, his face and body rigid, eyes wide. Then the terror goes, and he remains haggard, disheveled, and soddenly drunk. He slides off the bed with some creaking of the mattress, and Emily Ann opens her eyes. He crosses the room to the chest of drawers, hardly aware of Emily Ann's presence, takes one of the fifths of whisky sitting on the chest of drawers, looks around for a glass, sees it on the floor by the bed, gets it, pours himself a half tumblerful, sits down on the bed again, sipping his drink and examining his naked toes.

Emily Ann watches him, wary, her face worn and exhausted. He notes her briefly. The silence unnerves Emily Ann.

EMILY ANN You was laying out in the street there on Jackson Street in the rain and all, so we brought you up here.

He doesn't seem to have heard her.

EMILY ANN Are you really the son of John Tower?

She would prattle on, but in one quick gesture young Tower has sent the bottle of whisky he is holding crashing against the wall, the jagged pieces of glass spraying around, the liquor draining down the wall in small streams. Emily Ann sits petrified. Young Tower studies his glass of whisky.

TOWER *(his speech heavy and thick)* I can't even get myself a floozie without using my old man for a reference. *(He stands unsteadily and moves aimlessly around the room in his bare feet, muttering indistinguishable imprecations, his face swollen and hostile.)* I had plenty of women. I don't need my father. When I was seventeen I used to steal his women. *(He turns abruptly, goes back to the bed, sits down. After a moment, he mutters quietly.)* You can infer, if you wish, that I don't particularly care for my father.

Emily Ann stands a little uncertainly.

EMILY ANN *(mumbling)* As long as you're all right...

TOWER What did you say?

EMILY ANN *(louder)* I said, I just wanted to make sure you was all right, so as long as you're all right, I guess I'll be going.

TOWER *(standing again disjointedly, looks around the room for his jacket)* Don't leave me now. I won't do anything terrible, except possibly commit suicide. That's what I came up here for, you know. Drown myself in the bathtub. Go look in there. The bath is full. I got blind as a coot last night and staggered in stark naked and fell in the tub and put my head under the water, and I almost did it. I can't describe to you the absolute tranquility. But way back in the empty hollow some persistent hammer of life clunked away, and, at the last minute, I pulled my head up and gasped in the air and I lay on the dirty, cold, wet tiles twitching like a fish in the bottom of a boat. I just don't have the talent for suicide. I took seventeen sleeping pills in the Ashford Hotel in New York, but they rushed up the stairs with a stomach pump, and I spent the night in Bellevue. I tried gas, but all I got was color in my cheeks. I just don't have the knack. *(suddenly leans to her)* What are you living for? Be honest now. Tell me. What's it going to add up to, this sixty, seventy years you're going to flounder around this earth? One day you'll be necking in the back of the car with one of the boys from town, and because all your friends are getting married, you'll get married. You'll put on weight, and your husband will take up with a waitress in a hotel in Chattanooga. You'll have babies and visit your in-laws in the evening, and your husband will get sick, and you'll fret about the rent. Your hair will gray, and you'll suddenly look back and say, "What happened? It's all over." Your friends will die and you'll sink into melancholic hours, sitting by a window, peering with unseeing eyes through white chintz curtains, and finally they'll drop your long wooden box into the moldering grave. And what was it all about except worry and tears? Am I lying? Isn't that it? Slings and arrows. A tale told by an idiot. Why bother? It all ends up in the grave. You might as well make an honest effort to get there.

He turns away from her and lurches back to the bed. He sits down heavily, stares with swollen, sullen red eyes at the tumbler of whisky in his hand.

TOWER What would you know about it anyway, a frump in a hick town? You don't know what loneliness is. You think it's not having a date on Saturday night. You don't know the great, ultimate ache of desolation. I'm cold. Close the window or something.

He lies back on the bed now, staring up at the ceiling through wide, drunken, tear-filled eyes, crying quietly and without constraint now.

TOWER The last time I saw my father was six years ago. He was sitting in the living room of that barn he has in Sherman Oaks, playing solitaire, guzzling wine because he's too miser cheap to buy a decent fifth of Irish whisky, half hidden behind a thin blanket of cigarette smoke. The house was empty. My mother had a nervous breakdown when I was eleven. My older brother, Tom—my old man drove him years ago into an insane asylum, where he walks around picking up imaginary strings off the floor. My father said, "Where have you been the last couple of weeks?" Last couple of weeks! I had been gone for a year and a half in the Spanish Civil War. I said, "Pa, I need psychiatric help. I'm lost. I have to fight sometimes to keep myself from jumping out of windows. I'm asking you to be kind to me." He said, "I'm supporting one crazy son, and that's enough for me." That's my old man, star of stage, screen and radio, and a host of favorites.

He lies on the bed, quietly, unmoving, his eyes open.

TOWER *(after a moment)* You wouldn't understand, you wouldn't understand. You don't know what loneliness means. All you ever cried at was a Street and Smith love story.

CAMERA PANS SLOWLY to Emily Ann sitting hunched over on the soft chair. Tears make wet little paths down her cheeks. She has been quietly crying for some time.

DISSOLVE to some time later, ACROSS the bed, still a tempest of sheets and spread and blankets. The sun is high in the sky now; it's a very hot noon. On the bed, a fully dressed Emily Ann and young Tower, dressed as in the previous scene, lie clutched in embrace. Emily Ann is sleeping in the young man's arms.

He is awake, looking down at the full, soft young face with ineffable tenderness. The sun streams in through the window, almost whitening their faces and bleaching away the abject tawdriness of the room.

A HILLY LANDSCAPE. DAY.

LONG SHOT looking across the pretty countryside of Maryland with its clumps of trees and high grassy slopes, almost Renoiresque in warm pastel

*charm. The sun is high and strong. Way off in the distance, but visible, a sol-
dier and a girl are seated by a picnic basket.*

*CLOSER LONG SHOT looking through thickets and bushes, the sun glint-
ing and quivering through the leaves. We can see Emily Ann and young
Tower clearly enough, but they are too far away to be overheard too well.
They are romping—warm, sensual, tickling, laughing, muffled, intimate
enjoyment. Young Tower stands, and we can hear Emily Ann's laughter.*

*Through the bracken and bramble, we see Emily Ann on her haunches gath-
ering the wax paper and other remnants of the picnic into a pile so she can
set it afire. She is laughing as she goes about this. Tower is standing, his shirt
collar open, his tie dangling loosely as he expostulates.*

TOWER I am! I am! I'm tongue-tied, inarticulate. Silent to the point of
brooding! What are you laughing at? It's true. *(He laughs.)*

Emily Ann bursts into laughter again.

TOWER *(can't resist smiling himself)* Come on!

Her laughter is too infectious; he finds himself laughing with her.

EMILY ANN John, you haven't stopped talking since I met you.

*Tower has stopped laughing and is regarding her with a quick, sudden
warmth.*

TOWER When I was twelve years old, I was in Andover prep school. Very
fancy. My father sent me to one fancy boarding school after another.
I got thrown out of all of them. But when I was in Andover I knew a
boy—we shared a room together—a blond boy named Elliot
Sherman, and we used to sit up all night long talking about everything. He was the only boy I ever met who had read as much as I had.
You can't imagine what I had read by the time I was twelve. My father
had thousands and thousands of books. He bought this huge shack out
in Sherman Oaks, California, and the library came with it. He never

read a one of them; I read them all. Lucretius and Sophocles—all the great, desolate dramas of antiquity. I wore out Shakespeare and Macaulay and Gibbon, the fat sprawling histories of the Victorians, obscure poetry by B.V. Thompson and the elegant jaded sensuality of the Pre-Raphaelites. I used to lie all alone in the bleak, shadowed living room and read until my head fell on the books. Mark Twain. I adored him. That's all I own now are a few slim volumes of Mark Twain's black little pessimism, *Pudd'nhead Wilson's Notebook*, *What Is Man?*, and a collection of Eugene O'Neill, that great Irish peddler of death. I was twelve years old, mind you, and I used to stand in that empty living room quoting the sonorous despair of Edwin Arlington Robinson and the biting contempt of Jeffers. My father was out chasing some tart, and my sixteen-year-old brother was out wandering the streets, half demented. What a family, huh? Well, anyway, there was this boy in Andover when I was twelve years old, and we used to talk all night long. And to this day, you're the only other person I've ever talked like that with.

Emily Ann, squatting by the little pile of refuse, looks up at him standing beside her, and he looks down at her, both tenuously aware that this is somehow a declaration of love. After a moment he sits, staring at the ground, and then sprawls on his side. She lights a match and sets the little pile of papers in front of her ablaze. She sits in front of the small fire and studies her hands, nervously twitching in her lap.

EMILY ANN *(quietly)* I love you so much, John. I can't tell you how much I love you. If the Army ever stations you somewhere else, I think I'll die. I'll follow you. I swear I will. I wish we was married. I'll make you a good wife. I swear I will. You'll never be sorry. Never.

Tower rolls over on his back away from her. Emily props herself up on an elbow.

EMILY ANN I'll follow you. I mean it. I will. I wish we was married, John. I'd make you a good wife, I'll make you a good home. You'll never regret it—never.

Tower sits up now, his back almost to her. His eyes cloud and his features assume a rigid blandness. Emily Ann is keenly and miserably aware of the change.

EMILY ANN You don't care about me at all, do you?

TOWER That's not true.

EMILY ANN I'm just somebody to spend the weekend with because you can have your way with her.

TOWER That's not true.

EMILY ANN You keep me waiting in front of that hotel every week, an hour, an hour and a half. I never know if you're going to come. G.I.s come by, making cracks at me till I think I'll burst. Why do I do it? Who's he? He don't even care about me. I cry myself to sleep every night, thinking about you. I think about how you been hurt all your life, and I want to take care of you and give you a good home. And I'm just some girl for lack of any other to you.

TOWER *(avoiding her eyes)* That's not true, Emmy. You're the only person I have in my life. You're very dear to me. What do you think, I'm a big lover, I go around scraping women off my sleeves? You're the first girl I've talked to in months. I lie in my barracks, so lonely I can hardly keep from getting up and running across the street to the rec hall to call you on the phone.

She stares at him, her eyes suddenly welling with tears.

EMILY ANN Oh, Johnny, I wish you had—I wish you had!

TOWER I destroy everything that means anything to me. I always have.

EMILY ANN *(furiously in love)* That's not true. I never been so happy in all my life from what you just told me.

TOWER   I'm too damaged for you, Emily.

EMILY ANN   I want to hold you in my arms, John.

TOWER   Emmy, what are we kidding ourselves? I love you now. In half an
hour I'll wonder how I ever got into this. You have a passion for
respectability, and I have a horror of loneliness—that's love! See! I've
destroyed it already! A sweet feeling poked its head up out of my
morose solitude and I stomped it out fast. I always do. The worst thing
that could happen to us is if we get married. I'd hate you before the
blush of the ceremony had gone from your cheeks.

EMILY ANN   I'll make you a good wife, Johnny. I'll make you a good
home.

TOWER   I love you, Emmy.

They kneel, regarding each other with deep sweetness.

EMILY ANN'S APARTMENT.

*GROUP SHOT of a wedding ceremony, looking across the minister's back.
We see Emily Ann, silent and solemn, wearing a white bridal costume and
veil; young Tower, his face implacably expressionless. Around them are the
mother, the aunt, the uncle in a blue woolen serge suit, two girls of Emily
Ann's age dressed in cheap organdy frocks, and a G.I., apparently the best
man. There is a homemade wedding cake on the kitchen table which has been
brought into the living room. There is also a punch bowl. The most striking
aspect of this ceremony is the cheerlessness of it, the stern Baptist faces. Young
Tower, in particular, seems troubled. The minister intones the service.*

OUTSIDE EMILY ANN'S APARTMENT. NIGHT.

*LONG SHOT looking up to the second-floor landing. In the foreground, the
wedding party of the best man, the two bridesmaids, the mother, the aunt, the
uncle, either standing on the sidewalk looking up or getting into the various*

automobiles parked there. Three ghetto kids are fascinated spectators. On the balcony stands Emily Ann, a gay, white figure. She is waving goodby and shouting to the departing guests.

EMILY ANN *(shouting)* I want to thank you all very much! I want to thank you all very much! Saranne! I'll call you Monday morning!

THE UNCLE *(calling back)* Don't go to sleep too late!

This Rabelaisian advice brings a guffaw from the aunt and a giggle from one of the bridesmaids.

EMILY ANN *(calling)* I'm so excited! I'm so excited! I just can't tell you!

REVERSE SHOT from Emily Ann to the people down on the sidewalk.

EMILY ANN I want to thank you all for the presents and all!

BRIDESMAID *(calling back)* Call me up tomorrow and let me know how you feel!

Laughter from some of the wedding party and giggles from the neighborhood children. The G.I. who has climbed into one of the cars hollers.

THE BEST MAN Can I give anybody a lift?

THE MOTHER Goodby, honey!

EMILY ANN Goodby, Ma, goodby! See you Monday!

The mother gets into the uncle's car, the last to get in. The door closes behind her. The cars start off. Emily Ann watches them disappear, then stands a moment pensive, a little troubled, then turns, opens the screen door and goes into the apartment.

EMILY ANN'S LIVING ROOM.

Emily Ann comes back in. Tower is at the punch bowl pouring himself a glass.

He is dressed neatly in his olive drabs, sober but distant, detached, isolated, inside himself. She regards him a little anxiously.

EMILY ANN   I want to thank you very much for going through with the ceremony, the formalities, the minister and all that. I know how you despise little formalities like that, but they are deeply important to me, and I appreciate... *(She breaks off.)*

Tower merely nods, sips his punch, looks vaguely around the shabby little room, all the more shabby for the half-eaten wedding cake, the plates with portions of cake left on them, the glasses and tumblers here and there. He goes to the porch door, stands. There is a feeling of hostility in him.

EMILY ANN   I expect I better clean up a little bit now.

She gathers a few plates and starts for the kitchen. Before she reaches the doorway, she pauses and looks at her husband. He is examining his glass of punch. She is anxiously aware of his coldness.

EMILY ANN   Are you all right? Do you feel all right?

TOWER   I feel fine.

EMILY ANN   What are you thinking about?

TOWER   Nothing.

EMILY ANN   Give me a chance, Johnny.

TOWER   *(whirling to face her, his eyes blazing)* I said I feel fine! Go clean up the dishes or whatever you're doing!

He turns angrily back to looking out through the screen door, and the room is suddenly still, thick with the hush of restrained hatred. After a moment, Emily Ann moves a few steps into the room, afraid to look at him.

EMILY ANN   Don't turn your back on me. Give me a chance.

TOWER   Just leave me alone right now, Emmy. That would be the best thing for you to do.

She doesn't move. She stands in the middle of the room, afraid to let go of the fumbling moment of contact she has made.

TOWER   Leave me alone right now. Let me find my own way. I'll try to make this work out. Just leave me alone right now.

ACROSS the sad little half-eaten wedding cake, past Emily Ann standing in the middle of the room, her eyes closed, her shoulders slumped, her stomach taut, her heart cold, to Tower standing rigidly at the porch screen door staring stonily out into the night. And so they were married. Hold this tableau for a moment.

STREET OUTSIDE EMILY ANN'S HOUSE. DAY.

Four rowdy little kids dressed in winter clothes, interrupted in their play, look down the street.

KIDS' P.O.V.: Looking down the shabby, unsidewalked street with its uneven row of old frame houses, some of them unpainted. It is not quite dusk; the sun is low in the west, and there is a heavy golden sheen in the air. What the little kids are fascinated by is Tower soddenly drunk, lurching down the street toward the house he now lives in. His Army greatcoat is unbuttoned and flaps limply as he staggers along. He passes the kids; they eye him covertly. He turns into the house and starts climbing up the stairs with the painfully meticulous caution of the very drunk.

EMILY ANN'S APARTMENT. DAY.

Tower opens the door, then the screen door, then poising in the open doorway to make sure of his balance.

REVERSE SHOT of Emily Ann, eight months pregnant, full and swollen, crossing to the kitchen. We see enough of Tower's face to see the sodden distaste he has for this bulging, waddling girl.

He lumbers across the gray, shadowed living room to the kitchen doorway. Still across his shoulder we see Emily Ann and her mother at work in the kitchen preparing the evening meal: the mother a frumpy woman of forty, in a torn house dress and flapping slippers, one stocking loose and hanging on one leg, singing softly her inevitable hymns, and the very pregnant girl, sallow and without make-up. The mother stands at the stove absently watching a saucepan of boiling water.

Emily Ann is at the cupboard pouring her shelled peas into a saucepan. She places her hand on her swollen stomach as the baby kicks hard within her. Neither of them cares to acknowledge Tower's presence.

TOWER   Well, I finally got myself transferred to a combat outfit. I leave a week from Tuesday. I hope I get killed.

Emily Ann looks at him, the cold hatred manifest in her eyes.

EMILY ANN   I hope so too.

She turns to an opened package of chopped meat and begins rolling the meat into patties. Tower turns after a moment, crosses the living room and goes out the door.

The four kids watch Tower lurching back into the street he had just come down. We watch him with the kids for a moment, until he is quite down the block.

A STREET. NIGHT.

Tower sits on the curb of this quiet, dark residential street, staring out with drunken blankness. It is drizzling, and his face is moist, his greatcoat soggy wet. He closes his eyes and then slowly allows his weary, besotted body to slide into a reclining position. His knees curl up, and he lies, a grotesque, wet embryo of a man, half on the curb, half in the gutter, sleeping in the drizzle.

EMILY ANN'S LIVING ROOM.

Emily Ann lies on the floor of the living room reading movie magazines.

They are all around her: Modern Screen, Photoplay, *etc. She wears a skirt, sloppy-Joe sweater and saddle shoes and looks even younger than her eighteen years. She is no longer pregnant. The apartment is quiet. There are a few slight changes. On the walls hang portrait upon portrait of movie stars of that day, carefully scissored from the magazines—Ann Sheridan, Cary Grant, Deanna Durbin, Ann Rutherford, Mickey Rooney, Gene Tierney, Paulette Goddard, John Payne, Betty Grable, Errol Flynn, Victor Mature, etc.*

A baby cries faintly off in another room. Emily Ann cocks her head, waits to hear if it will continue. The baby cries plaintively again, and Emily Ann gets to her feet with a small sign of exasperation. The baby now begins to cry fully. Emily Ann moves to the bedroom.

THE BEDROOM.

ACROSS AND THROUGH the bars of a crib to the door of the bedroom as Emily Ann enters. There is a very small baby, hardly the size of your forearm, lying under a thin receiving blanket, only its face showing, crying lustily. Emily Ann moves to the crib, a soft smile edging her lips. She murmurs soothing endearments as she approaches.

EMILY ANN All right, sweetie baby. All right, sweetie baby. Don't you worry now. Mommie's going to kiss you.

She picks up the crying baby, receiving blanket and all, and presses it to her. Her eyes close and she hugs it in a flush of love for the child.

EMILY ANN Sweet baby, sweet baby, sweet baby...

The baby continues to cry. Emily Ann walks around with it.

EMILY ANN What do you want, baby? What do you want? You just had your bottle. Baby, baby, baby, baby.

The shrill thin screams begin to get on Emily Ann's nerves. She is clearly distressed.

EMILY ANN *(with no real vigor)* Shut up, shut up, shut up.

She goes out the bedroom, across the living room, into the kitchen. The baby's cry continues without pause, a disturbing, thin wail.

EMILY ANN Come on, I'll give you the rest of the bottle. You want the rest of the bottle?

There is a half-filled baby bottle on the cupboard shelf. She picks it up. The baby's cry is becoming nerve-wracking.

EMILY ANN *(losing her patience)* What's the matter? What's the matter? *(She feels the baby's rump under the blanket.)* Are you wet? What is it? *(The nerve-wracking little cry continues.)* Do you want the bottle? Here. Do you want the bottle? *(The baby cries.)* Shut up, shut up, shut up. *(Crying out.)* What do you want? *(The angry voice only makes the baby cry louder. Emily Ann is on the verge of tears herself, screams out.)* Shut up! Shut up! Leave me alone! Leave me alone!

She goes out of the kitchen, across the living room again, and walks aimlessly around the living room. She is crying now in desperation. The baby is crying with almost unbearable shrillness. Emily Ann moves up and down the bare living room, holding the screaming baby, crying.

EMILY ANN *(whimpering)* Please... please... please...

She clenches her eyes against the baby's screaming and rambles back to the bedroom.

EMILY ANN Oh, my God, my God, my God!

She puts the baby back into the crib, where it lies squalling. It has now been crying in this piercing fashion for at least a minute. It is unbearable. Emily Ann sits down, stares aghast around the room, shaking her head nervously, crying.

THE KITCHEN.

Emily Ann stands by the window on the far wall, staring out with hostile bleakness. The sun is strong, and there is an edge of frost on the window. Together, these effects combine almost to whiten Emily Ann's face like an overexposed snapshot. She turns at the sound of the door being opened.

Emily Ann turns to the doorway through which her mother, bundled in a winter coat, is now entering. The mother, vaguely aware something is amiss, looks across to her daughter through steel-rimmed glasses.

EMILY ANN   I'm getting out of here. I'm getting out of this town. I want to leave the baby with you, Ma. It's too much for me. I can't stand it no more.

THE MOTHER   What's the matter?

EMILY ANN   *(crying out)* I'm only eighteen years old! I got a good figure! I turn lots of heads when I go down the street. I want to have some fun!

THE MOTHER   What about the baby?

EMILY ANN   *(shrilly)* I don't want it! I don't want it! I didn't want it when it was born and I don't want her now!

TWO SHOT across the mother's face to Emily Ann by the window. The familiarity of Emily Ann's words bring an expression of deep pain to the mother's rock-ribbed face. The cycle is complete.

Emily Ann stands by the window, her face bleached by the white glare of the snow outside and the fierce stream of sunlight, her chin quivering with a terrified desperation.

EMILY ANN   I want to be happy.

FADE OUT.

FADE IN:

HOLLYWOOD, SUNSET BOULEVARD, LAUREL CANYON.

It is a bright, warm hazy Hollywood day looking down Sunset Boulevard in the direction of Highland Avenue. For orientation purposes, if we were to turn around we would see Schwab's drugstore and the parking lot where the old Actor's Lab used to be. Right now we see a row of gasoline stations in the background, a dry-cleaning store, a delicatessen, and some other stores.

We also single out Rita Shawn, Hollywood starlet (nee Emily Ann Faulkner), walking toward us. She is twenty-one years old by now, a little too blond. The black dress is too tight around the hips; the high heels are too high. She seems brassier, bolder, less vulnerable. She carries a large flat port-folio, the sort artists' models carry to show their pictures. Over this, the following legend:

PART TWO
Portrait of a Young Woman

CAMERA PANS with Rita as she walks indolently toward us and then past us. Her dress buttons high on the neck and is demurely topped by a Peter Pan collar, but the hips undulate more than necessary and her breasts are strain-ing against the material. The dress, frankly, was bought at Jack's on Wilshire, and it is a carefully selected size too small. Her blond hair falls in determinedly casual waves over her shoulders, and her lips glisten and sparkle.

We watch her undulate away from us toward the Ham and Eggery on the corner of Laurel Canyon Drive. By the time she turns into the Ham and Eggery, we all know that this is a Hollywood starlet.

Over this, the following legend:

HOLLYWOOD, CALIFORNIA
1947

THE HAM AND EGGERY. DAY.

Rita enters the restaurant. This is one of those waffle joints that flourished briefly in Hollywood right after the war. The overhead ceiling fixture is in the shape of a huge skillet, and the eggs are served in a hot frying pan right off the fire. There are five rows of booths and a counter that runs up the length of one side. At the end of the counter there is an alcove that leads into the sudden darkness of a bar. The bar to this day is called the Black Watch.

It is lunchtime and the place is crowded. All the patrons are actors, writers, or in some way connected with the movies. They are dressed after the casual fashion of Hollywood. The men wear sports shirts and slacks; the women wear men's shirts and slacks. There are a few dirndls and a few sports jackets. There is a noticeable sprinkling of sweat shirts and jeans, indicating that members of the Actor's Lab, a very serious school of acting, also patronize the place.

There is a great deal of talking going on. The talk is angry, bitter, hostile and loud. Most of these people are regularly unemployed. Even the jokes are rancorous, the laughter harsh.

Rita makes her way down an aisle toward a rear booth. In the foreground is a booth occupied by three young men and two young actresses. This is a contingent of the sweat-shirt brigade, and the discussions at tables like this stem from two major issues—the commercial mediocrity of Hollywood and the paranoid insistence that the whole society is preventing these chaps from getting their big break. The chap holding forth at the moment is a writer who writes one-act plays of studied social content crackling with violent pungencies of dialogue. Actually, he talks a great deal more than he writes. He is talking now.

THE WRITER   Name one good picture made in the United States in the last five years! Go ahead! Name one. I mean a good picture! Have we had one *Open City*? One *Shoeshine*? We don't have a director in this country to compare to Rossellini! De Sica! How can you compare American pictures to foreign pictures?

AN ACTOR   How about *Oxbow Incident*?

THE WRITER   All right. One good picture. All right. Name another.

ANOTHER ACTOR   *Lost Weekend.*

THE WRITER   All right. Two good pictures.

FIRST ACTOR   *Grapes of Wrath.*

THE WRITER   All right. Three good pictures. *(He is losing interest in the argument.)*

Rita approaches a rear-wall table at which sit two other starlets, one blonde and one brunette. The blonde's name is HILLARY and the brunette's name is JOANNA. They are both dressed in blouses and slacks. The blonde is a vapid type with undistinguished features.

The brunette is an enormously sad girl. She stares down at a shot of liquor with naked distaste for the liquor and all of life itself. She appears to have had a bad night the night before, a night of strange dreams; some of the horror is still with her. Both girls are in their late twenties. They look up briefly as Rita approaches. There is an exchange of hellos.

RITA   Where is everybody?

JOANNA   *(darkly into her drink)*   Dutch Seymour called you about ten minutes after you left the house.

RITA   *(amiably)*   I better call him.

HILLARY   *(offering a copy of a newspaper to Rita)*   You're in Ed Sullivan's column again today.

RITA   *(sitting at the table)*   Yeah, I know. *(to Joanna)*   Was Dutch mad?

JOANNA   *(not looking up)*   My mother answered the phone.

HILLARY   *(pointing to the paper)*   Where it says "Boxing champ Dutch Seymour is talking wedding bells to starlet Rita Shawn, who used to be Emily Ann Faulkner of Beacon City, Maryland." What did he put all that in for?

RITA *(brightly)* Oh, I called Joe Glass yesterday. I said, "Joe, Dutch Seymour has been asking me to marry him. Is that worth an item somewhere?" So I said, "Joe, if you get it into some column," I said, "ask them to put my real name down. Because my mother—I called her last week—she says nobody back in Beacon City believes all the clippings I sent back is really me. It always says starlet Rita Shawn." So I said, "Put down that my real name was Emily Ann Faulkner." My mama didn't even know who Dutch was. I said, "Ma, Dutch Seymour is an all-time boxing great. He was middleweight champ, retired undefeated and beat Slapsie Maxie Rosenbloom for the light heavy-weight crown, fighting out of his own weight class." So my mama said, "Slapsie Maxie who, precious?" *(To Joanna, who stands now and starts off for the bar.)* How do you feel, Joanna, after last night?

Joanna doesn't seem to have heard. She moves off into the blackness of the bar. Rita regards the empty glass on the table.

RITA Well, she's drinking before lunch now, I see.

HILLARY Oh, she's had about five shots already.

Rita has spotted somebody up in front of the restaurant and is gaily waving at him.

RITA *(broad smile, gay)* Hiya, Alex! *(turns to Hillary, the smile disappearing. She darts a quick look at the bar.)* You should have seen Joanna last night. She's been drinking something terrible. It's just breaking her mother's heart. I'm going to move out of there. There's just nothing but screaming going on in that house all the time. Who you rooming with now, Hillary?

HILLARY I'm rooming with Sandra Steele.

RITA Oh, I thought she was rooming with Sharlene.

HILLARY They had a fight.

RITA *(intense whisper)* I came home last night. I was out with Martin
   Charles, who's doing an independent with all unknowns. There's a
   nice little part in that picture, four days' work at least, a Nazi girl who
   hides out the aviator on her father's farm when he's running away from
   the Storm Troopers. Anyway, Martin Charles took me to my door.
   He's got big eyes for me. I think I'll get that part. Anyway, I came in
   the house. It was two A.M. Joanna was sitting in the living room with
   all the shades up, wearing just about nothing, talking to herself. She
   was so drunk, she didn't know I was there. She made me think of my
   first husband. Did I tell you my final divorce papers came through?

HILLARY Does Dutch Seymour really want to marry you?

RITA *(She suddenly beams and waves brightly to somebody off stage.)* I don't
   know what he sees in me. I only been in seven pictures, and only two
   of those was speaking parts. I must say, however, that ever since that
   item appeared in Ed Sullivan's this morning, I got four calls. I just
   come back from Hal King at Metro. I'm going up to see Burt Harres
   at Paramount in about forty minutes. His secretary called this morning.

HILLARY Well, if you're going up to see Burt Harres, I wouldn't wear anything so high in the neck.

RITA I just thought I'd try something demure for a change.

HILLARY I know a couple of girls been out with Dutch Seymour, and they
   say he's pretty dull.

RITA Oh, he's been out with about every girl in Hollywood. He's a lost
   soul. He really is. It's hard for a man to be a big athletic celebrity for
   so many years and then retire and be nothing. He don't know what to
   do with himself. He wanders around the country making speeches to
   Boy Scouts. He sits there in that hotel room of his, calling his friends
   on the telephone all day long. He calls me twice a day. I thought about
   marrying him, because it would be wonderful for my career. *(She*

stands.) I better call Dutch. *(She suddenly spots another familiar face off stage and waves and beams.)* Watch my portfolio, will you, Hillary? *(She moves off into the bar.)*

THE BAR OF THE HAM AND EGGERY.

Rita comes into the bar, erect and undulating, the professional half-formed smile nailed on her face. The bar is dark, with only a few little hidden lights by the bar mirror. There are about three people in it, the bar having just opened. At the end of the bar by the telephone booths is Joanna, standing hunched over her drink. She watches Rita as she comes to the phone booth.

JOANNA *(a girl who can drink for hours without showing it)* Where are you going this afternoon?

RITA *(sliding into the phone booth and fishing change out of her purse)* Well, I'm up for a part at Burt Harres' at Columbia at two-thirty.

JOANNA I'll drive over with you.

RITA *(inserting a dime and dialing)* Fine, if you want to, Joanna. *(She finishes dialing, waits.)*

JOANNA There's a letter from your husband.

RITA Yes, I saw it. *(on phone)* Room 417, please. Mr. Dutch Seymour. *(to Joanna)* Usual letter. He's fine. My little daughter's fine. He's working in a publishing house now. He's getting married again. He's being psychoanalyzed. *(on phone)* Hiya, Dutch? Dutch, this is Rita.... Well, I just...Dutch, I don't know who put that item in Ed Sullivan's. I didn't tell anybody, not even Joanna and her mother. *(She makes a move at Joanna, rolls her eyes at the ceiling, sighs with impatience.)* Well, maybe you told somebody, and it was overheard. You know how you can't say a word around this town without it getting in the papers.

STREET INSIDE COLUMBIA STUDIOS.

Rita and Joanna sit in a Ford convertible. The car is parked at the curb. The blank white stucco sound stages and studio buildings rise monolithically and blankly all around them. There is a desultory pedestrian traffic, a person here and there on the hot sunny streets. The girls both sit silently, disturbed, depressed.

RITA *(after a moment)* You need any money?

JOANNA No, my mother's alimony came in yesterday. I swiped twenty bucks.

RITA I got about a hundred dollars you can have if you want it. What's eating you, Joanna? You been going on like this for ever so long.

JOANNA Don't you ever get depressed?

RITA Sure.

JOANNA *(with growing surliness)* When I first met you, you were about one step away from picking men off the street. You were going to throw yourself off the top of the May Building. You don't remember that, do you? You just got fired, and you didn't have any money, and you kept talking about going up to the personnel manager's office and throwing yourself out of the window. That's how you were going to show him for firing you. Well, that's how I feel. I feel so tired I can hardly get out of bed in the morning. The only reason I get up at all is I just couldn't stand staying home with my mother. You better get upstairs. You're going to be late for Burt Harres.

RITA I got ten minutes.

JOANNA Well, just don't tell me to stop drinking all the time.

She stares desolately out at the glaring bright white stucco of the studio buildings. Rita sits uncomfortably.

JOANNA *(abruptly)* When I was eight years old, I won the Prettiest Child at the Missouri State County Fair, and that's all my mother had to hear. She whisked me up to New York, and she had me taking ballet lessons at Carnegie Hall. Whole bunch of us little girls prancing around on our skinny legs. She had me modeling for John Robert Powers when I was fifteen years old. I made eleven thousand dollars when I was fifteen years old. Well, I been out here eleven years now, and it's about time she realizes she ain't never going to be the mother of a big movie star. If you don't make it by the time you're twenty-eight, you never make it. I'm taking extra calls now, standing on line, making eyes at some assistant director. I don't know how to get out of this, don't you understand? I don't know where to go. I keep dreaming I'll meet some man who will marry me and take me away. Who, Eddie Rogers? I been going with him for four months, and I don't even like him. He's a vicious drunk; I never know what he's going to do. And after him somebody just like him. I wish I could just go to sleep and sleep and sleep.

RITA   You want to go to the beach this afternoon? I think Valerie and Marilyn went there.

JOANNA   It's two-thirty now.

They sit in stiff silence again. Joanna darts a quick look at her young friend.

JOANNA   I really do believe you are concerned about me.

RITA   I am, Joanna.

JOANNA   You'd really give me that hundred dollars, wouldn't you? Where would you get a hundred dollars anyway? Dutch Seymour give you money? Why don't you marry him? Don't you like him at all?

RITA   Sure, I like him. I like him a lot. He's a kind man. I just don't want to get involved, that's all.

JOANNA   I'd marry him in a minute.

RITA   Joanna, I never had it so good as right now. I got a lot of friends, and I go to a lot of parties, and I got nice clothes. My mother writes me I'm the hero of my home town. Everybody is following my career like I was a football player from the high school who went on to Notre Dame. We had a boy like that. My, how we all talked about him. What do I want to get married for? I'm having a fine time just the way I am.

JOANNA It's better than drinking yourself to sleep.

RITA Well, the day I find myself with nothing else to do but drink myself to sleep, I'll get married. I never drank in my life. I can't stand the taste of it. I saw what my first husband was like, and I won't even sip a cocktail at a party.

JOANNA Well, I hope you never have to start.

RITA I never will, don't you worry.

JOANNA Don't be mad at me, Rita.

A sudden swift compassion sweeps over Rita's angry little face. She leans toward her friend in a flush of warmth.

RITA *(sincerely)* I ain't mad at you, Joanna. You're the only person I know I feel something for, and it makes me sick to see you as miserable as you are.

JOANNA *(touched)* You better get up to see Burt Harres.

RITA *(peering at her friend)* Joanna...

JOANNA Could you lend me ten bucks, something like that?

RITA *(promptly opening her purse)* Sure.

A portly, middle-aged man comes out of the building behind the car, preoccupied, starts walking down the street. His appearance transforms the dejected Joanna into a brightly smiling young woman, her mouth somewhat ajar in the now common conception of sensuality.

JOANNA *(brightly)* Hiya, Mr. Cummings!

Rita looks up, her face automatically registering a vivid, flashing smile.

RITA   Hiya, Mr. Cummings!

Mr. Cummings turns, nods, and continues on his way. Camera stays on the two young starlets, their faces a study in facile gaiety.

BURT HARRES' OUTER OFFICE.

Rita and four other girls, all blond, all cut from the same cloth, almost indistinguishable from each other, sit on the long brown leather office couch or on the comfortable soft brown leather easy chair or standing against the wall.

All the girls are dressed fit to kill according to their own lights. For the most part, this consists of daring necklines and much too tight skirts. They all have large artists' models' portfolios or smaller books of pictures of themselves. They all sit with a determined jadedness, unmoving, their skirts arranged over their knees.

A gray-haired secretary sits behind the desk, drinking coffee from a container and jabbering indistinct words to a friend over the telephone. There are some prints on the wall, Japanese silks and hunting scenes, and a framed poster of Mr. Harres' last picture, an effort entitled Give Me My Blood. *Next to the poster is a mounted bronze plaque which is a box-office award for the aforementioned picture distributed by one of the innumerable organizations that bestow box-office awards.*

The door to the inner office opens, and still another pretty blond girl comes out, expressionless except for a thin little smile. She looks at one of her friends sitting on the couch and makes a small moue to indicate something every one of these girls understands. The girl she made the face at, sitting two away from Rita, offers the girl who just came out a cigarette.

THE GIRL WHO JUST CAME OUT   It ain't worth it. The part's about that big.

She indicates how big the part is by her thumb and forefinger held one inch apart. Rita stands, goes to the secretary's desk.

RITA *(to the secretary)* Rita Shawn.

SECRETARY All right, honey.

She goes to the door to the inner office, raps lightly, opens it, sticks her head in.

BURT HARRES' INTERIOR OFFICE.

ACROSS BURT HARRES' bulky back to the doorway where Rita stands. She peers in with a big smile.

RITA Can I come in?

HARRES Come on in.

Rita comes in, closes the door. Mr. Harres' office is precisely the same as his secretary's except that there is an air conditioner that clogs up his window. The window has white nylon curtains through which the Hollywood sun filters. There is a picture of Mr. Harres' wife and two children, aged sixteen and nine, on Mr. Harres' desk.

Mr. Harres himself is a tall, well-groomed, balding man in his fifties, dressed in impeccable business costume, a gray striped suit. He looks up briefly at Rita's entrance and then goes back to pacing the room with executive ponderousness. He keeps his right hand in his jacket pocket and talks in measured basso tones. There are several scripts on the desk, variously colored, and a small vase containing innumerable finely sharpened pencils. Rita advances with her portfolio.

RITA I have my pictures with me, if you'd like to see them, Mr. Harres. I had a very nice part in my last picture at Columbia. Michael Sillman directed. *The Wayward Angel*. I play a sweet sort of Southern girl type. I think...

HARRES I got a small part in my picture. A barmaid in a Western town. I've had my eye on you for some time, Miss... *(He looks quickly at a sheet of paper on his desk.)* Miss Shawn. You'd be just right for it. You be nice to me, and I'll see that you get billing. It'll be a good credit for you.

RITA   *(the smile gone from her face, all business)* How nice do I have to be?

HARRES   *(His face suddenly brightens into a smile.)* You're Dutch Seymour's girl. That's right. Sure. You'll get the part. We'll talk about it tonight. Rita Shawn. Sure.

RITA   *(smiling)* Are you going to pick me up or do I have to meet you somewheres?

HARRES   Why don't you meet me at the Ready Room. Seven o'clock.

Rita nods, gathers up her portfolio, and reaches for the doorknob.

HOLLYWOOD, NORTH CHEROKEE. NIGHT.

Down the hill of North Cherokee we see Hollywood at night—with a small six-story apartment house in foreground. There are some lights on.

BURT HARRES' APARTMENT, LIVING ROOM. NIGHT.

Burt Harres moves slowly, restlessly around the room. He is wearing a dressing gown over his clothes. He is detached, perhaps even cold. He seems unpleasantly preoccupied. His right hand is stiffly placed in the pocket of the robe.

Two standing lamps illumine the room. Through the Venetian blinds we can see that it is night outside. The room itself is furnished after the usual style of studio apartments, several day beds, soft chairs, an Eames chair, a portable bar with bottles of liquor and a variety of glasses, wallpaper showing small sporting scenes, a pipe rack running almost the length of the wall.

Burt Harres moves slowly around the room, right hand in pocket, the perpetual executive pacing his conference.

The door to another room opens, and Rita comes out. She is wearing a party dress. She seems calm, detached, a cigarette dangling listlessly from her lips. Neither of them looks at the other.

HARRES *(coldly)* I called a cab for you. Wait downstairs for it.

RITA *(squeezing her feet into her pumps, all business)* I told my agent I had the part. He'll call you in the morning, discuss terms.

HARRES Hundred dollars a day. Two days' shooting. There's nothing to discuss.

RITA When's my shooting date? *(Picking up a script from off a studio couch)* Is this the script? I'll take it home and study the part. I'll tell my agent to call you in the morning.

Rita picks her summer stole off the back of one of the chairs, and her tiny beaded purse.

RITA *(smiling amiably)* Well, thank you for a very pleasant evening. I enjoyed the dinner very much. Is this my cab money? *(She smiles pleasantly, scoops up a bill from off the coffee table.)* Goodby now.

Harres says nothing, is slowly pacing the room. Rita fits her stole over her shoulders and disappears into the shadows of the front corridor.

NORTH CHEROKEE STREET OUTSIDE THE APARTMENT.

Looking down the hill of North Cherokee with Rita standing, her arms folded across her chest, pulling the stole tight across her shoulders. Looking past her, we can see all the way to Sunset Boulevard. It is eleven o'clock at night, and the endless swishing parade of automobile lights moves back and forth on the boulevards. Some of the store fronts in the distance are still lighted, and neons blink in the dark night.

A taxicab has rounded the corner at the bottom of the hill. It pulls quickly up to where she stands in front of the small white apartment house.

Rita gets into the cab. She sits down and then just sits for a moment. The driver finally turns around.

DRIVER   Where to?

RITA   I don't know.

She stares listlessly at the floor of the cab.

THE HAM AND EGGERY. NIGHT.

*WIDE GROUP SHOT of a booth containing three young actors and two
girls. One of the girls is Rita; she seems quite tired. She rests her face on her
right hand and rubs the corners of her eyes. In the background we see that
the restaurant is jumping, filled with people, loud voices, loud laughs.*

*One of the three men in the booth is the writer of the previous Ham and
Eggery scene. Some of this restaurant's patrons never leave the joint, smoking, drinking coffee, and talking all day long right up to closing time at one
A.M. The writer is one of these fellows. He is in full blast of discussion as we
cut in.*

THE WRITER   Acting! You call that acting? A smile—that's joy? A
frown—that's tragedy?

*The other girl in the booth, an intense little brunette with a mop of hair and
disdainfully dressed in a sweat shirt and dungarees, leans toward Rita.*

THE GIRL   You want a Dexedrine Spansule?

RITA   Yeah, you got one?

*The girl fishes a little tin out of her pocket and gives Rita a Spansule, which
she gulps down with her coffee. She sits slumped in her seat, her face resting
heavily on the palm of her hand.*

*Camera begins to dolly slowly back and away from the booth. The writer's
words begin to fade into the over-all jumble of the restaurant just as this particular booth begins to get lost among all the other booths.*

THE WRITER All right, wise guy. Name me one good picture made in the United States in the last five years. Name me one picture to compare with *Open City* or *Shoeshine*. Name me one picture that's got guts. Right now, I'm writing a play that exposes this stinking industry for what it is.

ACTOR When do you write, George? You're here gassing away all day and night.

LONG SHOT looking down on the restaurant, only half filled with tired and driven people. In particular, we see Rita hunched in her seat, exhausted and spent, her face too weary to feign any cheerfulness.

THE HAM AND EGGERY BAR. NIGHT.

Rita is in the dark bar, which is jammed. Actors, actresses—old, young, middle-aged—assistant directors, writers, grips, gaffers, and prop men block the aisle and make it almost impassable. Rita has joined a huddled group at the end of the bar. There are two starlets sitting on stools sipping drinks, surrounded by four men. Rita is beaming, hyper-ebullient, hysterically gay. She wraps her arms around two of the men in a burst of effusive camaraderie.

Somebody offers her a drink. She says, "No, thanks. I don't drink." Her face is radiant, almost hysterically so. The two starlets on the stools say something. Rita bends down to hear it, then throws her head back and laughs and laughs and laughs.

NORTH SIERRA BONITA. NIGHT.

HIGH ANGLE SHOT looking down on the dark, deserted, silent little street of pretty little one-family houses. For a long moment, the absolute stillness hangs so that we know it is very late at night. Not a light in any window. All is quiet.

Then a taxi edges slowly into our view, moving along at the curb, looking for a particular house. The taxi stops. The door opens and Rita gets out of the cab, closes the door behind her. The click of the door is clearly audible in the night hush. The cab pulls away with a murmur of gears and motor.

Rita hurries up the little white walk to the front door of the house, fishing out her key from her purse. She inserts the key and opens the door. We can perhaps detect through the white chintz curtains that a lamp is on deep in the living room.

RITA'S HOME. NIGHT.

Rita comes into the house, closing the door behind her. She turns; the house is quiet, but the vague indication of light makes her turn from the small entrance foyer and take a few steps into the living room.

RITA'S P.O.V.: The living room is dark except for one small reading lamp at the far end. Its thin light throws a vague illumination over the modest room, which is half dining and half living room. The furniture is Victorian, uncomfortable-looking chairs on spindly legs and an uncomfortable couch. A small mahogany dining table is surrounded by small mahogany dining chairs.

Sprawled in one of the soft chairs is Joanna, soddenly, heavily drunk. Her shoes are off and lie on their sides in front of her. One of her stockings makes a wispy bundle on the shadowy floor. Her blouse is unbuttoned and hangs loosely outside of her slacks. On the floor lies a bottle of gin on its side, half of it spilled onto the rug in an ugly blotch. There is also an ice-cube container from the refrigerator on the floor, and beside Joanna's chair is a highball glass containing one ice cube. She regards Rita's entrance through swollen, heavy-lidded eyes. Her face is thick with drunken pain. The light of the lamp falls fitfully on her features, shadowing and distorting them.

REACTION SHOT OF RITA. Expressionless. Rita watches her friend. Then she sidles slowly across the room toward Joanna, who is now looking down at the floor. Rita sinks onto the couch, which forms an el to the chair Joanna sits in. For a moment she just sits there.

Rita bends down, picks up the gin bottle and pours some into the highball glass on the end table. Then she takes the glass and begins to sip it. Her face remains expressionless throughout all this. Now she kicks off her shoes, leans back and stretches her feet out in front of her. Her eyes close. She sips the drink.

LONG SHOT looking down the length of the living room to the two star-lets sprawled on their seats, the small disarray of a small drunken binge on the carpet in front of them. Not a word is said for a long moment.

Then Rita stands, holding her drink, sipping it as she walks down the living room toward the telephone sitting on the coffee table directly in front of cam-era. She sits down in the chair beside the phone, lifts the receiver, sets it down on the coffee table, dials, sipping her gin throughout. She picks up the receiv-er, holds it to her ear, looks vaguely, even with boredom, around the room.

RITA *(on phone)* Room 417, please. Mr. Dutch Seymour. *(She waits, making short sighs of frustration and tenseness, and then suddenly downs the rest of her drink in one gulp. The taste is forbidding and she clenches her eyes against it. Then, with her eyes still closed)* Well, hello, Dutch. This is Rita. I hope I didn't wake you up. I know how you stay up late read-ing all the time.... No, I just got in.... Well, I tell you, Dutch... *(She looks up at the ceiling, bored, tired)* I feel like getting married. Do you still want to marry me, Dutch? Yeah, sure, any time. I promise you I'll make you a very good wife. Dutch...

GRAUMAN'S CHINESE THEATER. NIGHT.

Rita and Dutch sweep up to the entrance of the theater. This is a premiere, and there are a number of excitable spectators flanking the entrance walk. Rita beams at them, waves, clutches her husband's arm. He is a tall, somber, well-built, lighthaired man of thirty-eight. He smiles at his wife's childlike excitement.

INSIDE GRAUMAN'S CHINESE THEATER.

Rita and Dutch seated off the aisle. A small bespectacled man is bent over them.

CLOSE UP of Rita being interviewed by the small bespectacled man.

RITA I never been so happy in all my life! We had a wonderful time in Acapulco on our honeymoon! I am absolutely deliriously happy.

INTERVIEWER Do you believe marriage will interfere with your career?

RITA   Dutch and I think we are two intelligent people, and we see no
reason why I can't have a career and be a wife too.

*She darts a quick, nervous glance at her husband at her side. He is listening
silently to a man at his side. Rita turns back to the interviewer with a
patient, waiting smile.*

BEVERLY HILLS HOTEL. DAY.

*ESTABLISHING SHOT of the hotel entrance: considerable activity, cars
pulling in and out, people waiting to be picked up.*

BEVERLY HILLS HOTEL LOBBY.

*MEDIUM LONG SHOT showing the crowded lobby. CLOSE SHOT of
switchboard with crowded lobby in background.*

SWITCHBOARD OPERATOR   Mr. Seymour isn't taking any calls yet.

BEVERLY HILLS HOTEL, SUITE.

*MEDIUM LONG SHOT noting Rita and Dutch asleep on their respective
twin beds. The Venetian blinds are drawn tightly and the room seems dark
and close. The sun, as we have seen in previous shots, is very strong today, and
the close air of the bedroom seems muggy. Rita sleeps with only a sheet cover-
ing her. Dutch has a light blanket over him, one bare, hairy arm visible over
it.*

*One of the bedspreads has been piled loosely on a soft chair; the other lies in a
heap on the floor at the foot of the bed. Clothes seem to have been left at ran-
dom here and there—a shirt, Rita's stockings, Dutch's shoes, a woman's white
silk blouse. The total effect is one of heat and disorder and discomfort.*

CLOSE SHOT of Rita waking up with Dutch sleeping in background. She wakes up conscious of the closeness of the air, her eyes red, not fully rested. She lies quietly for a moment, conscious of an unpleasant taste in her mouth and a sad, amorphous weight in her stomach. She sits up after a moment and lets her legs dangle over the side of her bed. She faces her husband's bed and watches him without betraying any emotion for a moment. She wears limp, blue pajamas, clinging in small patches to her wet skin.

She picks up the house phone, waits a moment.

RITA *(low murmur into phone)* What time is it?...As late as that? Think I can still get some breakfast out of room service?...No, I'll call later.

She hangs up and stands, stiff and yet not aching, with more of a feeling of desolation rather than physical discomfort. She creeps on her bare feet across the green carpeting to the windows, opens one blind, reaches out and opens the window. This effort exhausts her, and she stands limply, catching her breath. The sudden sunlight streaming in through the one blind bleaches her face.

Rita looks out over the palmetto and yucca trees to the busy, chattering activity at the car entrance to the hotel. Her face reveals a sad distaste for herself, the cluttered hotel room, the busy, bright sunlight. Behind her, her husband's voice reaches into the murky, slow movement of her thoughts.

DUTCH *(muttering)* What time is it?

She turns. REVERSE SHOT across her shoulder. Her husband lies silently on the bed. He has thrown back his covers, revealing a strong, brown, hirsute chest. He, too, seems drained.

RITA Half past one.

DUTCH Boy, it's hot.

She moves silently back to her bed, sits down facing her husband, looks down at a copy of Look *magazine on the floor by her bare feet.*

RITA I feel blue. I hate waking up with half the day gone already.

DUTCH We ought to get up eight o'clock in the morning.

RITA What'll we do eight o'clock in the morning?

DUTCH I don't know. Go to the beach.

RITA I'm sick of going to the beach. *(rubs her temples. A dense, close silence fills the room)* You know how I feel? When I first came out here, I didn't know anybody. I used to stay up till two, three, four o'clock in the morning reading magazines. I wrote a letter to my father-in-law, care of the studio, but he never answered me. I used to sleep till one, two o'clock in the afternoon every day. I used to wake up sick in my heart. It's funny. I haven't thought about that in years. I hate waking up this late. I feel real blue. I really do. *(She lies back on her bed, stares up at the ceiling)* You ever feel that way, Dutch?

DUTCH Sure.

RITA You know what I used to do when I first came out here? I used to go into bars and let men think they could pick me up. Just to talk to somebody. I never drank in those days. I just used to sit with these guys till they got drunk and then I'd go home and read. Sometimes I'd fall asleep sitting up reading. I had a little room with an old Greek couple on South Orange Drive. I was so lonely I used to have the shakes like I had Parkinson's disease. But I never went home with any of those men. I just couldn't stand the thought of somebody touching me. I came close to going crazy in those days.

DUTCH *(likewise lying on his bed staring up at the ceiling)* You know, before we got married, I started to go to pieces myself. I used to take awful good care of myself. Every morning a shower and a shave. I couldn't stand it if my shoes weren't shiny. My people are St. Louis German, you know. We're awful clean. But the last half year or so I began going to pieces. Sometimes I wouldn't leave my hotel room for two days. I wouldn't shave. I used to look at the toothpaste. I couldn't stand the idea of the taste.

RITA   Why's that, Dutch?

DUTCH   Well, you know. Doing nothing all day, it eats up a man. That's
no life. I don't know what I want to do, but I want to do something.
Get into some business. You can be a retired sports star just so long.
What do you think I ought to do?

RITA   I don't know. I'd like to get out of Hollywood though.

Dutch gets up on one elbow.

DUTCH   Would you, really?

RITA   I'm not getting anywheres here, Dutch. I mean, why kid myself?

*He examines her as she lies on her bed, a troubled blond girl in rumpled blue
pajamas, her eyes closed now against the warmth of the room. After a
moment, he lies back, staring at the ceiling.*

DUTCH   Would you like to go back to St. Louis with me?

She turns her head on her pillow so that she can see him.

RITA   What would we do there, Dutch?

DUTCH   *(afraid to look at her, he stares at the ceiling)* Well, my father died.
My brother's running the contracting business. They're doing very
nicely. He's always writing me, my brother, to come back, get in the
business. As a kid, I always liked hanging around my father, the
cement and the mortar and the big trucks full of steel rods. I'd like to
go back, I think, get into the business. I'm pretty important in St.
Louis. People like me there. We'll get a nice house, have people to
dinner. My mother's kind of nosy, but if she gives you any trouble, just
tell me. I'll straighten her out. You met my brother at the wedding. He
liked you very much. I think that would be nice. It's real, you know,
instead of floating around in mid-air like we are now.

He looks over to his wife and is a little startled to see that her eyes are filled with tears. He sits up, moves over to her bed, looks down at her with concerned tenderness.

DUTCH   It'll be nice, Rita. You'll like it.

She is suddenly in his arms, clutching at him, pressing her tear-streaked face against his chest.

RITA   Oh, Dutch, do you love me?

DUTCH   Sure.

RITA   Do you love me, Dutch?

DUTCH   *(holds her)* I love you, Rita.

RITA   Let's do that, Dutch! Let's go to St. Louis. I got kin in St. Louis. I never met them.

He is holding her tightly, kissing her neck, her shoulders. She holds onto him almost desperately, asking over and over again, "Do you love me, Dutch? Do you love me? Do you love me, Dutch?"....

DISSOLVE TO:

DUTCH AND RITA'S SUITE. DUSK.

Rita lies in bed. The room is still in a state of disorder. It is dusk. A small breeze gently wafts the draperies; the windows are opened. Rita lies in bed, her bare shoulders and arms over the light blanket. A glass ash tray balances precariously on her stomach; she smokes a cigarette. She watches her husband as he moves across the room, a strong lithe man in pajama trousers. He goes into the bathroom, comes out again. She watches his every move with a growing sense of apprehension. He looks into his chest of drawers for underwear and socks. He is also smoking a cigarette.

RITA *(abruptly)* What do you mean you love me, Dutch?

He looks at her briefly.

RITA What did I ever do for you? You know hundreds of girls. Why me?
I'm not especially pretty. Why should anybody love me? I don't think
very much of myself. If I was a man, I couldn't love me. In many ways,
I'm a terrible girl. I have a three-year-old daughter, and I just gave her
away to my first husband without even arguing. He sent me a paper in
the mail, and I signed her entire custody away without even reading
what the paper said. I never went to New York to visit her. I keep her
out of my mind, I'm so ashamed of myself. I think I'm ugly. I'm dirty.
I don't understand why you love me. I don't believe you. I don't think
you love me. I think you're physically attracted to me. I don't even
know why that. Why'd you marry me, Dutch? I came over any time
you called me anyhow.

DUTCH *(moving back across the room to the bathroom, carrying shorts and socks;
amiably)* I don't know what you're talking about.

He goes into the bathroom. Rita regards the open doorway.

RITA What's it like when you love somebody, Dutch?

DUTCH *(off-screen in bathroom)* Ain't you ever loved anybody?

RITA Nobody ever loved me before. Why should you love me?

*Dutch appears in the bathroom doorway. He is wearing a silk polka-dotted
robe. His bare legs protrude below it.*

DUTCH You always try to act so tough, but you're like a little kid. That's
the truth. I always liked little kids. My brother's kids, I'm crazy about
them. I'm going to take a shower. We'll have dinner downstairs, then
we're supposed to go to Burt Lancaster's.

*He disappears back into the bathroom. Rita leans on one elbow, holding the
sheet against her, regards the door to the bathroom.*

RITA I don't know what love is, Dutch. I find you very physically attractive, and I guess you find me very physically attractive, but that ain't going to last very long, Dutch.

The rush of the shower interrupts her. She calls out.

RITA Dutch...

He obviously doesn't hear her; she sinks back onto the bed, her pretty little face twisted into a thoughtful, anxious frown. She reaches around for the ash tray now at her side, drops a long ash into it.

BEVERLY HILLS HOTEL, POLO LOUNGE. EVENING.

Rita and Dutch are at dinner, with the restaurant in the background. Their dinner is about over; they are on their coffee and dessert. A tall man in a sports jacket is bending over Dutch, talking inaudibly to him. Dutch is listening with a thin smile. Rita sits, her feeling of apprehension deepening to the point of being obviously disturbed. Behind them, the dinner hour is in full progress, jangle and jammer. Dutch notes his wife's distracted mood.

DUTCH Something wrong, honey?

She smiles nervously, shakes her head, but the dark mood promptly returns to her face. The man talking to Dutch goes. Dutch looks at his wife again, purses his lips, wonders what's up.

RITA *(suddenly)* Let's go upstairs again, Dutch.

DUTCH Don't you want to go to Lancaster's?

RITA *(standing and starting away)* Let's go upstairs.

DUTCH AND RITA'S SUITE.

Rita is in tears, in panic. Dutch listens to her with the patient fondness of a father. Through the window we can see it is night outside. The lamps in the room are lit.

RITA *(in tears)* I don't want to go to St. Louis, Dutch!

DUTCH *(consolingly)* All right, honey, we won't go.

RITA You'll get tired of me.

DUTCH What are you talking about?

He moves to her, tries to hold her, but she moves away from him in panic.

RITA You'll leave me, you'll desert me. What would you want with me? I'm just a little tramp. You like me now, but you'll get tired. You'll be sorry you brought me. You'll be ashamed of me. Your family ain't going to like me.

DUTCH Honey...

RITA *(crying out)* Why should they like me? I'm a nothing! Give me a little more chance at my career, Dutch! If I was a star, then everybody would like me. Then I would go to St. Louis with you, and you'd see, all your friends would like me. See, then you could be proud of me. I know you'll leave me, Dutch. I know you will.

DUTCH *(holding her now)* You're like a little baby.

RITA *(weeping on his chest)* I'm sorry, Dutch. I'm sorry.

DUTCH *(with deep parental calm and affection)* Take it easy now. Take it easy.

RITA I'm no good. I'm no good.

He holds her, rocking a little back and forth, patting her head gently, very much as if he were calming a frightened baby.

WESTWOOD MOVIE THEATER. NIGHT.

LONG SHOT looking toward the entrance of the theater. In the foreground stands a Santa Claus in shirt sleeves and red trousers, ringing a bell. This, and the fact that people on the sidewalks wear light topcoats, is the only indication that it is winter. Some people come out of the theater; two of them are Rita and Dutch.

CAMERA PANS with them as they come toward us and past us, long enough for us to see that much of the warmth of their earlier relationship has drained away over the months. They walk silently, not particularly interested in each other, toward a Cadillac convertible parked down the street a bit. She opens the door on her side and gets in; he walks around to his side and gets in.

INSIDE CAR. NIGHT.

PROCESS SHOT as they drive along darkened Sunset Boulevard back to their hotel, the dark landscape gliding along behind them, occasional cars on the highway. They sit silently, unrelated. Rita is looking vaguely at the passing landscape. Dutch stares at the road ahead.

BEVERLY HILLS HOTEL LOBBY.

Rita and Dutch come into the lobby. It is deserted; it is quite late at night. Dutch pauses at the desk for messages; there are none. Rita waits in the middle of the lobby for him to rejoin her. He goes to her and they start wordlessly off for the elevators.

DUTCH AND RITA'S HOTEL SUITE. NIGHT.

The door opens; a shadow of hall light shoots into the black room. Rita and Dutch are two black, bulky silhouettes in the doorway for a moment. Then Dutch turns the entrance light on. He moves farther into the room, turning on the room light and pocketing the key as he goes.

Rita closes the door and comes slowly into the room after him. Dutch removes his coat, hangs it up in the closet, yawns, rubs the back of his neck. Rita goes to the window, closes the Venetian blinds. Dutch sits down on a soft chair, removes his shoes. Rita lets her cloth stole drop onto another chair, goes off to the bathroom, turns on the light, closes the door.

Dutch takes off his black silk socks now. He tucks them into his shoes, bends, picks the shoes up, stands, carries them to the side of the room, puts them down. Camera pans with him. He wriggles his arms free of his jacket, which he drops on a chair, and then slides out of his suspender straps.

BATHROOM OF DUTCH AND RITA'S SUITE.

Rita enters the bathroom, surrounded by gleaming white tile. She is slipping out of her dress. She hangs it on a hook on the door. She is wearing a corset-like undergarment with a starched underslip. She opens the door and calls dully out to her husband.

RITA   You want to give me my robe?

She leaves the door slightly ajar, sits down on the edge of the tub, begins ungartering her stockings. A moment later the bathroom door opens and her husband appears, proffering a pink lace peignoir. She takes it from him without rising and lets it fall loosely over the edge of the tub, so that the sleeves and collar form a soft puddle on the bottom of the tub. She goes back to ungartering her stockings, looks up, notes her husband, now in undershirt and trousers, standing, looking at her. She looks down at her other stocking and starts to ungarter that.

After a moment she reaches over with one foot and closes the bathroom door in her husband's face. She strips off her second stocking and stands, leaving the two stockings in wispy heaps on the bathroom floor. She stands in front of the full-length mirror regarding herself with no evident expression. She reaches behind herself and begins to unhook the corset-like undergarment.

BEDROOM.

Dutch, in pajama bottoms, moves back to the small entrance hallway to turn off the light there. His suit lies carelessly draped over the back of a soft chair. After he turns off the entrance light, he moves around the room, turning off

*the lamps, leaving only a reading lamp by the soft chair on which Rita's stole
lies. He finds a copy of* Life *on the bed table between the twin beds, carries it
to the soft chair, moves the stole aside, sits and begins thumbing through the
magazine. He is a strong, lithe, muscular man, his chest thick with blond
hair, somberly looking at the pictures in* Life.

*After a moment the bathroom door opens and Rita appears, carrying her
dress, which she throws over Dutch's suit on the soft chair. She is wearing the
pink peignoir. She puts a handful of jewelry, a choker and a bracelet, on the
chest of drawers, sits down on one of the twin beds and examines her fingernails. Dutch rises, comes over to her, sits down beside her, begins kissing her
neck.*

RITA *(examining her nails)* Aren't you going to brush your teeth or wash
up or anything?

*Dutch rises a little sullenly and goes into the bathroom, leaving the door ajar.
Camera stays on Rita. She lies back on the bed now and stares up at the ceiling. Behind her, off-screen, we hear the sound of rushing water, then off, and
Dutch comes out of the bathroom, stands looking down at her. She closes her
eyes.*

*He lies down on the bed beside her, reaches over and grips her limp body, and
kisses her on the mouth. His face is emotionless, even cold. His head moves to
kiss her neck and we see Rita's face close up over his shoulder. She is staring
at the ceiling. Then her eyes close again, and she prepares to suffer through
the experience.*

DISSOLVE TO:

THE HOTEL ROOM. NIGHT.

*Dutch sleeps heavily on his twin bed. The room is dark now except for the
lights of the patio and the moonlight, which brings a vague, white light into
the room, drawing a thin white outline along the furniture pieces. Camera
pans slowly across the room, noting that the other bed has been occupied but
is not now, and eventually finding Rita sitting in the soft chair by the now
slightly opened Venetian blinds. She is wearing her peignoir and smoking a
cigarette, sipping a highball.*

The bottle of liquor is on the chest of drawers at her elbow. She is a little drunk. She is staring bleakly down at the carpeting.

HOTEL SUITE. SOME TIME LATER.

DISSOLVE to their hotel suite. Dutch stands in his pajama trousers, unshaven for two days, hair unkempt; he has obviously just awakened and not from a particularly good sleep. His eyes are slitted with cold fury, and he is brandishing a magazine.

DUTCH You have to pose for these kind of pictures!

He flings the magazine in the direction of the bathroom door. It flaps against the wall and slithers to the floor. Rita is standing in the bathroom doorway. She wears an overly chic cocktail dress, which is still unzipped under her armpits and hangs loosely about her. She has not put on her shoes yet and stands in her stocking feet. She is fixing her hair, which is loose. There is a slatternly feeling about her. She is in a black rage herself.

RITA I didn't know he was going to sell them to that magazine. He told me the pictures were for *Esquire.*

He turns away, his anger thick within him, an inarticulate, unexplored anger, really against himself, but no less intense for that. He sits down, stares at his toes, absently rubs his unshaven cheeks. Rita has gone back into the bathroom. We can see her from the back, standing in front of the wall mirror over the basin, angrily bobby-pinning her hair. She turns now, comes back to the open doorway, surveys her husband with sullen distaste.

RITA You coming with me or not?

DUTCH Where?

RITA You know where.

DUTCH I never know where you go any more.

RITA Lester Brackman is giving a party because they finished shooting the picture this morning. Lester Brachman says my bit was the stand-out bit of the whole picture. He told me R.M. Lucas, Vice President in Charge of Production, saw the rushes, says I'm going to steal the whole picture. They're having a party on the set. Are you coming?

Dutch says nothing, sits heavily in swollen, dull anger. Rita waits for an answer. Then, still fixing her hair, she moves across the room, a little squat-ly in her stocking feet. She opens a closet door.

RITA   I don't like this dress. I'm going to change it.   Draw the blinds, Dutch.

DUTCH   What for? All anybody has to do is buy that magazine.

She turns and regards her husband with cold dislike.

RITA   I never cheated on you once, Dutch, in the eleven months we've been married. Not even for business. I could have had a contract with Lester Brackman a hundred times. All I had to do was say a word. But I told him, "Mr. Brackman, I'm a married woman. I don't do that kind of thing any more." I never cheated on you once. That's more than you can say.

The point is a telling one. He looks away.

RITA   Just don't cheat with girls I know, Dutch, because it gets back to me.

She zips her dress with angry, sharp movements of her hands, finds a pair of shoes lying on the carpeting by the closet door, straightens them with her toe, slides her feet into them.

RITA   Why don't you shave? You haven't been out this room in two days. You better get a hold yourself. You sleep till one, two o'clock every day now.

She crosses coldly back to the bathroom, stands in front of the bathroom mir-

ror, examining herself. The basin below the mirror is covered with endless jars of cosmetics and lipstick tubes. In the living room, Dutch sits, holding in his own anger.

DUTCH *(eyes down, muttering)* Maybe if I had a wife who was a wife... *(looks up as Rita starts back into the room)* You don't care about me. You never cared about me. *(His voice has begun to rise.)*

RITA *(her own voice suddenly shrill)* Any time you wanted me, I submitted to you.

They are suddenly shouting at each other, drowning out each other's words.

DUTCH Oh, shut up!

RITA Why don't you leave me alone?

DUTCH Shut up! Shut up! Shut up!

RITA You sit there watching television all night long.

DUTCH You married me to get your name in the papers.

RITA Why'd you marry me?

DUTCH Two-bit tramp!

RITA I never understood that! Just tell me!

DUTCH I have to send my own clothes to the cleaners!

RITA Just tell me that!

DUTCH *(crying out)* What? What? What do you want?

RITA *(staring out the window)* All right, quiet. Everybody'll hear you.

He stands and moves quickly away because he is horrified to find that he is about to cry.

DUTCH Because I thought you was a nice girl! I thought you liked me!

He sits down on the bed. A cold, unresolved silence fills the room, a silence thick with hatred and unspoken violence.

DUTCH I'd like to get out of this town. I don't know what keeps me here. I don't know where to go. I don't know what to do.

Rita stands, much more deeply disturbed by their sudden flurry of hatred than she herself knows. She hopes he will continue talking, but he just sits, a somehow disheveled and beaten man, frightened even to look at the intense, flinty woman he has married. After a moment she speaks.

RITA *(hoping he will agree)* You coming or not? I'll wait for you if you want to get dressed.

He says nothing, stares at the floor. She stands, her entire body taut with the feeling of her trapped marriage, aching to leave with some feeling of resolution but completely unequipped to deal with the matter.

After a moment she turns and takes two steps toward the door and then stops.

RITA I'm going. Okay?

He says nothing. She turns wearily and goes out the door.

Dutch stands promptly upon the closing click of the door, walks a few aimless paces around the room. He turns and meanders barefoot to the telephone table between the beds, perches on the welter of bedsheets and blankets on one bed, lifts the phone.

DUTCH *(into phone)* You got any messages for me?...Okay...Yeah, yeah, will you get Mr. Kleiner for me, please? Thanks.... Sports desk, please.... Hello, Allie, this is Dutch. I got a message you called me.... No, I just woke up.... No, I don't want to go.... Ah, I feel lousy...I don't

know, I just feel like sitting around the room.... She went to a party
down at the studio. They just finished her picture.... What do I want
to go to the fights for? ...Who else is going?... Ah, they'll just keep asking me who's better, Canzoneri or Barney Ross.... Listen, whyn't you
bring them over here and we'll watch it on TV or something....

HOTEL SUITE LIVING ROOM. NIGHT.

*Dutch Seymour and three other men in the living room of Dutch and Rita's
hotel suite. The FIRST MAN is fifty-odd, the SECOND MAN forty-odd.
They are both unmistakably of pugilistic background, a little given to weight.
The THIRD MAN is a reasonably intelligent-looking fellow—a newspaper-
man. They are involved in one of those endless, familiar bull sessions that ex-
boxers fall into.*

*They are all vaguely bored, but this is all they have to talk about. They have
heard the stories a hundred times, but they still summon enough energy to
laugh. Dutch is removed from it all—detached from the talk, bored by the
baseball game showing on the television set, deep within his own pained
thoughts.*

SECOND MAN You guys remember Baldy Hoffman?

FIRST MAN Baldy Hoffman? Hey, Dutch, I ever tell you, Dutch—hey,
Dutch—about the time, Dutch—hey, Dutch—about the time Baldy
Hoffman was fighting Oscar the Turk? Hey, Dutch, he was no more
a Turk than you or me, Dutch Hey, Dutch, he was an Irishman from
Fall River, Mass.

SECOND MAN You guys remember Baldy Hoffman with those big feet of
his?

FIRST MAN Used to fight 1921, 1922, around that time. He had hair all
over him. He looked like a gorilla.

SECOND MAN Hey, Rocky, you mind if I tell a story?

FIRST MAN What? What?

SECOND MAN   I can't get a word in edgewise with this guy here.

FIRST MAN   Hey, Dutch...

Dutch turns a dutiful interest to the persistent sound of his name.

FIRST MAN   I ever tell you, Dutch, about the time Baldy Hoffman—he got the biggest feet in Boston, you know—I ever tell you guys—hey, Dutch, I ever tell you guys about the time Baldy Hoffman, he can't find his fighting shoes?

The other two men have begun to laugh. The Second Man, who has heard this story endless times already, begins rocking back and forth in his seat, shaking with silent merriment.

FIRST MAN   Well he can't borrow a pair. Man, there's nobody in Boston gotta pair o' shoes Baldy can wear. So he has to fight barefooted. By the third round he got so many blisters from the canvas, Dutch—hey, Dutch—he gotta cool off his feet in a pail of water, Dutch. Hey, Dutch...

Everybody but Dutch is absolutely choking with laughter now.

FIRST MAN   *(roaring with laughter himself)*   Hey, Dutch, that Baldy, he got such big feet he can't get them in the pail!

Dutch works up a thin smile for the story.

FIRST MAN   *(he can hardly get the words out, he is laughing so much)*   He says, "Hey! I can't get my feet inna pail!" *(screams of laughter)* He finally gets one of his feet in, he can't get the foot out!

This is too much for the Second Man. He gets up and walks around in little circles, clutching his aching sides. Dutch abruptly stands.

DUTCH   I don't feel so hot. You guys stay here.

He turns sharply and exits. The laughter drains out of the others. The news-paperman looks worried seeing Dutch departing that way.

A STUDIO SOUND STAGE.

A wrap party is going on. An improvised buffet has been set up on two car-penter's horses, and about thirty people stand loosely around in the huge, sprawling area, holding drinks and paper plates covered with cold cuts, occa-sionally laughing. Most of the party are crew members and are in their shirt sleeves and work clothes. There are about eight or nine women; a few men in jackets and neckties. It is not a particularly gay affair.

Dutch picks his way past a flat and joins the large opened area where the party is quietly going on. He stands on the fringe, watching the party.

DUTCH'S P.O.V.: The desultory party. At the far end of the long shot we see Rita gaily chatting with two men wearing jackets and ties. She holds a drink. She has noted Dutch's entrance. She is one of those girls who always have one eye on the entrance to see who's coming. When she thinks she has caught Dutch's eye, she smiles and waves a little. He does not respond; instead, he turns away and moves a few paces to an impeccably dressed man in his late forties with an intelligent but determinedly sardonic face. The man is talking to another man in shirt sleeves. He watches Dutch approach with a smile.

DUTCH   Hello, Lester, how are you?

BRACKMAN   Hello, Dutch. Want a drink?

Dutch shakes his head. Lester returns his attention to the man he is talking to.

BRACKMAN   Well, I don't know, Joe. I think you'll be free by the end of the week. It looks pretty good to me. Maybe one, two days of retakes. We'll know that by Wednesday.

DUTCH   Lester... *(Brackman bends to hear Dutch's quiet, tense words.)* Lester, my wife got any talent at all?

BRACKMAN Well, she's got something, Dutch. She's very good in this
picture. She's going to attract a lot of attention. She's got what I call
the quality of availability. She's not particularly pretty. It's a kind of
warmth that some women have that makes all the men in the audience
think they could make her if they only knew her. She don't act—she's
no Olivia de Havilland—but there's a lot of big stars in this town who
ain't Olivia de Havilland. If you're asking me as a producer whether I
think she's going to get somewheres, I'd say yeah, I'd like to sign her.
You know, we've been getting about five or six hundred letters a week
on this girl on her last picture. And the fan magazines are picking her
up. There's apparently something about your wife, Dutch. R.M. Lucas
saw her dailies. He's very excited about her. He wants to sign her, do
a lot of publicity, a whole campaign.

DUTCH (*without looking at the man*) Lester, I understand you're trying
to make my wife. I'll bust your head open if I hear that again.

*He turns and moves slowly off, picking his way past the flat he passed com-
ing in. Lester Brackman stands pursing his lips.*

A MOVIE. DARK.

*Dutch sitting in the darkened movie theater. The diffuse gray light emanat-
ing from the screen far up ahead makes changing shadows on his face. He is
watching the picture with no response. Then his attention wanders downward
and he stares at the back of the seat in front of him.*

SANTA MONICA BOULEVARD. NIGHT.

*We see the deserted boulevard at one o'clock in the morning. An occasional car
shoots by. Otherwise, the dusky little shop fronts are empty and dark and
bare. We see Dutch walking slowly, almost purposelessly, down the street.*

*CAMERA WAITS for him to pass it. He gets near enough for us to see he
carries a dull weight of pain inside him, and the ever-controlled muscles of his
face are released enough to show this.*

BEVERLY HILLS HOTEL. LOBBY.

Dutch slowly crosses the deserted lobby on his way to the elevators.

DUTCH AND RITA'S SUITE.

Dutch's bulky silhouette blocks the light issuing from the hallway. The room itself is dark. With a sudden rush, Rita is upon him, flinging her arms around his neck and pressing herself to him.

Rita and Dutch clutch each other in the opened doorway of their suite. The sudden unexpected explosion of love from his wife has ripped the last of Dutch's reserve away. He stares over his wife's head, tears rolling slowly out of wide-opened eyes. He presses his wife to him slowly, his cheek against the softness of her hair. Their words come in mumbles and whispers and with great effort.

DUTCH I want to go back to St. Louis, Rita. I want to go back to St. Louis.

RITA I love you, Dutch. I love you. I love you.

DUTCH Please come with me. Please...

RITA Anything you say, Dutch.

DUTCH Holy Jesus, Mary, Mother of Christ...

They hold each other in a desperate embrace.

DISSOLVE TO:

THE HOTEL SUITE. DAWN.

Rita and Dutch sleep in their respective beds. It is dawn now, and the room is alight but gray. Dutch's robe lies on the floor in front of his bed. One of the bed pillows is on the soft chair. The bedspreads have been piled loosely on other chairs.

Dutch sleeps peacefully on his side. Rita sleeps rigidly, her face almost stiff with control. Her sheets are twisted and one of the blankets is half off the bed. Suddenly she sits bolt upright, her eyes wide, staring. For a moment she just sits this way.

Then she gets her feet over the side and sits holding her face in her hands and shaking her head as if to clear it of its suddenly turbulent thoughts. She gets up. She is wearing pajamas now, and she steps barefoot to the window and looks out on the dawning day.

Then she turns and looks at her husband, a blanketed hump, one hairy bare arm over the covers, his face pressed deep in the pillows. She stares at him for a long moment, then sits down on a soft chair on top of a piled bedspread. She seems exhausted. Her shoulders slump wearily and her hands fall slackly between her knees. She stares abjectly at the floor.

THE HOTEL SUITE. MORNING.

MEDIUM SHOT looking across Rita's shoulders, sitting as she was in the last shot, toward Dutch's bed. He is just waking up. He shifts under his covers and eventually opens his eyes. After a moment, he sits up, dressed only in pajama bottoms. The sun is bright in the room.

He looks quickly over to Rita sitting in the chair and knows instantly that whatever moment they had the night before has gone. He looks back at the floor, assembling himself, a chill gathering in his stomach.

Rita sits in the chair void of reaction. Dutch stands. He hobbles around the bed, past Rita, and plods off to the bathroom. He tries a quick look at his wife again and then goes into the bathroom. He closes the door.

Rita gets to her feet with some effort. Her mind is going lickety-split. Her face is one condensed mass of concentration as she assembles her words, arguments, points of discussion. She moves to the closed bathroom door, takes another moment to think before she speaks.

RITA   *(to the bathroom door)*   Dutch, let's stay here just another couple of weeks. What's another couple of weeks? Lester Brackman wants me to come over to his office this morning. I'm entitled to my chance. We could live in St. Louis. I would make a two-picture deal and just fly out here to make the pictures. But we could live in St. Louis.

The sound of rushing water in the bathroom interrupts her. She turns a little, exasperated, sits on her bed by the bathroom door, waits till the sound of water stops.

RITA   *(suddenly crying out)*   Dutch! I can't live in St. Louis and just be a nothing! I can't! You'll be tired of me in three months! You'll be sorry you brought me! I ain't no housewife. I wouldn't know what to do in a kitchen! I'll go crazy there, doing nothing all day long. I'm sorry, Dutch! I swear I'm sorry! I don't know why you put up with me at all!

Only silence greets her from behind the bathroom door. She waits a moment, then turns and begins to pace restlessly around. As she starts to say something, she becomes aware of muffled sounds behind the door. After a moment, she realizes that her husband is crying, and the sounds are deep, shuddering sobs.

She wheels away from the door, clutching her hands, her face screwed into the most intense expression of pain. She stands, her eyes squeezed tight, every feature twisted into an agony she couldn't explain herself. Behind her, her husband's sobs come clearly through the door.

MAJOR STUDIO LOT. DAY.

HIGH ANGLE SHOT looking down on the deserted studio street. The street is absolutely empty except for Rita striding briskly across the street from the blazingly bright side into the deep shadow cast by one of the executive buildings. She is overdressed just a little, as usual, everything a little too tight. She is the same brassy little starlet we met at the beginning of this part of the story.

BRACKMAN'S RECEPTION ROOM.

WIDE SHOT showing Rita sitting composed and stiff on a wooden chair and a bespectacled SECRETARY busy tapping away at her desk. It is the same sort of reception room that Burt Harres had except there is more of everything, including space and awards and picture posters hanging on the wall. Rita is the only one waiting. The intercom buzzes on the secretary's desk. She picks up one of the three phones on her desk, nods, looks at Rita.

SECRETARY You can go in, Miss Shawn.

The secretary puts the receiver back on the hook, returns to her typing. Rita rises and crosses to the door leading to the inner office.

BRACKMAN'S OFFICE.

Rita enters, closing the door behind her.

The office is a corner one, obviously a prominent producer's office. It is done in the most impeccable taste. It is unbearably well furnished. Lester Brackman stands at a window. There is a man in his late sixties, portly, bland, pince-nezed, wearing a baggy blue suit with a vest, standing at the other window. An extremely large desk, covered with all the evidence of a busy producer carefully arranged all over it, dominates the center of the room.

RITA *(smiling at Lester)* Hello, Lester.

The two men smile at her.

BRACKMAN *(detaching himself from his window)* Rita, I don't have to tell you who this is. *(He indicates the sixty-five-year-old man.)* This is Mr. R.M. Lucas, one of our vice-presidents.

RITA I'm very honored to meet you, sir.

BRACKMAN Mr. Lucas saw the picture last night. He's very excited about your little scene.

Having concluded the introductions, Brackman retires diplomatically into a corner of the office, easing himself out of the way and onto a radiator cover. Mr. Lucas regards Rita blandly out of pale-blue eyes.

LUCAS You're a very attractive girl. You screen very well. You're a strange type, but you're exciting. Audience response to you has been very interesting. Martin Charles, your director, says you have real talent. We think you're going to be very big. Got a very nice part for you, six weeks' work. Your agent will tell you to jump at it. Give Lester his name. We'll send him a script. We'd like to have you under contract, young lady. We'll make very nice terms for you. Why don't you come to my house tonight? We'll discuss the whole matter.

A thin smile forms on Lester Brackman's saturnine face.

LUCAS I eat at eight o'clock. I'm sure you'll enjoy the food.

Rita looks knowingly at the old man, a little wearily.

RITA Shall I dress or is it informal?

LUCAS What does it matter? Mr. Brackman will give you the address. Give my best to your husband. A very fine fellow.

Rita, dismissed, smiles, turns, and goes out the door. A moment's pause hangs between the two men. Mr. Lucas regards his broad-toed shoes. Mr. Brackman exhales a breath of smoke. After a moment, Mr. Brackman makes a wry face.

BRACKMAN A star is born.

FADE OUT.

A STREET IN BEL AIR. DAY.

ACROSS a rolling expanse of a house in Bel Air. The house is Spanish Monterey style, surrounded by flowering gardens, with a curved driveway leading to and away from the high, heavy oak front door. It is obviously a big house, a rich house, a high-style house.

Over this, the following legend:

PART THREE

Portrait of a Goddess

RITA'S HOME.

Several shots show the large entrance foyer reaching two stories up, with a wide, curved stairway leading up to the second floor and a huge crystal chandelier dangling from the second-floor ceiling; the very large, rather old-fashioned kitchen with wall refrigerators, and a Negro man and a woman, middle-aged, working at the preparation of a meal.

LONG SHOT looking out the lanai windows, out across the flat red stones of the patio, the outdoor furniture, across a large expanse of green terrace that slopes down to a white Grecian colonnade and then to the pool. The whole area is surrounded by flower gardens, in which an occasional spouting statue stands.

Over this, the following legend:

HOLLYWOOD, CALIFORNIA
1952

RITA'S HOME, BACK TERRACE.

A man and a woman come out of the den doors onto the patio. They start across the long green terrace toward the pool. The man is tall, grayhaired, casually dressed. The woman is in her late thirties, chic in a casual summer dress and high heels.

The couple, whose name is WOOLSY reach the white Greek banister and railing that separate the terrace from the pool. They wave to the lovely blond young woman sitting on a beach chair at the pool, who now stands to greet them.

This is Rita Shawn, 1952, twenty-six years old, bronzed under the California sun, her hair a gleaming ashen blond, her body full in the white bathing suit. Behind her the undisturbed waters of the pool glisten green in the sunlight. Sitting erectly in a white wrought-iron chair is her mother, soberly dressed in a simple, formless print dress, bespectacled, reading. The mother is now forty-eight. She has a stern face, austerely pale, as if every instinct in her is resisting the sun.

ANOTHER ANGLE favoring Rita as the Woolsys come down to the pool. We are aware now of edges of restlessness in Rita. She seems to be in constant small movement, flicking her cigarette, crossing her legs, sitting, standing, moving nervously about. Her eyes shift incessantly to the pool, to the fringe of high palms surrounding the gardens, to the baked red tiles at her feet, to whoever is talking. When she talks, there is an urgency in her words, as if she is not sure she is making her meaning clear.

We see the vague harrows of troubled nights turning down the corners of her mouth and shadowing her eyes. One gets the feeling of a looseness of flesh, of too full a bosom, of long formless days of drinking and deep, gray mornings of despair. She is delighted to be roused from the silence that had hung between herself and her mother. She is on her feet instantly, in the furious flurry of introductions.

RITA This is my mother, Mrs. Faulkner. This is Mr. and Mrs. Joe Woolsy. Joe and Sally Woolsy. My mother just came in yesterday.

MRS. WOOLSY Isn't that wonderful? How do you do.

The mother smiles and nods, looks up from her book.

RITA My mother read in the paper how I had my nervous breakdown, and she called me long distance. Well, I told you, I had that long talk with my mother—it cost eighty-one dollars, that one call—well, I told you all that, about her coming out here.

MRS. WOOLSY How long do you intend staying, Mrs. Faulkner?

RITA Well, she thinks she's just out here for a couple of weeks, but she's really here to stay, because this is her home from now on. I been try-ing to get her out of that little old shack—she lives with my aunt and uncle—for years, and now that I got her out here, I ain't going to let her go. Ma, Mr. Woolsy is the producer of the picture on which I had my breakdown, and they been at my side all through the experience. They are my oldest and dearest friends. I thought I had a lot of friends, but these two here visited me every day at the sanitarium, and they were the only two, I might add. Except Shirley Donehoe. She's my hairdresser. She's been my hairdresser on every picture since 1949. I wouldn't do a picture without her. But all my other so-called friends, why, they didn't know I was alive, which just goes to show you something. I don't know what. Why don't you all sit down?

MRS. WOOLSY Well, actually, we just stopped by to see if you would have lunch with us. We're going....

RITA Well, I just think I'll stay here and have lunch with my mother. I haven't seen her in eight years. Eight years! My heavens, that's no way for a mother and daughter to be. Did I tell you, Abe Silverman called in a state yesterday. He just found out I wasn't seeing that psychiatrist any more.

MRS. WOOLSY Yes, we know.

RITA I said, "Abe, I'm not crazy. I don't need any psychiatrist." Why don't you all stay with us for lunch?

MRS. WOOLSY No, Rita dear, we...

RITA (starting abruptly for the stairs to the terrace) I'll go tell the cook that...

MRS. WOOLSY Rita, we're having lunch with Arlene Hugo at Frascati's.

RITA Well, I'll go check and see what's holding it up anyways.

She hurries, in her almost frantic fashion, up the stairs and the green, neatly mowed terrace to the house. An uncomfortable pause falls between the Woolsys and the mother.

THE MOTHER (after a moment) I want to thank you for all you did for my daughter in her time of need. She speaks of your friendship with the deepest affection.

WOOLSY *(seriously)* Mrs. Faulkner, we hardly know your daughter. I never met her till she was assigned to my picture four months ago. She only met my wife three weeks ago. I visited her at the sanitarium because she was holding up my picture for thirteen days. Cost me well over a hundred and fifty thousand dollars. It makes me very sad to feel she considers us her best friends. I think it's very good that you're out here, Mrs. Faulkner. I think she needs somebody very much. Try to talk her into going back to her psychiatrist.

THE MOTHER Well, I'm sure I don't know.

WOOLSY You talk to her, Mrs. Faulkner. She needs a psychiatrist. You talk to her.

RITA'S HOME, THE DEN. AFTERNOON.

FULL SHOT of Rita standing in the den dressed in a casual frock now, smoking a cigarette, giving a directed but not really interested attention to the television set. The GOP political convention is going on. She moves nervously, restlessly around the room, dropping her ashes in various ash trays.

Then she moves in her sandalled feet out into the main entrance foyer and then into the lanai, pausing a moment to look out through the windows across her patio and sloping green terrace. Her cigarette has been smoked down to the filter, and she turns and crushes it out in an ash tray on the lanai table. She promptly lights another one.

She rambles over into the butler's pantry, where she smiles briefly at the woman servant, hard at work preparing dinner now. She peeks into the kitchen, which is empty.

RITA *(to the woman servant)* How's everything?

The woman smiles. Rita moves with a brief sigh back into the lanai, back into the entrance foyer, and starts up the wide curved stairway. A Siamese cat slinks silently down the stairs past her.

UPSTAIRS LANDING.

FULL SHOT of Rita coming to the top of the carpeted stairway, pausing a moment to look down the length of the corridor to her left.

REVERSE SHOT at the far end of the corridor. We can see into what seems to be a darkened bedroom—dark, that is, in relation to the brightness of the other rooms. Her mother is sitting, dressed as she was before, in a stiff arm-chair, reading her Bible. After a moment, Rita moves down the corridor to her mother.

THE MOTHER'S BEDROOM.

RITA   How do you feel, Ma?

THE MOTHER   Oh, everything's just fine. This is about the biggest house I think I ever saw.

RITA   I guess you could put Mrs. Phillips' house on Union Street which she was so arrogant about right inside that living room.

THE MOTHER   I guess you could.

RITA   I made inquiries about an Adventist congregation here in Los Angeles, and there is one. I'll drive you down there tomorrow.

THE MOTHER   Fine, because I do not want to miss Friday-night Sabbath.

Rita moves into the room, silently gliding to the opposing wall, and sits down on a second soft chair.

RITA   You go on with your praying, Ma. I'll just sit here.

The mother, who has already turned her attention back to her Bible, her lips moving silently, smiles briefly even as she prays. For a long, long moment the

room is hushed and still between the two women—the older woman by the
window, softly murmuring over the Scriptures, the younger woman huddled
in the far-corner soft chair watching her with wide eyes.

RITA *(suddenly)* I make four thousand dollars a week. Did I ever tell you
that, Ma? You know what the studio got for me when they lent me out
to Columbia for that Cary Grant picture? A quarter of a million dollars, but they got me on that staff contract, so all I got was my four
thousand a week. Did you see the latest *Film Daily* listings? Well, I'm
in the top eight in *Film Daily* box-office ratings. Do you know the kind
of business my last picture, *Stardust Girl*, did on opening day in New
York? We opened at the Roxy in New York, and we did fourteen thousand dollars, and that was a house record for an opening day. We did
a boff one hundred and fifty-eight thousand for the week. What do
you think of your little girl now?

THE MOTHER Well, that's very nice.

RITA What are you reading, Ma?

THE MOTHER *(looks briefly at her Bible, then turns to her daughter and recites*
amiably from memory) "And ye shall know that I am the Lord, when I
have opened your graves, O my people, and brought you up out of
your graves, and shall put my Spirit in you, and ye shall live, and I shall
place you in your own land; then shall ye know that I the Lord have
spoken it, and performed it, saith the Lord."

Tears well in Rita's eyes as she stares at her mother.

RITA I'm so glad you came, Ma, because I was like to go crazy just
wandering around this house all by myself.

THE MOTHER I meant to come the day I read in the papers about your
nervous breakdown, but the doctor...

RITA *(The words pour out of her.)* I don't know what's the matter with me.
I have these black moods when I'm like to kill myself. I'm really like
to kill myself. I had this nervous breakdown. They tell me I began to

scream right on the set about this cat. Somebody had brought a cat on the set, and I just began to scream to take it away from me. And I love cats. I got these two big Siamese—you seen them. But my nerves were at the breaking point. I'd been drinking heavily. I confess to the sin of drinking. Oh, my God, I was arrested twice for drunken driving. I just feel, Ma, I'm losing all control of myself. I feel I'm going crazy. Sometimes I wake up in the morning, I don't know what I done the night before, and I feel I'm going right out of my mind. I can't bear to be alone. I can't bear it. I've taken men home with me who I didn't rightly know for more than an hour because I can't bear to be alone at night. I wake up in the middle of the night in a sweat and my heart pounding, and I've gone down and awakened my servants and made them sit with me till morning. Life just seems unbearable to me. I need you, Ma. I need you to be here with me because I'm like to go insane. I feel I'm going insane.

THE MOTHER We are all put on this earth to suffer.

RITA I'm going to take care of you. Wherever I go. I'm going to take you with me. You will always be at my side.

THE MOTHER I spoke to you on the phone last week, and I hung up, and I turned to Elliot Wainwright, who is an elder, and to your aunt, who was sitting there, and I said, "Riches and fame mean nothing, for here is my daughter, the envy of her generation, who like to cry her heart out over the phone. She is a lost soul, and all the glory of her life is just vanity. King Solomon had all the wealth of the world, and queens of mighty nations rode miles of sand and desert to see him, and what did he say but 'It is all vanity.'" I said, "My daughter is approaching her cataclysm. She has lived a life of sin and torment. She has borne the mark of the beast upon her. And surely she will be redeemed just as all men shall be redeemed from the curse as his corpse molders back to his mother earth."

She stands, stares at her daughter, her eyes wide with fervent intensity, but her words are gentle.

THE MOTHER Wipe away the red stains of sin and clothe yourself in dignity. Your body is the temple of the Holy Spirit, and you must keep yourself in modesty. Let righteousness into you, honey. Open your soul, open your arms, and just let Jesus Christ in you. Don't hold back a thought. Just let Him fill your body and your soul, and ye shall be transported into Peace and Love. *(Her eyes are closed now as she experiences something of the rapture she describes.)* O Lord, O Lord, I yield myself without reservation, and I feel the sweet, sweet warmth and peace.

In the corner soft chair, Rita sits bunched, bent almost double, stirred by some physical anguish she has never felt before. Her face is contorted with pain, her eyes clenched shut, her knuckles white as her hands grip each other.

RITA   I feel Him near me. I feel Him near me.

THE MOTHER   Without reservation. Ye must open your heart and your soul.

RITA   Oh, my God, my God!

THE MOTHER   Without reservation...

RITA   Oh, my God, my God!

THE MOTHER   Life is pain and sin and torment, and Jesus Christ absolves you, and there ain't no pain, and there ain't no sin, and there ain't no torment because your body is filled with His eternal love and His eternal compassion. Just open your arms and let Christ come in to every part of you.

Suddenly Rita falls from her contorted position on the soft chair onto the thickly carpeted floor, falling softly on her knees, her back bent in an arch of trembling and supplication. She is sobbing rather from the extraordinary exhilaration that suffuses her than from a sense of pain. Her eyes are open, brimming with tears, and she stares through the wet film of her tears at the carpet before her.

Her mother regards her with deep and gentle compassion. She creeps quietly to her daughter's bent figure and strokes her hair. She kneels down beside her and begins to pray quietly. Rita suddenly clutches at her mother, and the two women hold each other in passionate embrace.

RITA'S HOME, FOYER.

LONG SHOT looking straight at the heavy oaken front door of the house, which opens now to admit Rita with her mother right behind her. Rita seems in the best of spirits. She wears a sober dress and flat-heeled shoes. Her face is devoid of any make-up. She comes hurrying across the entrance hall to the lanai, calling out.

RITA Joe!

She crosses into the lanai to the screen doors leading out onto the patio.

RITA'S HOUSE, PATIO.

FULL SHOT of Rita coming out onto the patio. Joe and Mrs. Woolsy are slouched on the porch furniture. They are reading newspapers and smoking. Woolsy stands as Rita comes out.

RITA I'm sorry to be so late, but the time just flew. *(calling back to the house)* We're out here, Ma. *(to the Woolsys)* I'll go check dinner. We went for a long ride. I took my mother out to Encino and Sherman Oaks. I showed my mother John E. Tower's home, the father of my first husband. I wonder who's living there now. They got some pretty big ranches out that way. We saw a pretty good-size herd of cattle. *(looking at screen door)* I guess she went upstairs to wash.

WOOLSY It's nice to see you looking so well, Rita.

RITA Well, now, Joe, I'm happy. I have found God. I truly have. I tell this to you and Sally because I don't think you would mock me. But last Wednesday night, I woke up in the middle of the night with my old panic. Joe, you was at my side when I tried to kill myself on location in Arizona when I had my breakdown, so you know how I was. Well, Wednesday night, I woke up and went in to my mother and woke her and up, we prayed. I prayed to God to save my soul. I held my mother's hand. I remember her fingers tight on mine, and that's what saved me, her holding my hand that way. Because I can tell you now just what I feel when I have these nightmares and get drunk like I used to. It's the most awful loneliness in the world. I remember my first husband telling me about this awful loneliness he used to feel. Now, I know what he meant. It's like all the world is off somewheres else like an echo. It must be the loneliness a crying infant feels when it's left all alone. It's just so unbearable. I can't describe it. And I remember holding onto my mother's hand and praying. And I tell you, it went away. I felt so light and relieved from pain and trouble. I couldn't sleep the rest of the night. I just sat with my mother, and we talked and talked. And dawn came up—it was the most beautiful dawn, fiery red-like flame, like God was saying to me, "It's all right," like He personally was saying that to me. And I like to burst, I felt so fine. Oh, glory, it's so fine to have my mother with me!

There is a radiance to her face now that deeply touches her two friends.

MRS. WOOLSY Well, it's wonderful to see you this way, Rita.

RITA I feel I'm ready to go back to work, Joe. I'm going to call Abe Silverman and tell him to inform the studio I am ready to read any scripts they care to send me.

DISSOLVE TO:

RITA'S PATIO. MONTHS LATER.

A considerable amount of time has passed, and the mother sits alone on a straightbacked, wrought-iron garden chair. It is not a rocker, but the mother rocks lightly back and forth as if it were. Her hands are folded in her lap. She is visible in the dark summer night because the lights of the patio are on. Around her, the night is still except for the chirp of crickets.

CLOSE-UP of the mother on the patio, rocking back and forth. She is the picture of profound resignation, but her face is troubled. After a moment she stands disquieted, and goes through the lanai screen doors into the dark lanai.

RITA'S HOME, LANAI.

The mother comes into the dark lanai, her outline visible because of the patio lights and the lights in the butler's pantry. She pauses a moment, framed against the lanai windows, and then moves into...

THE BUTLER'S PANTRY.

The middle-aged black cook is at the sink silently washing some lettuce. The mother stands at the far end of the pantry, watching her tentatively for a moment.

THE MOTHER Well, she's just coming home later and later.

THE COOK Sometimes she don't come home till eleven, twelve o'clock at night when she's making a picture. I can set your plate if you're hungry.

THE MOTHER No, no. I'll just wait on my daughter.

She looks down at the floor, uncertain and still. The cook goes back to unleafing the lettuce.

THE MOTHER Well, maybe I'll just rustle myself up something. Don't you pay no mind to me. I don't feel comfortable having somebody serving me, waiting on me hand and foot. *(She's at the wall refrigerator, poking her head in, looking for some appetizer.)* I do all my own cooking at home. I cook for my brother and my sister-in-law. I live with them. My brother George is more in bed than out, he is that sick, and my sister-in-law is at the store most of the day. We have a grocery and fruit store. I work there a couple of hours a day too. I have a very busy day back there in Beacon City. Sometimes I just drop in my bed exhausted at the end of the day. I'll just take some of this here cheese.

THE COOK You go right ahead and take some of that cheese, ma'am.

The mother has found some American cheese. She unfolds a strip from the pack and nibbles at it.

THE MOTHER *(after a moment)* I'm so very lonely out here. I'm like to go out of my mind.

THE COOK   Well, it's hard to get to know somebody out here.

THE MOTHER   My daughter's away all day, and most of the night. She's gone at seven in the morning. I just walk around from one room to another. I just don't know what to do with myself. My daughter and I went down to a church meeting, but the congregation was mostly colored.

She bites her lip even as she says the words, mortified with embarrassment.

THE MOTHER   I didn't mean to say that.

THE COOK   *(wryly)* That's all right, Mrs. Faulkner.

An embarrassed silence falls between the two women for a moment.

THE MOTHER   I got another letter from my sister-in-law. They all miss me very much. She writes how the Schefflers—he's the cashier in the supermarket—and their two little boys was over the other night, and they was watching the boys catching fireflies. It's so lovely in Maryland about this time of year in the evening, and the smell of jasmine and honeysuckle is sweet enough to just breathe into your whole body. Oh, I do admit I am homesick. I just ache with it. It's awful hard for a woman of my years to just uproot herself and come live somewheres else. I lived twenty-two years in Beacon City.

THE COOK   Well, it's hard to leave home, no matter how old you are.

THE MOTHER   Yes, it is.

There are tears in her eyes, and she turns away sadly and moves back into the dark lanai, nibbling on her cheese. She stands silhouetted against the windows of the lanai, an aging little woman with wet eyes.

THE MOTHER'S ROOM.

*ACROSS Rita to the bathroom door. Rita still wears a sober dress and no lip-
stick. She seems in a temper. Her mother is just coming out of the bathroom,
wiping her hands on a towel. She is dressed in what would seem to be her one
dress, the formless print. Religious pictures and calendars have been pinned
on the wall. There is one battered valise open on the bed.*

RITA *(with repressed fury)* I ain't going to pay your railroad fare. If you're
thinking I'm going to pay your railroad fare back, you're crazy. I ain't
even going to take you down to the station and buy you tickets. You
just find your own way down to the station. I ain't going to send you
no more money. I ain't going to send you nothing.

THE MOTHER   Honey, I told you when I first came out here...

RITA   All I know is...

THE MOTHER   I didn't expect I would stay more than two or three weeks.

RITA   I done everything I can to make you happy.

THE MOTHER   I been out here more than two months now.

RITA   I gave a ten-thousand-dollar tithe for the furthering of missionary
work.

THE MOTHER   Honey, your Uncle George is more in bed than out, he is
that sick, and Alice Marie tends the store, and they can hardly make
do without me.

*The feeling of some unexpressed hatred suffuses Rita's body in a wave of
almost physical heat. Sweat appears in beads on her brow, and her face swells,
and the words she says are bitter and unrestrained in their venom.*

RITA *(viciously)*   Nothing I do pleases you. Nothing I ever did pleases
you. All you know is to run off on me. I hate you so much I can't find
words to tell you how much. You never cared whether I lived or died.

Well, just get out of my house. I never want to see you again, not even in your grave. I hope your heart just explodes. I hope you die. I just want you to know that.

She turns on her heel and stalks out of the room. The mother stands with her head bowed, the towel hanging slackly from one hand, patiently resigned.

DISSOLVE TO:

RITA'S BEDROOM.

FULL SHOT of Rita standing by her bedroom window looking out through the white nylon curtains. The sun streams in, whitening her face.

RITA'S P.O.V.: Looking down to the front of the house. There is a Yellow Cab parked in the driveway in front of the big oaken door. The driver stands waiting for the mother to come out through the door, which is open. When the mother appears in her dark shapeless topcoat, the driver hurries to help her with her valise.

ANGLE SHOT looking up past the driver as he loads the valise on and, as the mother gets into the cab, to Rita's window. She is desperately opening one of the casements of her window, pushing the curtains aside.

RITA *(screaming)* There ain't no God! You hear what I said? There ain't no God!

The driver nervously gets into his seat of the cab and starts the car quickly.

RITA *(screaming)* There ain't no God! Can you hear me?

The taxi curves off down the driveway and wheels into the street and moves out of sight. Rita screams at its departing fumes of unburned oil.

RITA *(screaming)* There ain't no God!

Rita turns from the window. She sits down on a bedroom chair, slumped for-

ward, her arms dangling between her knees, her eyes open, staring blankly at the wall ahead of her. She seems entirely spent, weary, exhausted. Suddenly one of her big Siamese cats swishes silently into the room and moves with feline restlessness around the room. Rita watches it, benumbed. As it moves to rub against her leg, she reaches out and grabs it and presses it against her face.

CLOSE-UP of Rita's anguished face pressed against the endlessly smooth pale fur of the terrified cat.

RITA *(muttering to the cat)* There ain't no God.

The cat wriggles free and sprints out of the room. Rita remains seated, stumped and exhausted, devoid of any expression.

                                                        FADE OUT.

FADE IN:

BEACON CITY, MARYLAND. 1957.

VERY HIGH ANGLE SHOT showing Beacon City, lolling quietly on its hill on a hot August morning. The sun beats down on the sidewalks and most of the people are off in the shade of their homes and stores. Most of the people, that is, except for the seventy or eighty that are congregated outside a gray frame house on one of the hills. We may remember this to be the aunt's and uncle's home. There is also a number of cars lined up outside the home.

Over this the following legend:

BEACON CITY, MARYLAND
1957

CLOSER SHOTS show the people outside on the sidewalks, milling sweatily in the street, a shirt-sleeved crowd but quite respectful. There is no unruliness, just a quiet curiosity. It is apparently a funeral procession that is lined up on the street, for there are a hearse and two black limousines and seven other private cars.

Suddenly there is a murmur and a press of movement in the people hanging around the house, and the pallbearers appear coming out of the front door bearing a coffin on their shoulders. They move slowly, sweating, down the front path to the hearse outside the house.

The crowd is much more concerned with the people following the coffin out of the house—the elder, a spare young man in sober black suit, and then Rita Shawn in a black suit, black hat and veil, and black gloves. She seems faint, being held on one arm by her aunt, now a graying lady also in black, and on the other arm by her SECRETARY, a rather chic woman in her late forties wearing a blue suit.

FULL SHOT of Rita being helped into the limousine by her aunt and the other woman. The elder stands by the open door of the limousine, watching them. After Rita is deposited in the car, he turns to the woman in the blue suit, who stands wiping the sweat off her brow.

THE ELDER I hope all these people here believe she is grief-stricken, but God knows she came to her mother's funeral drunk as a lord.

THE SECRETARY   It's no sign of disrespect, Elder. She's always a little drunk. *(She climbs into the limousine.)*

BEACON CITY STREETS. DAY.

VARIOUS ANGLES of the funeral procession wending its slow way through the town. On the hot sidewalks, a few hardy souls stand and watch; others look out of windows.

INSIDE THE LIMOUSINE.

Group shot of the four occupants. Rita and her aunt sit in the rear seat. The elder and the secretary sit on the jump seats. The windows are all open, but the heat inside the car is oppressive.

Rita stares through heavy-lidded eyes at the slowly passing store fronts of Main Street. Sweat gathers in beads on everyone's face. They ride stolidly, silently, squinting against the glaring blind spots on the shiny doors and chrome finishings.

After a moment Rita, her voice slightly blurred, and without looking away from the passing scene, speaks.

RITA   I just suddenly had a picture of myself twenty-five years ago, a little girl with high ankle shoes and a middy blouse, walking down the street here.

There are suddenly tears in her eyes, and she stares helplessly around her. Then she lapses back into her vague, lost study of the passing scene. The others ride silently. The aunt wipes her neck.

THE AUNT   My soul, it's hot.

They ride slowly on.

CEMETERY.

LONG SHOT showing the funeral procession pulling to a halt outside the iron-railing fence of the cemetery. There is a crowd on the walk outside the cemetery, perhaps a hundred and fifty people. It parts into a respectful path for the transference of the coffin into the cemetery. There are six or seven people already waiting on a small knoll by an open grave.

The fresh earth is piled on either side of the grave. The air is humid and dense. The people get out of the cars, form a disorganized line behind the four pallbearers and straggle through the headstones of the small cemetery to join the small group waiting at the grave.

Among this group there is a thin, graying man in his late thirties and a girl of thirteen. We may recognize the man as John Tower, Jr. As the procession comes close to him and the girl, he speaks.

TOWER   Hello, Emily Ann.

Something in the quiet greeting frightens her, and she whirls to the voice. For a moment she just stares at Tower, and then the shock of recognition floods over her face. Then she brings herself under control.

RITA Hello, John. I hardly expected you here. John, you remember my aunt Alice Marie, and this is my secretary, Miss Haywood. This is my first husband, Mr. Tower. Will you excuse us, please?

They all nod their greetings. The secretary seems particularly hostile. Rita, supported by the two women, moves on farther to the grave into which the coffin is now being lowered. There is a moment of silence.

CLOSE SHOT of Rita flanked by her aunt and secretary standing by the grave. All around her are gravestones and crosses. The sun beats down on her. She moves her veil down over her face, and then darts a quick look back to Tower and the girl.

RITA'S P.O.V.: Tower and his daughter, a not particularly distinguished-looking girl of thirteen among the fifteen-odd people around the grave. Over this shot, the elder begins his reading from the Bible, quiet and sonorous.

ACROSS RITA'S SHOULDER looking across the elder reading, past Tower and the daughter, past the rows of gravestones, to the hundred and fifty-odd people staring at her through the iron railings of the fence.

CLOSE-UP of Rita, rubbing her eyes against the heat, the elder's words droning on behind her. Beside Rita we see the aunt's bowed head, the ever-present background of gravestones. The heat is beginning to get to Rita. Her eyes close, and her head shakes a little. Suddenly she begins to wail, screaming out into the hot afternoon sky.

RITA I want to die! I want to die! I can't stand it no more! I can't stand it! Leave me alone! I want to die!

The secretary moves quickly, slaps Rita sharply. Rita's panic abruptly subsides and her knees buckle. The secretary holds her tightly to prevent her from falling. A murmur rustles through the crowd outside the gate. The elder pauses in his reading. The secretary and the aunt, aided by one of the pall-bearers, manage to move Rita away from the grave and back to the entrance of the cemetery.

LONG SHOT looking past Tower and the daughter as Rita is being helped away. We can see enough of their faces to see the sad compassion on Tower's face and the wide-eyed fascination on the daughter's.

AUNT'S HOUSE, PORCH. DUSK.

The secretary and the aunt rock quietly on the porch. The secretary has taken off her jacket and unbuttoned her blouse collar. There is still a curious group of about twenty people, mostly teenagers, straggled along the sidewalk across from the house.

LONG SHOT of Tower coming up the street to the house, opening the gate and walking up the path to the porch.

THE AUNT   Come on up here in the shade.

Tower climbs slowly up to the porch.

THE AUNT   I never expected to see you here.

THE SECRETARY   *(with evident coldness)*   Neither did I.

THE AUNT   It was very nice of you and the girl to come to the funeral.

TOWER   My daughter wanted very much to come.

THE SECRETARY   *(coldly)*   She's asleep, Mr. Tower. I gave her some pills, and she went off.

TOWER   Do you think she'd like to see us?

THE SECRETARY   Not after the last time.

TOWER   My daughter would like to meet her very much.

THE SECRETARY   I don't think I'll let you see her, Mr. Tower.

TOWER   *(smoking nervously)* I'm not sure just what you have to say about all this, Miss Haywood.

THE SECRETARY   I've been with Miss Shawn for three years; I'm very fond of her. If there's anything that'll stay in my mind till the day I die, it's that picture of you sitting in that lawyer's office two years ago while that hysterical woman pleaded with you on her knees to see her daughter, and you just kept saying, "No."

TOWER   I didn't think it was a good idea for my daughter to spend two weeks with a hysterical woman.

THE SECRETARY   You destroyed that poor girl, Mr. Tower. You...

TOWER   She was destroyed long before then.

THE SECRETARY   Did you know she tried to kill herself that night?

TOWER   Miss Haywood, this is none of your business. *(Disapprovingly, he nervously crushes his cigarette out with his foot.)* It is your job, Miss Haywood, to hover over that poor desolate woman upstairs. My job is to give my daughter some love of life. I don't really care about Rita Shawn any more. Or myself. We are a gutted generation, born in the depression and obsessed with prosperity. Well, we got prosperity, and what have we got? A hysterical woman upstairs who needs barbiturates to put her to sleep, Dexedrine Spansules to wake her up, and tranquilizers to keep her numb, who has a nervous breakdown once a year and has tried to kill herself at least four times that the public knows. I don't want my daughter to grow up like that. Or like me. A twisted, loveless man, patched together by psychoanalysis. My daughter was a very strange little girl for a long time, well on her way to continuing the desolate pattern of her parents, her grandparents, and all the generations before her, the long parade of history that has brought us to this year of suicide and insanity. Do you think I would take this frightened little girl and send her for two weeks with a meaningless mother, to be devoured by this wandering panther of a woman as she prowls through life looking for some reason for living? My daughter has a reason for living. She's not going to scream out in a hot cemetery that she wants to die. She wants to see her mother very much. She is a sweet girl. She has given me the little importance in life that I have. I thought she might give Rita a little of that.

THE SECRETARY You worry about your girl, Mr. Tower. I'll worry about mine.

TOWER *(murmurs)* So she finally found a mother. *(takes out his cigarette pack to light another)* I'll come back later.

THE SECRETARY You might as well sit here. She'll be up soon. I better go upstairs. She likes me to be in the room when she wakes up.

She turns and goes back through the screen door into the house. Tower finds a chair on the porch and sits, loosening his collar.

UPSTAIRS BEDROOM.

CLOSE SHOT of Rita asleep on the bed. The shades are drawn, and the room is hushed and quiet. It is the same room she slept in when her mother first brought her to this house twenty-seven years ago. Camera dollies back to show the whole room. An electric fan whirs silently, fluttering the white lace fringes on the bed.

Rita lies sleeping sweetly, like a child. Sitting perched on the window sill is the secretary, quietly studying the lovely blond girl on the bed in her long, white, childlike nightgown. After a moment Rita opens her eyes and lies without movement, looking vaguely up at the ceiling. From the small portion of the window not covered by the shade we can see that it is getting dark outside.

THE SECRETARY *(gently)* Hello, baby.

Rita turns her head on the pillow and regards her secretary.

RITA Let's get out of here.

THE SECRETARY We don't have to be back on the Coast till Monday.

RITA Let's just get out of this town. I've been sick ever since we got here.

THE SECRETARY   Okay. We can take the eleven o'clock flight to New York. Your husband, Mr. Tower, is downstairs.

RITA Is the girl with him?

THE SECRETARY No.

RITA Okay, let him come up. What time is it?

THE SECRETARY About a quarter to eight.

RITA Give me a drink.

THE SECRETARY I want you to eat something first.

THE RITA Okay. Confirm those reservations. I want to get out of here. I feel I'm getting nervous again.

THE SECRETARY All right, baby. Take it easy.

RITA *(panic rising in her)* We never should have come here. We never should have come here.

THE SECRETARY *(sharply)* Rita!

The little flurry of panic subsides. The secretary stands, crosses to the old-fashioned chest of drawers, opens her large shoulder bag, takes out a medicine bottle.

THE SECRETARY *(unscrewing cap of bottle)* Do you want a pill if you're going to see your husband? *(She lets a flat capsule fall into her palm.)* There's a condolence telegram came for you from Joe and Sally Woolsy.

RITA   Who are they? Oh, yeah. Whatever happened to them? *(She suddenly begins to cry.)* Oh, I don't know, I don't know. *(She lies on the bed, a handsome blond woman, childlike in a long white cotton nightgown, crying quietly.)* We never should have come here, Horty. It's the same old town, the same old town. You'd have thought it would have changed in thirteen years. But just some more cars and a couple of new neons, and the dime store got a new front window, but it's all the same. It's worse, even. I always thought this house was a pretty house, but it's a shabby old place, a shabby, shabby little wooden house. Did you see that place where I used to live? Oh, my God! It was an ugly, ugly childhood. Ugly and dirty and lonesome. Oh, my God! I can feel it now! That lonely little girl with her high ankle shoes! Oh, I don't know. Life never changes. I'm the same as I was then, and I'll always be the same, the same miserable little girl wandering through ugly streets in her high ankle shoes. I wish I could just sleep the rest of my life.

She is crying quite fully now. The secretary, who has listened patiently, even compassionately, now brings Rita the tranquilizer pill and a glass of water that was sitting on the chest of drawers. Rita gets up on one elbow, takes the pill. The secretary helps her drink the water.

RITA   *(the panic momentarily over)* You got any sleeping pills there?

THE SECRETARY   Yeah.

RITA   Maybe I ought to take one of those too.

THE SECRETARY   Okay.

The secretary goes to her large bag on the chest of drawers and takes out a larger bottle and starts to unscrew the cap. A quick look of cunning crosses Rita's face.

RITA   Why don't you go down and tell my husband to come on up? I'll take the pill after he goes. Then I could sleep on the plane.

THE SECRETARY *(screwing the cap back on and returning the bottle to her bag)*
Okay. You want a sandwich?

RITA That'll be fine.

The secretary goes out of the bedroom, Rita watching her with sly caution. After a moment, Rita gets out of the bed and looks out the doorway and then moves quickly on her bare feet to her secretary's bag, filches the bottle of sleeping pills, and moves back to her bed, putting the bottle under her pillow. She sits patiently now, dominated by some feeling of immense achievement, deeply calm. She seems unaware of muffled footsteps on the stairs outside. Tower comes a few tentative steps into the room.

TOWER Hello, Emmy.

She smiles briefly at him, almost as if she didn't know who he was, as if her mind was on other, more profoundly moving things.

RITA I was just thinking that life is really a fraud, isn't it? There's really nothing to it at all. I'm thirty-one years old, and I look back on it all, and all I feel like saying is "So what?" I think of all that heartache and fretting.

TOWER Slings and arrows...

RITA I got a handsome house with gardens as far as your eye can see, filled with red flowers of paradise and tulips. And I can hardly get out of a taxicab in New York but there's hundreds of people crowding around the door, screaming how much they love me. I've known men, hundreds of men, just blank faces—I can't remember them at all. I don't believe there's anything in this world I haven't tried once. All the things that are supposed to be fun really ain't no fun, and all the things that are supposed to be important really ain't nothing at all. For the life of me, I can't think of any reason to get up tomorrow morning. I can't think of anything I want or look forward to. It's all a fraud, isn't it, John?

TOWER No.

She lies back on the bed and looks up at the ceiling, quiet with an almost drunken feeling of omnipotent knowledge.

RITA   Why, I remember you, drunk as sin in that dirty little room in the Hotel Montgomery, shouting these very things at me, quoting all the great poets.

TOWER   "All life is weariness," saith the preacher. "No man can utter it."

RITA   I remember when I was a little girl I used to dream of drowning all the time.

TOWER   "The dark tideless floods of nothingness, where all who know may drown."

RITA   *(staring up at the ceiling)*   That seems to me an awful nice feeling, to just float and let the water come up over you, for I can't bear this life no more. I can't. You wouldn't understand.

TOWER   Sure I would.

There is something so gentle in his voice that she looks at him. He is regarding her with great sweetness.

RITA   How have you been, John? I never did get to talk to you too much the last time we met.

TOWER   Oh, still in one piece.

RITA   How kind you look!

TOWER   I was just thinking you're so unchanged. I wish I were meeting you now for the first time.

She is suddenly pressing herself against him, her face against his chest.

RITA   Hold me, John.

He holds her gently.

RITA   I never loved anybody but you.

TOWER   *(holding her gently)*   You never loved me either, Emmy. You needed me, but you never loved me. You never knew what love was. Whoever taught it to you?

She is crying, and he holds her, caught himself in a surge of emotion.

TOWER   Life is unbearable if you don't love something, Emmy. Don't I know that as well as you? Come with me now. Put on your clothes and come with me. The girl is waiting at the bottom of the hill. I want you to meet her. People like us can never love anything but our children. But that's something. She's given me moments of great pleasure—moments when I can see that life is fine. She wants to meet you so much.

RITA   *(face pressed against his chest)*   I can't. I can't!

TOWER   That's the reason we came down here, because she wanted to meet you so much.

RITA   *(in panic)*   I can't face her! She despises me!

TOWER   Emmy...

RITA   *(flinging herself away from him)*   Leave me alone!

From the open doorway of the bedroom we hear the secretary's voice.

THE SECRETARY   Leave her alone.

Tower turns to look at the secretary.

RITA   *(in full panic)*   I'm no good! I'm no good!

TOWER   *(to the secretary)*   Would you rather she clutches at life for half hours in cheap hotel rooms?

RITA   *(sobbing)*   I had my mother in labor for seventeen hours and I been nothing but pain to everybody since!

THE SECRETARY   *(moving to her)*   Rita...

RITA   Leave me alone.

THE SECRETARY   *(to Rita)*   Give me the bottle. Where'd you put it?

RITA   Leave me alone.

THE SECRETARY   Where'd you put the bottle of sleeping pills, Rita?

RITA   Save me, save me, save me!

The secretary slaps her sharply, and the panic subsides as abruptly as it began. Rita stands in the middle of the room, her hair awry, fingering her long white nightgown. Tower regards her with deep, pained compassion. The secretary caresses her hair gently.

THE SECRETARY   *(kindly)*   Where's the bottle, baby?

RITA   *(murmuring)*   Under the pillow.

The secretary leans over the bed and extracts the bottle of sleeping pills from under the pillow.

THE SECRETARY   Lie down, baby. I have a sandwich for you outside.

Rita moves silently, like a punished child, to the bed and lies down. The secretary sidles over to Tower and looks at him in an oddly pleading way.

THE SECRETARY   *(to Tower)*   We got her to a psychiatrist for four months. Then he said to me we were wasting our money. She's a dead woman, emotionally dead. She could keep coming every day for an hour and pour out her heart, and this would relieve the immediate tensions, but she would never really respond to treatment. I'll take her back to California, and she'll go on making movies, because that's all she knows to do, and whatever happens after that happens. But I kind of love her, and I'll take good care of her.

TOWER All right. *(He smiles at Rita.)* I'll see you, Emmy.

RITA *(smiling from the bed)* Please call me if you get out to the Coast.

TOWER Of course. *(He turns and goes out onto the landing.)*

LANDING OUTSIDE THE BEDROOM.

Tower goes down the stairs.

STREET OUTSIDE THE AUNT'S HOME. NIGHT.

Tower comes out of the house. He goes down the walk and out to the sidewalk. He begins to walk quickly down the hill. There is a feeling of pain and urgency and deeply stirred emotions in Tower.

CLOSE SHOT across Tower's shoulders as he reaches the bottom of the hill where it joins Main Street. There is an ice-cream parlor sandwiched between several other stores facing him across the street.

Standing in the lighted doorway is his daughter. He stops and stares at the girl, his face almost bursting with the pain of his love for her. Then he comes to her, takes her hand, and leads her briskly farther down Main Street to the little jumble of lights that constitutes the heart of town.

TOWER She never had a chance, honey. She never had a chance from the beginning.

They go off down the dark hill into the scattering of lights in the heart of town. Soon they are swallowed up in the darkness.

THE END

THE AMERICANIZATION
OF EMILY

1964

Screenplay by **PADDY CHAYEFSKY**
based on the novel by **WILLIAM BRADFORD HUIE**

Produced by **MARTIN RANSOHOFF**

Directed by **ARTHUR HILLER**

CAST CREDITS

LT. COMMANDER CHARLES E. MADISON	James Garner
EMILY BARHAM	Julie Andrews
REAR ADMIRAL WILLIAM JESSUP	Melvyn Douglas
LT. COMMANDER "BUS" CUMMINGS	James Coburn
MRS. BARHAM	Joyce Grenfell
ADMIRAL THOMAS HEALEY	Edward Binns
SHEILA	Liz Fraser
OLD SAILOR	Keenan Wynn
CAPTAIN HARRY SPAULDING	William Windom
CHIEF PETTY OFFICER PAUL ADAMS	John Crawford
CAPTAIN MARVIN ELLENDER	Douglas Henderson
ADMIRAL HOYLE	Edmond Ryan
YOUNG SAILOR	Steve Franken
GENERAL WILLIAM HALLERTON	Paul Newlan
LIEUTENANT VICTOR WADE	Gary Cockrell

FADE IN TO THE ROLLING OF DRUMS.

HENDON AIRPORT. NIGHT.

LONG WIDE ANGLE ESTABLISHING SHOT of the airport. A high-level military mission is about to arrive. Three black official cars wait on the grass by a landing strip. Their drivers, three young uniformed ENGLISH-WOMEN, lounge in a group by one of the cars, smoking, chatting among themselves. A Captain of the U.S. Navy, SPAULDING, hurries down to the three women drivers, calls something to them. They quickly step on their cigarettes, and each hurries to stand at attention by her car. Now a DC-4 taxies slowly out of the darkness.

The following legend appears briefly over this:

HENDON AIRPORT, ENGLAND
MAY 4, 1944
MIDNIGHT

ANOTHER ANGLE across the three drivers FAVORING EMILY BARHAM, a handsome Englishwoman of 24. In background, the DC-4 has come to a halt. REAR ADMIRAL WILLIAM JESSUP and his team—CAPTAIN MARVIN ELLENDER, LIEUTENANT COMMANDER STANLEY "BUS" CUMMINGS, LIEUTENANT COMMANDER CHARLES MADISON, and CHIEF PETTY OFFICER PAUL ADAMS—disembark from the plane, each carrying an attaché case. Spaulding moves quickly forward to greet them. There is a brisk exchange of salutes and hand-shakes. The Admiral, Ellender and Cummings follow Spaulding to the cars.

ANOTHER ANGLE, ACROSS Emily. A jeep and a 3/4-ton truck roll up to the plane out of the darkness. Four sailors begin unloading cases and cartons of everyone's luggage from the plane. In particular, there is an enormous crate that requires the strength of all four sailors and two of the DC-4 crew to carry. Lt. Commander Madison, supervising the distribution of the baggage to the separate cars, busily signs bills of lading and other official documents. He shouts out greetings and dispenses last minute instructions to the staff.

MADISON Hi, Harry. Is everything set at the hotel? *(to Admiral Jessup)* I'll only be a few moments, sir. *(to crew)* Put that hand luggage in the automobile. *(to Adams)* Paul, put the footlockers in the jeep. Everything else goes in the two-and-a-half. Unloading shouldn't take long, so you'll only be a few minutes behind us. I'll see you back at the hotel.

As Chief Petty Officer Adams approaches Emily's car, lugging valises, sea bags and other duffle, she hurries to open the trunk of her car for him. Madison exchanges a few words with Admiral Jessup, already seated in the first of the cars, and then comes strolling down to Emily's car.

We see now that Madison is an agreeable young Navy officer in his late thirties. There is, however, something raffish about him which is not at all in key with the somber weightiness of this midnight mission. Indeed, as he passes the DRIVER of the second car, he gives her a good-natured pat.

SECOND DRIVER *(smiles, whispers)* Hiya, Charlie.

Emily's eyebrows shoot up at this.

MADISON *(across Emily to Adams)* All right, let's go.

Adams SLAMS the trunk shut.

LONG SHOT: three cars turn on the airstrip and drive off. The loading of the truck and jeep continues in background.

LONDON. NIGHT.

Our convoy of military vehicles heads toward the hotel, passing areas of blitz damage to streets and buildings.

WESTCHESTER HOTEL. NIGHT.

The mission pulls up to the hotel. MPs and soldiers hurry out from the hotel to help with the luggage.

ACROSS Emily, Madison dismisses the drivers of the other two cars. As he passes the DRIVER of the first car, he amiably pats her, too.

FIRST DRIVER *(smiles at Madison)* Glad you're back, Charlie.

Emily's eyebrows shoot up again.

MADISON *(calling to Adams in car)* Let's go around the back and wait for the truck. *(Adams nods.)*

HOTEL SERVICE ENTRANCE. NIGHT.

Truck being unloaded.

HOTEL BASEMENT.

Crates and cartons are carried by sweating sailors, with Madison directing the traffic to the service lifts.

HOTEL, SIXTH FLOOR HALLWAY.

Madison comes out of the service lift and strides to the Sixth Floor Kitchen. The Floor Service Captain, TOM, an Englishman in hotel livery, stands in the open doorway watching. A large refrigerator has just been uncrated and stands in lofty isolation in the middle of the kitchen floor. Madison pokes his head in.

MADISON *(to Floor Service Captain)* Hello, Tom.

TOM Nice to have you back in London, sir.

MADISON Thank you. *(opens refrigerator)* That's a crate of eggs, four pounds of bacon, four tins of coffee, six pounds of butter, assorted marmalades, and ten pounds of fresh oranges. Would you check those for bruises, Tom?

TOM I will, sir.

MADISON The Admiral breakfasts at seven-thirty tomorrow with Captain Ellender and Commander Cummings. I've scribbled down the way everyone likes their eggs.

TOM Thank you, sir.

Madison gives the Captain a piece of paper, turns to Adams, who is now directing more sailors and more crates down the hallway.

MADISON I'll sign us in. You get the wash and dry cleaning.

Adams nods. Madison hurries down the hallway as more sailors and crates pour out of the service lift.

HOTEL. NIGHT.

Emily stands by her car after the jeep and truck have been unloaded. Madison comes out of the hotel in the best of spirits. He signs the papers submitted to him by the drivers of the truck and jeep. As Emily watches him out of the corner of her eye, he stands on the sidewalk amiably drinking in the night air. After a moment, he ambles good-naturedly down to Emily, takes the trip-ticket she offers him and signs it, using a window of the car for a desk.

MADISON *(smiles affably)* Well, get some sleep.

As she bends to get into the car, Madison pats her bottom, more out of habit than anything else. However, this driver straightens and slaps his face a splendid, crisp slap. Emily gets back into her car and starts the motor.

TRUCK DRIVER You can't win them all, Commander.

Madison shrugs. Emily's car roars off into the night. Suddenly, the ululation of air raid SIRENS fills the night. The lights of the hotel quickly black out. Madison darts a nervous look at the sky and hurries back into the hotel.

To the ROLLING of drums and the EXPLOSION of bombs, a solemn legend rolls across the BLACK SCREEN:

In World War II, few men served
their countries more ably than a
small group of unheralded heroes
known as "The Dog-Robbers."

A "Dog-Robber" is the personal
attendant of a general or admiral,
and his job is to keep his general
or admiral well-clothed, well-fed,
and well-loved during the battle.

Every army and navy in the world
has its "Dog-Robbers," but, needless to say, ours were the best.

To these resolute procurers and
luftsmenschen, this film is gratefully dedicated.

With an enormous sweep of coronation MUSIC, the credits explode:

THE AMERICANIZATION OF EMILY

*Under the credits: EXTERIOR DAYLIGHT SHOTS of London in the
first week of May, 1944, showing the streets crowded with grim-faced, resolute military men, obviously carrying the weight of the Invasion on their
particular backs and in their particular attaché cases.*

NAVY BUILDING.

*CUT TO FULL SHOT of Madison entering the lobby which courses with
purposeful Navy personnel. We PAN him to the stairway.*

COMMANDER CUMMINGS' OFFICE.

*Madison enters. Cummings, bespectacled now, is busy behind his desk. Chief
Petty Officer Adams is unloading a box filled with packages of nylon stockings. Madison promptly begins stuffing his attaché case with these packages.*

CUMMINGS *(without looking up from his administrative chores)* Charlie, the Admiral's playing bridge tonight with Generals Hallerton and Waterson.

MADISON   General Waterson doesn't play bridge.

CUMMINGS   Yeah, but he'll want a partner anyway. Find a couple of someones to complete the foursome. Here's the menu. Dinner will be at six—steak, avocado salad, ice cream and the appropriate wines.

MADISON *(to Adams)* Call the Motor Pool and get me a driver.

CUMMINGS   We're going to stay put here in London for a while, Charlie, at least until the balloon goes up.

MADISON   What balloon?

CUMMINGS   D-Day.   The invasion of Europe.   So you might as well set up house.

MADISON   Okay.

ADAMS *(on phone)* Motor Pool, please.

MADISON   General Waterson likes red-headed partners, right? *(to Adams as he starts for the door)* Never mind, Paul. I'll go by the Motor Pool myself. *(exiting)* Avocado salad. That's a new one.

NAVY BUILDING, MOTOR POOL.

In the anteroom, the DISPATCHER, a uniformed woman of 40, sits at her desk, busy at her phone.

DISPATCHER   Motor Pool, Miss Simpson here . . .

She looks up as Madison enters, flutters her hand at him. He flutters his hand at her, continues on to the inner office where three uniformed young Englishwomen lounge about, on call. One, SHEILA, is a blazing blonde, a second is the driver of the evening before who slapped Madison's face. A brief cold look passes between Madison and this driver.

MADISON *(to the blazing blonde)* Sheila, could you be a redhead by five-thirty this afternoon?

SHEILA I could manage, love. Am I to dress, or am I to drive?

MADISON You'll have to dress. It's for dinner and a little bit of mauling. Two-star General who usually passes out about half-past eleven.

SHEILA Oooh, a Two-star General.

She follows Madison back into the dispatcher's office.

DISPATCHER *(calling to third driver)* Push on to SHAEF, Pat. Two Navy captains wait in front, here's your ticket.

PAT, the third driver, takes her trip-ticket.

PAT *(exiting)* Ta-ra Charlie. Nice that you're back.

MADISON Ta-ra. *(to Dispatcher)* I need a driver to take me to Hendon. How about Sheila?

DISPATCHER She's on call. *(calls to Emily in rear office)* Emily, dear, take Commander Madison to Hendon Airport, here's your ticket. *(The phone rings.)* Motor Pool, Miss Simpson here...

In the rear office, Emily looks up, puts her magazine down, comes out into the dispatcher's office to pick up her trip-ticket.

SHEILA *(to Madison)* If I'm to be a redhead, love, I shall need a new frock, don't you agree?

MADISON I'll be back at my room by lunch.

SHEILA Ah, you're a love, Charlie.

By now, the dispatcher has finished writing up Emily's trip-ticket. Emily takes it, exits through the door Madison holds open for her.

DISPATCHER   *(to Sheila)* This is yours, love.   Rear Admiral to go to Hammersmith.

SHEILA   Oooh, a Rear Admiral.   *(calls to exiting Madison)* I'll be up for my new dress during lunch, love.

DISSOLVE TO:

HENDON AIRPORT, ENTRANCE GATES. DAY.

The car pulls up to the gate. An M.P. SERGEANT comes forward to examine Madison's papers being offered through the rear window.

Madison and the M.P. Sergeant talk through the window.   The back of Emily's head can be seen.

MADISON   Is Lieutenant Haworth still Navy Supply Officer here, Sergeant?

M.P. SERGEANT   *(handing papers back)* No, sir, there's a Lieutenant Wade there now, sir.

Madison extracts a package of nylon hose from his attaché case, gives it to the Sergeant.

M.P. SERGEANT   Thank you sir.   It might help you to know, sir, this Lieutenant Wade is from Alabama.

MADISON   *(nods, then to Emily)* The Navy Supply enclosure.

The gates open.   Emily drives the car into the field.

NAVY SUPPLY DEPOT.

LT. VICTOR WADE, an Alabama boy of 28, sips his coffee.   The depot is a large quonset hut, filled with monstrous refrigerators called "reefers."

WADE This Admiral you're dog-robbing for, Madison, is he a good joe?

Madison, we suddenly discover, has a Southern drawl and reeks with the restrained charm of a Confederate gentleman.

MADISON He's from Virginia, boy. Two stars. Adjutant to the Secretary of the Navy. Highest echelon, policy level.

The REVERSE ANGLE, across them to open doorway, shows Emily waiting by her car outside.

WADE All those stories true about those lady volunteer drivers in the Navy Motor Pool?

MADISON Some of them.

WADE You think you could arrange one of those high echelon Navy Motor Pool drivers for me?

MADISON Come round the hotel tomorrow about three. I've got some bottles for you besides.

WADE What kind of bottles?

MADISON Now, what kind of bottles would I offer a Confederate kinsman in an alien land?

WADE Don't tell me.

MADISON I. W. Harper.

WADE Man, you can't get bourbon over here.

MADISON You've got three bottles.

WADE You're quite a dog-robber, ain't you, Madison?

MADISON Well, let's just make sure we read each other clear, Wade. I'll take care of you. But, Lieutenant, my Admiral sets a better table than anybody in the European Theater of Operations, including the Supreme Commander. I want the prime of everything you've got in here. When I ask for steak, I mean aged, two inches thick, corn-fed, that you can cut with a sharp look. I'm setting up house now. For today, I want six dozen sirloin strips, one crate of oranges, one crate of grapefruit, six rib roasts, three Swift's hams, six gallons of ice cream and one gallon of chocolate syrup. I expect to be favored, and, if any other Admiral's dog-robber complains, my Admiral'll cover for you all the way to the Secretary of the Navy. If you do right, I'll see you get the Legion of Merit with Clusters for your gallant service. But if you fink on my Admiral, man—well, my Admiral has a pet research project, the study of navigable waters in the Arctic Circle. The last supply officer who sent my Admiral a chewy steak is now up at the North Pole, doing polar research. You read me, Lieutenant?

WADE Oh, I read you, Commander.

He claps Madison on the back. Madison hands Wade a page from his notebook. They walk up the length of the quonset hut to the door.

WADE *(eyeing Emily)* If you just have that sweet young thing drive that Buick around to the dock, we'll load you up.

THE SUPPLY ENCLOSURE. DAY.

ACROSS Emily by her car, as sailors load it with cartons, crates and ice-cream containers. Madison stands by the trunk checking off the items. Wade stands by the door of the quonset hut, checking off his list. Emily regards it all with icy contempt.

COUNTRYSIDE, LONDON SUBURBS. DAY.

Inside the car as they drive back, Madison sits in the rear seat, crowded in by all the crates and cartons. He checks his watch, makes notes.

EMILY *(suddenly)* You Americans are really enjoying this war, aren't you?

MADISON Ma'am?

EMILY Most English families haven't seen that many oranges or eggs in five years, but it's all one big Shriners' Convention for you Yanks, isn't it?

Madison nods briefly, recognizing the type.

MADISON Yeah, well, that's swell, Miss...

EMILY Barham.

MADISON Yeah. On to the hotel, Miss Barham. It's nearly lunch.

He turns his attention back to his notes.

HOTEL, MADISON'S ROOM.

The entire bedroom has the look of a storeroom. There's hardly space to walk between all the crates and cartons. Chief Petty Officer Adams is still unpacking. The closets are jammed with frocks, the bed piled high with dress packages, and the bureau obscured by boxes of hosiery, lingerie, soap and soap flakes. The bathroom is crammed with cases of liquor, cartons of candy, racks of perfume bottles, and a half-size refrigerator for chilling wine. Madison is perched on his bed, talking on the phone and sipping coffee—his lunch.

MADISON *(on phone)* Avocado, avocado!...Demi-douzaine...since when did you start asking for ration coupons, Alfie...Oui, vingt minutes...*(hangs up, stands, mutters)* Well, that's the avocados. I need a blonde, a bridge-playing blonde. *(He looks out the window, down to the waiting cars.)*

MADISON'S P.O.V.: through the window to the sidewalk six floors below where Emily stands beside her car.

REVERSE SHOT across Madison shows Sheila lifting a black sheath dress from its package of tissue on the bed.

SHEILA Oh, it's too bloody gorgeous, Charlie.

MADISON I need a girl, Sheila, a bridge-playing girl, very crusty, elegant, with British diction calculated to bring out the upstart in any American, who can handle herself at a dinner table and play bridge like an assassin. Whatever happened to Alice Luddens?

SHEILA *(holds the sheath against herself)* She married off, love. To a lieutenant in the paratroops. Can't be choosy, I suppose, if you're a widow with two kids. May I try it on, Charlie?

Madison nods as he riffles through another of his countless notebooks. Sheila dashes off into the bathroom, unbuttoning her uniform, as Captain Harry Spaulding enters from the hall. He affects a cane. He pockets a bottle of perfume he finds on the dresser.

SPAULDING Well, the balloon's going up any day now.

MADISON *(looking down at Emily again)* What balloon?

SPAULDING *(with a cavalier twirl of his cane)* D-Day, old man. The invasion of Europe. Any day now, one million men are going to hit the beaches of France in the greatest battle in history.

MADISON Oh. Harry, do you know any girls who play a good game of bridge?

Sheila comes out of the bathroom dressed in her black sheath.

SHEILA What do you think, Charlie?

He suddenly reaches over and appropriates Spaulding's cane.

MADISON *(again looking down at Emily)* Yeah. It's worth a try. Harry, May I borrow this for a little while? *(He takes the cane.)*

SPAULDING Hey...!

MADISON   It's a matter of state.

He opens the door to the hallway and exits, suddenly walking with a notice-able limp, leaning heavily on the cane. A little startled, Spaulding watches him go.

HOTEL, PARK LANE SIDE. DAY.

WIDE ANGLE SHOT shows Emily leaning against the front fender of her car, smoking, as Madison comes out of the hotel. She is a little astonished to see him walking with his right leg stiff as a board and using a cane. So, for that matter, is a LIEUTENANT in the background, who is going into the hotel.

FULL SHOT of the Lieutenant going in and Madison coming out.

LIEUTENANT   Hey, Charlie, what happened to you?

MADISON   *(mutters)* Knock off.

Madison comes down to the car. Emily steps quickly on her cigarette and hur-ries to open the rear door. Madison makes a great show of pain.

EMILY   An old wound, Commander?

MADISON   *(grimaces)* Yes.   I caught a bit of flak flying for the RAF in 1940. It acts up every now and then.

EMILY   *(not unamused)* Pity.

Madison rubs his suddenly wounded thigh, regards Emily.

MADISON   Miss Barham, do you play bridge?

EMILY   Yes, I do. Why?

MADISON   Miss Barham, Admiral Jessup would like you to be his guest for dinner and bridge this evening.

EMILY Ah.

MADISON Just dinner and bridge, nothing else. I'll have you delivered back to your quarters by half past ten.

EMILY No, thank you. If you don't need me, Commander, may I take my lunch?

She hands him her trip-ticket. He signs it, gives it back.

MADISON You're something of a prig, Miss Barham.

Emily, who had started round the car to get to her own seat, pauses and turns.

EMILY I don't mean to be.

She frowns; continues round the front of the car.

TRANSIENT WOMEN'S QUARTERS.

HIGH ANGLE SHOT down on a large barracks-like room, lined with cots and filled with a variety of military women. WACS, WRENS, SPARS, etc. dress and undress—with much toweling, toiletting, lipsticking, etc.

Emily sinks down onto a cot next to one on which Sheila, swathed in towels, is dyeing her hair red with dabs of cotton. A small laboratory of bottles, vials, bowls and basins is spread out on the cot before her.

EMILY Do you think I'm a prig, Sheila?

SHEILA Oh, Lord, yes, love. You've been shattering us all with your virtue ever since you joined this Motor Pool.

EMILY Have I been that awful?

SHEILA Bloody virgin goddess herself.

EMILY Well, the fact is I'm anything but. I'm grotesquely sentimental. I fall in love at the drop of a hat. That's why I gave up hospital driving. All those men moaning in the back of the ambulance, especially the lot from Africa. I used to read to them in my off-hours. When they were healed and being sent back to the front, they'd come looking for me in the ambulance garage to spend their last nights of leave with them. Little hotel rooms, bed and breakfast for a guinea. I paid the guinea myself more often than not.

She lies back on the bed, suddenly weary.

EMILY But I couldn't say no to them, could I? I had just lost my husband *(almost cries)*—at Tobruk, and I was overwhelmed with tenderness for all dying men. As I say, I'm grotesquely sentimental—What on earth are you doing with your hair?

SHEILA I'm turning it red. I'm going to one of Charlie Madison's do's tonight.

EMILY Oh yes. I was just asked to that one. Does it require red hair?

SHEILA Oh, do come along, love. Charlie lays on smashing food. All sorts of meats, fruit, real cream, things we haven't seen in England for years. You'll probably get a new dress out of it. Have you ever been up to Madison's room?

EMILY No.

SHEILA Well, you've got to see it. It's the swankiest shop in town. He's got everything up there but the crown jewels.

EMILY Yes, so I've heard.

SHEILA *(pulls out a parcel from under her bed, extracts wisps of hosiery and lingerie)* Here, look at that. You can't buy that at Harrod's. That's nylon, love, and this is pure silk. I'd show you the new dress, but I don't want the others here to see. It's Bonwit Teller's. You've heard of that, I imagine.

EMILY You mean, he actually supplies you with a wardrobe?

SHEILA Oh, Charlie dresses you proper. Americans don't like to see their women in uniforms.

EMILY But it all ends in someone's bed, doesn't it? I mean, that's the point, isn't it?

SHEILA Well, look who's talking, after that lurid confession you just made.

EMILY Sorry. I'm rather a prig at that.

SHEILA I feel rather tender towards the poor beggars myself.

EMILY *(stands, on edge)* Well, I don't want to feel tender towards anyone, especially soldiers. *(slowly takes a few paces)* I've lost a husband, a father and a brother in this war. When my husband died, I almost went insane. I take these things badly. *(She sits, tears in her eyes.)* I fall in love too easily, and I shatter too easily. I don't want any more doomed men.

SHEILA Oh, do come tonight, love. *These* chaps aren't doomed. They'll never see any of the shooting, that's for sure. We'll have a few laughs. I've never seen anyone needing a few laughs as much as you do.

CLOSEUP of Emily. Her eyes close. A sigh shudders through her as she masters her tears.

HOTEL, ADMIRAL JESSUP'S SUITE, LIVING ROOM.

Madison is going over the dinner arrangements with the Floor Service Captain, Tom. A handsome table has been set up in the middle of the living room. Madison moves around it, checking every piece of silver, every plate.

MADISON *(examining a water glass)* Very nice crystal, Tom. Danish?

TOM   Of course.

MADISON   I don't much care for the centerpiece. You can take that out.

TOM   Yes, sir.

MADISON   *(fingering the table linen)* Italian. Very lovely.

TOM   Thank you.

Madison is suddenly aware he is being watched. He looks across to the doorway leading to his room.

MADISON'S P.O.V.: Emily stands in the doorway, fascinated by all that's going on.

ACROSS Madison to Emily, as Madison turns to the Floor Service Captain.

MADISON   Cocktails at five-thirty and heavy on the gin, Tom. Dinner at six promptly. Once you've cleared away, I'll manage from there.

TOM   Very good, sir.

EMILY   You're not limping, Commander.

She turns back into Madison's room. Madison follows her.

MADISON'S ROOM.

REVERSE ANGLE as Emily enters, followed by Madison.

EMILY   *(looking about the room wide-eyed)* It's the Arabian nights. Do you have chests of rubies in the bathroom?

MADISON   Just perfumes and liquor.

EMILY   *(walking about, looking at this case, that carton)* I've heard about this room, Commander. All the girls talk about it. But I simply couldn't believe it. Bergdorf-Goodman's, Saks Fifth Avenue, Lord and Taylor...Sheila's right. It's the swankiest shop in town. Good heavens! Arpège perfume! How did you ever manage Arpège perfume with the Germans in Paris? There are Germans in Paris, aren't there? There is a war on, I think. You Americans must have heard something about it, I'm sure.

Madison has found a cigar box among the things on the bureau. Now, he sits on a soft chair and lights a cigar.

MADISON *(regards Emily flatly)* Just pick out a dress, honey, and be back at five-thirty.

Emily turns, startled.

MADISON You American-haters bore me to tears, Miss Barham. I've dealt with Europeans all my life. I know all about us parvenus from the States, who come over here and race around your old cathedral towns with our cameras and Coca-Cola bottles, brawl in your pubs, paw your women and act like we own the world. We overtip, we talk too loud, we think we can buy anything with a Hershey bar. I've had Germans and Italians tell me how politically ingenuous we are. Perhaps so, but we haven't managed a Hitler or a Mussolini yet. I've had Frenchmen call me a savage, because I only took half an hour for lunch. Hell, Miss Barham, the only reason the French take two hours for lunch is because the service in their restaurants is lousy. And the most tedious of the lot are you British. We crass Americans didn't introduce war into your little island. This war, Miss Barham, to which we Americans are so insensitive, is the result of two thousand years of European greed, barbarism, superstition and stupidity. Don't blame it on our Coca-Cola bottles. Europe was a going brothel long before we came to town.

EMILY Dear me, what an outburst.

MADISON So, lay off, Mrs. Miniver. If you don't like our Hershey bars, don't take them. Pick yourself a frock or get out. It's not my job to listen to your sentimental contempt.

Emily appraises Madison with new eyes.

EMILY You know, I could almost believe you flew for the RAF.

MADISON I never flew for the RAF, and you know it.

EMILY You didn't expect me to believe you for a minute, did you?

MADISON Not for a minute.

EMILY But why, Commander?

MADISON You're here, Miss Barham.

EMILY *(looks quickly at him)* Yes, so I am. You're a complete rascal. I'll be back at five-thirty, Commander.

MADISON *(opening the door)* The Admiral will be delighted you're coming. If I can be of any service, Miss Barham.

EMILY Oh, I have my own clothes, Commander. I'll do without your Hershey bars.

TWO SHOT: For a moment, the two of them appraise each other silently, smiles pending on their lips, amused by the other.

EMILY *(smiling amiably)* Do you have a girl, Commander?

MADISON *(smiling just as amiably)* None of your damn business, Miss Barham.

They both smile at each other. Emily goes out. Madison closes the door.

DISSOLVE TO:

ADMIRAL JESSUP'S SUITE, LIVING ROOM.

The Admiral's cocktail party is in full swing. There are twenty-five people present, including a distinguished civilian, a RUSSIAN GENERAL, and officers from the various Allies: Free French, British Navy, etc.; some ladies and some not so.

Emily is in conversation with an American Army COLONEL of about forty and a British NAVAL OFFICER.

COLONEL   I don't much care for chamber music myself, but these Hungarians at the Princess are very good.

Emily's attention goes to Madison who makes his way among the guests. We follow his progress past...

ADMIRAL JESSUP *(in discourse with GENERAL HALLERTON)*   Listen, Willie, I don't like the way the Navy's publicity is being handled in Overlord.

GENERAL HALLERTON   Yeah, I figured that's what this party was about.

Madison notices Emily and, while steering another female guest in the direction of an officer, inquires if all is well. He looks at her appreciatively.

MADISON   Miss Barham...?   You must know somebody at Saks Fifth Avenue yourself.

EMILY   Oh, this old thing?

MADISON   If you need any assistance, I'll be near at hand.

Emily can't help but admire his gallantry and hospitality.

ADMIRAL JESSUP   We'll talk about it later.

GENERAL HALLERTON   You're wasting your time, Jessie.

PANNING, CAMERA picks up American and British officers again.

COLONEL I've been trying to get them American visas.

The Russian General, with a girl in tow, approaches Madison and group.

MADISON Horoshaw?

RUSSIAN GENERAL Ochen Horoshaw!

The Russian General makes some Russian comment. Madison laughs, and translates.

CUT TO:

Bus, NAMELESS BROAD, French Naval Officer, Air Force Officer and two other women.

NAMELESS BROAD Avocados! Really, I haven't seen an avocado in London for years!

BUS When the Admiral entertains, he likes to have a surprise or two for his guests.

NAMELESS BROAD But avocados...and out of season at that!

CUT TO:

Madison, continuing to translate for Russian.

BRITISH NAVAL OFFICER You can't leave decent musicians wandering around homeless. There are so few really good ones as it is.

An American MAJOR enters in background and goes to the bar. Madison spots him. On the way, Madison first gives instructions to Tom, then joins the major.

MADISON Let's keep the food moving, Tom. The Admiral wants the room cleared for bridge in two hours.

TOM As you wish, sir.

MADISON *(at bar)* Hello, Ted. I've been looking for you. I dropped in to see your wife at the hospital in Washington. She's really much stronger and says not to worry about her.

MAJOR *(as they move away)* Thank you Charlie. That was very thoughtful of you and I appreciate it.

ADMIRAL JESSUP'S LIVING ROOM. TWO HOURS LATER.

ACROSS the bridge foursome. The Admiral and Madison are paired against Hallerton and Emily. In the background, the party is getting sexier.

ADMIRAL JESSUP Doubled.

GENERAL HALLERTON Redoubled.

MADISON Pass.

EMILY Pass.

General Hallerton as dummy lays out his hand on the table. Emily winces.

GENERAL HALLERTON Did I overbid?

EMILY Well, let us just say you have unbridled courage.

Admiral Jessup leads a card. Emily slips a card from the dummy. The play goes quickly and expertly. Without losing a second's concentration, Jessup engages General Hallerton, now standing behind him, in conference.

ADMIRAL JESSUP Willie, I don't like the way the Navy's been left out of the publicity in Overlord. I want extreme measures taken to publicize the Navy's role in the Invasion. The President supports me in this.

GENERAL HALLERTON Yes, we got your cables, Jessie, but I don't know what you mean by extreme measures.

EMILY *(studying the cards)* Oh, dear, this is going to be a bloodbath.

ADMIRAL JESSUP I want a Marine division to be the first assault wave.

GENERAL HALLERTON Good Lord, you're not dragging that old chestnut in.

ADMIRAL JESSUP The Marines are the traditional shock troops, and you know it.

GENERAL HALLERTON Not in the European Theater of Operations, they're not. You Navy guys had all the headlines in the South Pacific, but Europe's an Army show. That's been clearly understood from the beginning, Jessie.

ADMIRAL JESSUP I've written the Supreme Commander about this.

GENERAL HALLERTON Yes, that's one of the reasons he's out of town. You must be off your nut, Jessie, if you think the assault plans are going to be changed at this stage of preparation. You know when the balloon's going up.

MADISON *(pondering his hand)* What balloon?

GENERAL HALLERTON I've been instructed to say we'll put on a few more Navy staff officers at Supreme Headquarters, and we're going to push the PRO people to send out more Navy releases. But the Supreme Commander wants it clear, Jessie, that he considers this inter-service competitiveness in very bad taste. He's having enough trouble keeping the English and French in line.

Admiral Jessup gathers in a trick and then lays the rest of his hand down.

ADMIRAL JESSUP You're down four, Willie, doubled, redoubled and vulnerable.

GENERAL HALLERTON *(sitting down, scowling)* A Marine division. You must be losing your mind, Jessie. Who deals?

ADMIRAL JESSUP'S LIVING ROOM. STILL LATER.

Admiral Jessup stands at the window looking out. The party is breaking up. The Admiral mumbles to himself, or at least it seems that way.

Madison comes out of the room. He starts to cross to the bridge table where General Hallerton sits, meticulously rechecking the scores of the games.

GENERAL HALLERTON *(standing unhappily)* Thirty-four bucks, all right.

Two waiters have entered from the hall. With a gesture, Madison indicates he wants the room cleared and begins his farewells to the last few guests.

MADISON General Waterson, your car's ready.

Cummings intercepts him.

CUMMINGS *(whispers)* The champagne, Charlie.

MADISON It's being chilled. I'll leave it outside your door in half an hour.

CUMMINGS *(looking around the room)* Where'd she go?

MADISON I sent her in.

Cummings nods and exits out the front door.

MADISON *(to General Hallerton)* At Admiral Jessup's request, I've had the Scotch House send you three yards of tweed, General. It's for Mrs. Hallerton.

GENERAL HALLERTON It won't get him his Marine division, Charlie, but it's generous of him anyway. Thank him for me. *(exits)*

By now, the last guests, General Waterson with Sheila and Emily, are congregating by the door, putting on the coats.

MADISON Good night, sir, Sheila.

They exit, with Emily the last straggler. Madison crosses to her.

MADISON There's a car downstairs for you, Miss Barham. If you'd like me to take you down?

EMILY No thank you. I'll manage. I had a lovely evening, Commander. Please ask me again.

She follows General Waterson and Sheila out. The waiters finish clearing away. Madison closes the door on them all. Admiral Jessup stands by the window, looking out. There's no doubt of it now. He is mumbling to himself.

MADISON Sir?

ADMIRAL JESSUP *(turns)* What?

MADISON I thought you said something to me, sir.

ADMIRAL JESSUP You're losing your mind, Charlie.

MADISON Yes, sir. I'll lay out your night clothes, sir.

He crosses to the Admiral's room. The Admiral turns back to the window.

ADMIRAL JESSUP'S BEDROOM.

Madison enters. He turns on the bed lamp, turns off the overhead light and turns down the bed with deft, familiar movements. He glides into the bathroom, draws the Admiral's tub. He comes out, extracts an old-fashioned nightshirt and sleeping cap from the bureau drawer, and lays them neatly across the bed. The Admiral enters, unbuttoning his jacket.

ADMIRAL JESSUP Was I very rude, leaving all the goodbyes to you, Charlie?

MADISON It wasn't noticed, sir.

Madison takes the Admiral's jacket, drapes it onto a hanger, slips it into the closet. He bends and retrieves the Admiral's slippers, whisks a bathrobe off a closet hook, and crosses back into the bathroom where he turns off the tub and leaves the robe and slippers. When he comes out, the Admiral has stripped off his shirt which Madison takes.

ADMIRAL JESSUP I've got the damnedest headache.

MADISON I'll fix you a drink before your bath, Admiral.

The Admiral strips off his undershirt. Madison takes it and neatly folds it and the shirt onto a chair. The Admiral straddles a hard-back chair, rests his chin on his forearms. Madison begins massaging the Admiral's shoulders.

ADMIRAL JESSUP Charlie, in seven weeks I've got to go back to Washington and testify before the Joint Committee on Military Affairs. On the agenda is a review of the Army's new Long-Range Bomber program and there'll be speculation as to whether that doesn't make carrier-based aircraft obsolete. In short, they're out to scrap the Navy again. Charlie, the Air Corps's coming out of this war as the darling of the services—the Army and its Air Corps. The Navy will be the runt of the litter. They'll scrap us like they do after every war. They'll limit our capital ships, reduce our crews to cadres, strip us back to Pearl Harbor level. And then they'll scream how ill-prepared we are when somebody hits us with another Pearl Harbor. All Washington is bug-eyed over this invasion of Europe, and this invasion of Europe is an all-Army show. That's why we're here, Charlie, to remind the Congress of the United States and the American public that this invasion is also a Navy show. *(chuckles)* I just threw in that Marine division for openers. They turned me down and now they owe me something. But what? I don't know what to shoot for, but I've got to come up with something. It's driving me crazy. Charlie, fix me something for this head. It's killing me.

MADISON Sure, Admiral.

Madison turns from his massaging and exits into the living room.

ADMIRAL JESSUP'S LIVING ROOM.

Madison enters, moving to the improvised bar. He quickly mixes a drink and returns to...

ADMIRAL JESSUP'S BEDROOM.

Madison enters with a drink. The Admiral moves about the darkish room, muttering to himself.

ADMIRAL JESSUP *(barely audible)* Sure, George, sure, sure—support that damned peanut—damn Chinese—Communist five years, George— five years the most.

MADISON *(extending the glass)* Here's your drink, sir.

The Admiral crosses past Madison and goes into the bathroom, muttering, seeming not to notice him.

ADMIRAL JESSUP —moderates, boy, moderates—you're on the nose there, George—land reform, take the steam out of it—only damn Army in China anyway—

He disappears into the bathroom, closing the door. Madison is left standing with an outstretched drink. He sets the glass on the bed table and calls out.

MADISON I'll leave your drink on the bedroom table, sir.

There is no answer. Madison shrugs and crosses back into the living room.

ADMIRAL JESSUP'S SUITE, LIVING ROOM.

Madison pauses to dump a loaded ashtray, overlooked by the waiters, into a trash can, then goes into his own room.

MADISON'S BEDROOM.

Madison enters the dark room, stops in the doorway, framed in the rectangle of light, his face registering mild surprise.

ACROSS Madison to his bed. Emily is perched on it, legs crossed and hands folded patiently in her lap. She smiles up at Madison in the doorway.

REVERSE ANGLE across Emily to Madison in the doorway.

MADISON Come to think of it, I don't have a girl.

CLOSE-UP of Emily.

EMILY I don't have a man. *(stands, smiles)* Do you think we can keep it on that level?

MADISON Not a chance. This is going to be just one of those things, you and I. I can see that.

EMILY I like your spirit, Commander.

She slips happily into his arms. They kiss many times. Madison kicks the door behind him shut. The room is now lit only by moonlight. Between kisses, they murmur.

MADISON I'm not your type, you know.

EMILY Like hell you're not.

They kiss, clutch at each other. It's a hungry scene.

MADISON I'd have thought you'd fancy heroes, and I'm yellow, honey, clear through.

EMILY *(whispering)* That's your most attractive quality.

They sink into bed.

EMILY I've had it with heroes, Charlie. Every man I've loved has died in this war, but you'll never get caught in the shooting. That's one thing I'm sure of. You can't imagine how attractive that makes you to me.

She tears at his tie and collar button so she can kiss his neck.

MADISON Easy, tiger, that's a tailored shirt.

EMILY *(affably)* Oh, shut up, and let me kiss you.

They wrap themselves ravenously around each other.

MADISON *(delighted)* What a savage.

For a moment, the screen is filled with the bobbing and weaving of the two heads and the four shoulders of the lovers as they assail each other with embraces.

Suddenly, the door to the hallway in background is thrust open, and a SHAFT of LIGHT shoots into the room, bathing Madison and Emily with light. The two lovers slowly extricate themselves from their sinuous embrace and turn to see what this interruption is.

Framed in the doorway against the light of the hall is the Admiral. He makes an odd figure, dressed as he is in an old-fashioned nightshirt, with sleeping cap askew on his brow, especially here as he shouts at the two startled lovers.

ADMIRAL JESSUP The first dead man on Omaha Beach must be a sailor! Do you read me, sir? The first dead man on Omaha Beach must be a sailor! Put your mind on that, sir!

He abruptly exits into the hallway, slamming the door behind him.

REVERSE ANGLE to Madison and Emily on the bed. They are both staring blankly at the CAMERA, where the Admiral had been standing.

EMILY Dear me, what was that about?

Madison sits up slowly.

MADISON *(befuddled)* What did he say?

EMILY I think he said the first dead man on Omaha Beach must be a sailor. That's a very piquant thing to say, don't you think?

MADISON *(stands)* Yes, I think I'd call that piquant.

He crosses to the doorway, opens it, peeks out into the hallway.

EMILY *(on the bed)* Does he do that often?

MADISON *(looking up and down the empty hallway)* No, I can't say I can ever remember him doing that before. Excuse me a minute, will you please.

HALLWAY OUTSIDE THE ADMIRAL'S SUITE.

Madison closes his bedroom door. He moves thoughtfully past the living room entry to the Admiral's door and knocks gently. There is no answer. After a moment, he opens the door tentatively.

The Admiral, in his nightshirt, sits on his bed. He looks up.

ADMIRAL JESSUP Hello, Charlie. The first dead man on Omaha Beach must be a sailor. Think about that for a minute.

MADISON *(closing the door)* In what reference, sir?

ADMIRAL JESSUP Yes, the unknown sailor. Let me kick that around in my own mind a bit. I want the whole team in my office at o-nine-hundred hours tomorrow morning to discuss just that.

MADISON To discuss just what, sir?

ADMIRAL JESSUP Arrange that, Charlie. O-nine-hundred hours, the whole team. Goodnight, Charlie.

The Admiral switches off his bed lamp, plunging the room into darkness, gets under the covers and goes promptly to sleep.

MADISON Yes, sir.

HALLWAY OUTSIDE ADMIRAL JESSUP'S SUITE.

Madison comes out, closing the door. He stands a moment, perplexed to say the least. Then, he moves still another door down, stops in front of Cummings' room, and KNOCKS sharply.

LT. COMMANDER CUMMINGS' ROOM.

The room is very dark, lit only by moonlight. Two bodies leap from the bed. They are Cummings with his clothes in disarray and a NAMELESS BROAD with no clothes on at all.

CUMMINGS *(stuffing his shirttails in)* Who is it?

NAMELESS BROAD *(muttering imprecations)* Ruddy Americans, always barging in in this ruddy hotel.

The door opens, and Madison takes a step into the room.

MADISON Bus, the screwiest thing just happened.

CUMMINGS For Pete's sakes, Charlie, close the door, will you?

The Nameless Broad, frantically trying to hide behind Cummings and look for her skirt at the same time, mutters.

NAMELESS BROAD Ruddy Americans, haven't got the ruddiest clue to what privacy means...

MADISON *(closing the door)* The Admiral just barged into my room in his nightshirt, Bus, and yelled at the top of his lungs: "The first dead man on Omaha Beach must be a sailor!"

CUMMINGS All right, Charlie, what's up? I mean, you see the obvious state of affairs here, Charlie.

MADISON I'm telling you. I think the Admiral's flipped a braid. He just came charging into my room, yelling: "The first dead man on—"

CUMMINGS Charlie, for Pete's sakes, I mean... *(He indicates the naked girl muttering behind him.)*

NAMELESS BROAD Ruddy circus, the whole ruddy place...

CUMMINGS Tomorrow morning, what do you say, Charlie?

MADISON Tomorrow morning, o-nine-hundred hours, the Admiral wants the whole team in his office to discuss "The first dead man on Omaha Beach must be a sailor."

CUMMINGS Yeah, swell, great. Tomorrow morning, Charlie.

NAMELESS BROAD Where's my ruddy shoes?

MADISON All right, I'll see you tomorrow.

He turns and exits. Cummings glowers. The Nameless Broad continues with her indistinguishable imprecations.

CUMMINGS *(to the Nameless Broad)* I think Charlie's flipped a screw.

NAMELESS BROAD This hotel's a ruddy circus, if you don't mind me saying...

                                                                    FADE OUT.

FADE IN:

GROSVENOR SQUARE. DAY.

WIDE ANGLE SHOT showing an endless convoy of Army trucks and Jeeps inching along South Audley Street.

NAVY BUILDING, ADMIRAL JESSUP'S OFFICE.

Admiral Jessup, spruce, shining and apparently sane, stands at the window looking down on the convoy. After a moment, he turns from the window.

REVERSE ANGLE ACROSS Admiral Jessup to his team: Captain Ellender, Lt. Commanders Cummings and Madison, and Chief Petty Officer Adams sitting about the office, a sparse room decorated with a picture of President Roosevelt and one of Admiral King on one wall. A second wall is entirely covered by a large map of Great Britain and Western Europe.

ADMIRAL JESSUP We've got about a month. *(He moves to the wall map.)* I want a movie made showing the Navy's contributions to D-Day, from the procurement of vessels to the actual landings. Gentlemen, four thousand ships and boats—battleships, destroyers, landing crafts, spitkits, excursion steamers, channel boats, private yachts, tugs, tubs and Chinese junks—four thousand vessels!—the greatest armada ever assembled by man!—is going to cross that channel. And what's more, they're going to have to do it at night, across one of the nastiest pieces of water in the world, the English Channel. And every inch of that channel is mined in the bargain. It'll be the most incredible Naval achievement in history. If Hitler could have done it, he'd have had the world in his pocket. It's the Navy that is the essence of victory in this invasion. I want a movie that makes that clear.

CUMMINGS Well, sir...

ADMIRAL JESSUP I especially want a movie to show the Navy Demolition Units who are going to be the first men in on those beaches. Casualties are estimated at fifty percent in the first waves. A lot of brave men are going to die on D-Day, gentlemen. I want a movie made that shows the first brave man to die on those beaches was a sailor.

The phone RINGS. Cummings picks it up.

CUMMINGS *(on phone)* This is Admiral Jessup's office.

ADMIRAL JESSUP   If that's Sir Roger Charlton's office, I'll be there directly.

CUMMINGS   *(on phone)* Yes, sir, he'll be there directly. He's leaving now, sir.

ADMIRAL JESSUP   *(putting on his hat)* Now, here's what I want done. I want a photography team assigned to the demolition engineers to record their activities on film right up to the beaches. I'm leaving this in your hands, Bus. I consider it urgent. Any questions?

He crosses to the door to Cummings' outer office, pauses. The members of his team purse their lips and avoid each other's eyes.

CUMMINGS   Well, sir, there are already six Navy photography teams assigned to the first assault wave.

ADMIRAL JESSUP   I don't care about any other photography teams. I want one of my own to record the heroism of those Navy engineers. I want this film made, Commander. Now, you get some Photographer's Mates and start making it.

CUMMINGS   Yes, sir.

ADMIRAL JESSUP   Any questions?

CUMMINGS   No, sir.

Nobody else says anything, so the Admiral exits. A moment of silence fills the room until the CLICK of the outer door is heard. Cummings stands.

CUMMINGS   Now, how's that for a cockamamie assignment?

ELLENDER   He's been getting these eccentric flashes ever since his wife died last year.

CUMMINGS   *(reaches for the phone)* Yeah. Well he's got something in the back of his mind. I better check around and see if there are any unattached Photographer's Mates around. *(to Madison, now leaving)* Where are *you* going?

Madison waves an airy goodby and exits.

CUMMINGS *(calling after him)* Call in around noon, Charlie.

LONDON STREET IN ST. JOHN'S WOODS. DAY.

It is an uncharacteristically sunny morning for London. Madison, carrying two candy boxes, comes down the street of pleasant middle-class houses, each embedded in charming gardens and isolated by neatly-chopped hedges. Half the peaceful street, however, has been shattered by bombing, and parts of walls are all that remain of some of the houses. At the near end of the street, Madison finds one that is still intact. He unlatches the gate and goes up the walk.

EMILY'S HOUSE. DAY.

Madison raps the clapper on the front door. The door behind Madison opens. He turns from looking at the neighborhood to face his hostess.

CLOSE-UP of Emily in the open doorway, smiling like a well-fed cat. She's clearly a woman in love.

MADISON Hello, Emily.

EMILY Hello, Charlie. You're just in time for tea.

CLOSE-UP of Madison. He's in love, too. Obviously, last night went off very well.

MADISON *(entering the house)* Thank you.

EMILY'S HOUSE, FOYER.

Madison comes into the darkish anteroom, and Emily closes the door.

EMILY *(notes the box he's carrying)* You've brought me some chocolates.

MADISON *(proffering the parcels)* Two boxes of Hershey bars.

EMILY *(annoyed)* Well, that's very American of you, Charlie. You just simply had to bring along some small token of opulence. Well, I don't want them.

She turns, annoyed, starts for the living room, then turns on the threshold.

EMILY You Yanks can't even show affection without buying something.

MADISON *(following her)* Well, don't get into a state over it. I just thought you liked chocolates.

EMILY I do. But my country's at war, and we're doing without chocolates for the while. And I don't want oranges or eggs or soap flakes either. Don't show me how profitable it will be to fall in love with you, Charlie. Don't Americanize me.

Madison stares into the living room.

MADISON'S P.O.V.: The living room is flooded with family photographs and portraits. On the piano alone are some ten framed photographs of various sizes, showing men in uniform for the most part. On the wall hangs a portrait of a stern, gray-haired man in his sixties, wearing sashes of honor across his chest and a variety of medals.

EMILY That's my father. He lost a leg in the first war. Got the Victoria Cross for that. He died in an air raid a week after that portrait was painted. That's my brother there. *(She indicates a photograph on the piano.)* His name was Charlie, too, by the way. He was shot down during the Blitz. Sacrificed himself to save his squadron. The one you're looking at now is my husband.

MADISON *(holding a photograph)* He looks like a rake.

EMILY Yes. He was very bawdy. I was insane about him. He died at

Tobruk. The rest of the lot there are cousins. There's two of them still living. I must say the family's been thinned out nicely one way or another.

She takes Madison's arm and speaks confidentially.

EMILY Charlie, before we go out to my mum, I must tell you she's just a bit mad. You'll like her very much, she's very funny. But she may yatter away about my father and my brother as though they were still alive. Just go along with her. You do understand.

MADISON Oh, I get the point. You don't want my Hershey bars.

EMILY Yes. I think it profane to enjoy this war.

She starts for the French doors to the garden. As she reaches for the knob, Madison stops her.

MADISON You know, I never realized what a sensual satisfaction grieving is for women.

EMILY *(stiffens)* I'm not sure that was a very tasteful thing for you to say.

MADISON I'm not sentimental about war. I see nothing noble in widows.

EMILY *(smiles)* You're jealous of my husband. I like that.

She opens the French doors, and they go out.

EMILY'S HOUSE, GARDEN.

Emily and Madison come into the garden. Emily's mother is seated at a small garden table, pouring tea. MRS. BARHAM is a tweedy lady in her fifties and as mad as the Hatter.

MRS. BARHAM You've brought chocolates! Two whole boxfuls. What a treasure trove!

EMILY I've already refused them, Mother. *(Everyone sits and gets comfortable.)*

MADISON On ascetic grounds.

MRS. BARHAM You're an absolute flagellant, Emily.

EMILY *(sipping tea)* Oh, take the things if you want them.

MRS. BARHAM Well, I shall have one later. I'll save the rest for your father. *(She whispers conspiratorially to Madison.)* I take it you're Emily's new lover, since she hasn't bothered to introduce us.

MADISON *(whispers)* You must be her mother.

MRS. BARHAM Ah, you've found the chink in my armor, have you? What are your religious beliefs, sir?

MADISON I'm a practicing coward.

MRS. BARHAM That *is* very fervent of you.

EMILY I should've known you two would get on. You're as dotty as she is, Charlie.

MADISON *(sipping tea)* Actually, before the war, I was an assistant night manager of a diplomatic hotel in Washington, D.C.

MRS. BARHAM Whatever made you say that?

EMILY Oh, Lord, I'm beginning to feel like Alice at the tea party.

MRS. BARHAM Shh. The Commander is about to tell us of a religious experience, I think.

MADISON Yes. Before the war, I was an assistant night manager of a diplomatic hotel in Washington, D.C. It was my job to arrange things for many of the great historical figures who came to Washington on great historical missions.

MRS. BARHAM What exactly did you arrange?

MADISON Usually, I arranged girls, but individual tastes varied, of course.

MRS. BARHAM Of course.

MADISON Well, it's useful work, anyway, especially in a war. I was offered all sorts of commissions in the Army and Navy, the one I have now, in fact. Admiral Jessup phoned me to join his staff. But, I had always been a little embarrassed by my job at the hotel and wanted to do something redeeming. Have you noticed that war is the only chance a man gets to do something redeeming? That's why war's so attractive.

MRS. BARHAM Yes, war is very handsome, I quite agree.

MADISON At any rate, I turned down Admiral Jessup's offer and enlisted in the Marines as a private. I even applied for combat service. My wife, to all appearance a perfectly sensible woman, encouraged me in this idiotic decision. Seven months later, I found myself invading the Solomon Islands. There I was, splashing away in the shoals of Guadalcanal. It suddenly occurred to me a man could get killed doing this kind of thing. The fact is, most of the men splashing along with me were screaming in agony and dying like flies. I don't think any of them wanted to die. Yet they had all volunteered for the Marines, and the odds on getting killed are pretty good in the Marines. To make it more grotesque, their wives, sweethearts and mothers had all applauded their acts of suicide, and their children were proud of them for it. It was then I realized how admirable war was, the most admirable act of man. Those were brave men dying there. In peacetime, they had all been normal, decent cowards, frightened of their wives, trembling before their bosses, terrified at the passing of the years. But war had made them gallant. They had been greedy men; now they were self-sacrificing. They had been selfish; now they were generous. Hell, war isn't hell at all. It's man at his best, the highest morality he is capable of.

He sits back, crosses his legs, sips his tea, pleased with his long statement. The women wait expectantly for him to go on, and after a moment, Mrs. Barham speaks up.

MRS. BARHAM   Well, you're not going to just leave us there, splashing at Guadalcanal?

EMILY   Never mind all that. What's all this about a wife?

Madison sets his teacup down, leans back, folds his hands across his chest, and studies the clear sky.

MADISON   That night, I sat in the jungles of Guadalcanal, sopping wet and waiting to be killed, and all because there's a madman in Berlin, a homicidal paranoid in Moscow, a manic buffoon in Rome and a group of obsessed generals in Tokyo.

MRS. BARHAM   By George, he's right. They're all batty.

MADISON   I said to myself, "Charlie, you're as nutty as they are. Worse. At least, they're not sitting here in a jungle, waiting to be killed." It was then I had my blinding revelation.

MRS. BARHAM   Ah!

MADISON   I discovered I was a coward. That's my new religion. I'm a big believer in it. Cowardice will save the world. You see, cowards don't fight wars. They run like rabbits at the first shot. If everybody obeyed their natural impulse and ran like rabbits at the first shot, I don't see how we could possibly get to the second shot.

MRS. BARHAM   That seems perfectly sensible to me.

EMILY   Mother, he's just being facile.

MADISON It's not war that's insane, you see; it's the morality of it. It's not greed and ambition that makes wars; it's goodness. Wars are always fought for the best of reasons, for liberation or manifest destiny, always against tyranny and always in the interests of humanity. So far this war, we've managed to butcher some ten million humans in the interest of humanity. The next war, it seems, we'll have to destroy all of man in order to preserve his damn dignity. It's not war that is unnatural to us; it's virtue. As long as valor remains a virtue, we shall have soldiers. So, I preach cowardice. Through cowardice, we shall all be saved.

MRS. BARHAM (stirred almost to tears) That was exalting, Commander! Absolutely occult!

EMILY Never mind the metaphysics, Commander. Let's get back to your wife.

MADISON (sipping his tea) Well, needless to say, that first night in the jungle, I wrote to Admiral Jessup, saying in essence, "For heaven's sakes, get me out of this!" Two weeks later, I was transferred back to Washington. I raced home to my wife...

EMILY And found her with another man.

MADISON Oh, Lord, no. My wife, who had deceived me before the war more times than I care to think about, was now having the time of her life being faithful. She was furious with me for coming back. There was no reason for her being virtuous anymore. She promptly sued me for divorce on the grounds of religious differences. I was a Self-Preservationist, you see, and she was a High Anglican Sentimentalist.

EMILY (satisfied) Well, you're fair game then.

MRS. BARHAM After every war, you know, we always find out how unnecessary it was. After this one, I'm sure all the generals will dash off to write books about the blunders made by other generals, and statesmen will publish their secret diaries, and it will show beyond a shadow of a doubt that the war could easily have been avoided in the first place.

The CAMERA EDGES IN on Mrs. Barham as her face suddenly clouds with pain. She is no longer the outlandish British dowager.

MRS. BARHAM *(murmurs)* And the rest of us are, of course, left with the job of bandaging the wounds and burying the dead.

MADISON I don't trust people who make bitter reflections about war, Mrs. Barham. It's always the generals with the bloodiest records who are the first to shout what a hell it is, and it's always the war widows who lead the Memorial Day parades.

EMILY That was unkind, Charlie, and very rude.

MADISON *(quite serious)* We shall never end wars, Mrs. Barham, by blaming it on ministers and generals or warmongering imperialists or all the other banal bogies. It's the rest of us who build statues to those generals and name boulevards after those ministers. It's the rest of us who make heroes of our dead and shrines of our battlefields. We wear our widow's weeds like nuns, Mrs. Barham, and perpetuate war by exalting its sacrifices. My brother died at Anzio...

EMILY I didn't know that, Charlie.

MADISON *(not taking his eyes from Mrs. Barham)* Yes. An everyday soldier's death, no special heroism involved. They buried what pieces they found of him. But my mother insists he died a brave death and pretends to be very proud.

MRS. BARHAM Perhaps your mother needs this pretense to endure your brother's death, Charlie.

MADISON He's dead, Mrs. Barham. He was killed at Anzio, an occasion for grief, even anger. But why pride?

MRS. BARHAM You're very hard on your mother, Charlie. It seems a harmless enough pretense to me.

MADISON No, Mrs. Barham. You see, now my other brother can't wait to reach enlistment age. That will be in September.

MRS. BARHAM Oh, Lord.

MADISON It may be ministers and generals who blunder us into wars, Mrs. Barham, but the least the rest of us can do is to resist honoring the institution. What has my mother got for pretending bravery was admirable? She is under constant sedation and terrified she might wake up one morning and find her last son has run off to be brave. I don't think I was rude or unkind before; do you, Mrs. Barham?

MRS. BARHAM *(perceptibly upset)* No. *(suddenly stands)* You'd better push off, Emily, if you've got to get to work.

EMILY *(starting off with Madison)* Give my best to father, then.

MRS. BARHAM *(standing by the tea table, beginning to cry)* Your father died in the Blitz, Emily.

Emily pauses on her way to the house, turning to regard her mother.

MRS. BARHAM And your brother died a brave and pointless death in December, nineteen forty. I've carried on much too long with all this as it is.

Emily takes a solicitous step to her mother.

MRS. BARHAM No, do go, Emily. I'd much rather be alone. I mean it.

She looks full face at Madison, her eyes filled with tears.

MRS. BARHAM You're a very kind man, Commander. I hope you'll come again.

MADISON Thank you, ma'am. I'd like to.

He turns, takes Emily's arm and leads her back to the French doors of the house. Madison and Emily go to the house. Emily keeps looking back at her mother who is standing now, head up, tears coursing down her cheeks, crying unashamedly.

GROSVENOR SQUARE, NAVY BUILDING. NIGHT.

ADMIRAL JESSUP'S OFFICE.

Admirals Jessup, Healy and Hoyle at the end of a long conference. They are in shirt sleeves, collars open, ties askew, drawn and exhausted. The desk, which serves as a conference table, is covered by documents, maps, charts, etc. The huge wall map is dotted with markers.

ADMIRAL HEALY ...at the same time, Jessie, it has to be a neap tide, so we can unload all the Army's heavy stuff with a minimum of open beach to cross. D-Day has to be June fifth or sixth. We won't repeat these tidal conditions for half a year—at least with a moon—and that'll put us into the winter—why don't we knock this briefing off, Jessie? We've been at it since three.

ADMIRAL JESSUP *(on verge of exhaustion)* Yes, I'm tired, George. It took me six months to get that portable port plan through the Pentagon, let alone the British. I haven't got but two, three hours' sleep a night since Florence died. I'm really worn out.

ADMIRAL HOYLE Why don't we get a couple of beers and get a decent night's sleep?

ADMIRAL JESSUP Yeah, let's really tie one on tonight.

Cummings, aide-de-camp, enters with more documents.

ADMIRAL JESSUP Bus, call Charlie Madison, and tell him to set up a little bar at the hotel.

CUMMINGS Yes, sir.

HOTEL, MADISON'S ROOM.

Madison is extracting two bottles of bourbon from a case while Emily sips tea.

MADISON *(going to the living room door)* Back in a minute.

ADMIRAL JESSUP'S SUITE, LIVING ROOM.

Madison enters with the liquor. Cummings is waiting for him, takes the bottles from him. Laughter issues from the Admiral's room.

CUMMINGS The old man's really tying one on tonight.

MADISON He's earned it.

More laughter comes out of the Admiral's room.

ADMIRAL JESSUP'S BEDROOM.

Cummings enters with bottles. The three Admirals are laughing so hard, they can hardly breathe. Admiral Hoyle is bent over, clutching his sides, stamping about. Admiral Healy is sitting on a hard-backed chair, a helpless heap of laughter. Admiral Jessup is weaving about the room, barely able to gasp out a story he is telling.

ADMIRAL JESSUP "Hey!" says this master-at-arms, "Hey, you cadets there in the bushes..."

This provokes a fresh wave of wheezing and grunting.

ADMIRAL JESSUP "Hey, you cadets!" this jimmy-legs says. We weren't called midshipmen then, remember? We were called Naval Cadets...

ADMIRAL HOYLE *(singing)* I've drunk your health in company, I've drunk your health alone...

ADMIRAL JESSUP This was before Bancroft Hall was turned into a dormitory because the O.O.D. was sitting in his...

Laughing too hard to go on, he is reduced to helpless head-shaking.

ADMIRAL HEALY Remember when they christened the Kansas with a bottle of water and...

ADMIRAL JESSUP Anyway...

ADMIRAL HOYLE *(singing)* I've drunk your health so many times, I've damn near ruined my own.

ADMIRAL JESSUP "Hey, you cadets!" this jimmy-legs says...

The three Admirals burst into a fresh wail of laughter. They sink back onto chairs and/or the bed, gasping for air.

ADMIRAL HEALY Oh!... Oh!... Oh!...

GROUP SHOT of the Admirals: Jessup and Healy slumped on the bed, Hoyle straddling a hard-backed chair. Three old bull walruses. Cummings enters the frame with a fresh drink for Admiral Jessup, disappears silently. A moment of pensive silence settles over the old Romans.

ADMIRAL HEALY Jessie, you think they're going to unify the services after the war?

ADMIRAL JESSUP Yeah, looks that way. The Joint Committee on Military Affairs is holding hearings at the end of June. Ostensibly, it's about the Army's new bombers, but it's really about the Army pushing to be the dominant service in the Military Establishment.

ADMIRAL HEALY A lot of talk about the Air Corps becoming a separate service.

ADMIRAL JESSUP Yeah. Every Senator in Washington is infatuated with strategic bombing. You don't win wars with strategic bombers! *(lurching to his feet)* If you did, Hitler would be sitting in this hotel instead of us.

ADMIRAL HOYLE Right!

ADMIRAL JESSUP Hitler ruled the skies. He had the greatest army in the world, but he couldn't cross thirty miles of English Channel! Hitler had everything except a Navy, and now he's finished!

He reels around the room, roaring with rage.

ADMIRAL JESSUP This planet is five-sixths water! God made it that way, and that's the way it's going to stay! In this world, you're as strong as your sea-power!

ADMIRAL HEALY *(beginning to laugh again)* You tell 'em Jessie!

Admiral Jessup has focused his blurred eye on poor Cummings, standing by his improvised bar on the wall table.

ADMIRAL JESSUP *(roaring)* Boy! My father was class of 1869! He beat Army two-to-nothing when they were still pitching baseball underhand!

ADMIRAL HEALY *(roaring with laughter)* I wish he was pitching for us this year, Jessie!

ADMIRAL JESSUP *(to Cummings)* My grandfather died slipping a sloop through the Union blockade at Charleston!

CUMMINGS Yes, sir.

ADMIRAL HOYLE I knew we'd get back to the Civil War all right!

ADMIRAL JESSUP *(riveting Cummings with a bleary eye)* My people shipped out for this country under sail, wood and diesel ever since

Captain John Smith left a Jessup to hold Jamestown in Sixteen Ten! And I'm damned if I'm going to see the Navy sucking runt's udder in my time, I'll tell you that!

CUMMINGS Yes, sir.

Admiral Jessup turns and exchanges looks with the other two Admirals. They promptly sail off into another flight of howling laughter.

ADMIRAL JESSUP Oh. By George! Oh! *(He smiles over to Cummings.)* Hey, Bus, how's that movie coming along?

CUMMINGS Movie, sir?

Suddenly, Admiral Jessup collapses.

CUMMINGS Sir, are you all right?

HOTEL, MADISON'S ROOM.

Madison is in a soft chair as Emily pours him tea. It's a vision of blissful domesticity.

MADISON You know something strange is happening to me. I'm beginning to like tea.

Cummings enters from the living room. In the background, we hear a muffled shouting.

CUMMINGS Charlie, you'd better come in here.

Cummings is sufficiently anxious to make Madison promptly follow him out.

MADISON What's the matter?

CUMMINGS C'mon, you'll see.

ADMIRAL JESSUP'S SUITE, LIVING ROOM.

Admiral Jessup, a sagging dead weight, is held up by Admirals Healy and Hoyle, framed in the doorway of the room. Admiral Jessup is staring gauntly, fixedly at the floor and shouting hoarsely.

ADMIRAL JESSUP Florence! Florence!

REVERSE ANGLE ACROSS the three Admirals as Cummings and Madison enter.

ADMIRAL HEALY *(to Jessup)* Take it easy, Jessie.

ADMIRAL JESSUP *(shouting)* Florence! Florence!

Madison relieves Admiral Healy, wrapping Admiral Jessup's arm around his own neck.

MADISON *(to Admiral Healy)* All right, I've got him, sir. *(to Cummings)* Help me get him on the bed, Bus.

Cummings relieves Admiral Hoyle.

ADMIRAL HEALY Think we ought to call a doctor?

MADISON No, he'll be all right, sir.

The two Commanders slowly bear their sagging Admiral to his bed.

ADMIRAL JESSUP'S BEDROOM.

The two aides bear the Admiral through the doorway into the dark bedroom.

MADISON What happened, Bus?

CUMMINGS I don't know. He asked me about that silly movie. I told him I couldn't locate any Photographer's Mates, and since he hadn't

brought the matter up again, I let it slide. He started yelling for his
wife. We couldn't stop him.

They get the Admiral onto the bed. Madison loosens the old man's collar.

MADISON Okay, Bus, I'll take care of him. You see to Admirals Healy and
Hoyle.

The Admiral opens his eyes. At the door, Cummings watches, concerned.

ADMIRAL JESSUP *(murmurs)* Charlie, I want you to make this movie for
me. I want you to take charge, Charlie. I want you to make this movie
for me.

*Madison looks up slowly as he removes the Admiral's shoes. He regards the
Admiral, first frowning, then with compassion.*

MADISON *(gently)* Sure, Admiral, you just leave it to me.

DISSOLVE TO:

CURZON STREET THEATRE. DAY.

*ESTABLISHING SHOT of movie house. The marquee is blank except for
the words: FOR MILITARY USE ONLY.*

CURZON STREET THEATRE, AUDITORIUM.

*Madison enters. Cummings and Ellender are slumped in their seats in an
otherwise empty auditorium.*

MADISON We might as well see some of this film before the Admiral
comes.

*The houselights go down. A shaft of light shoots out of the projection booth,
and on the screen, we see the leader running through.*

MADISON This is the combat engineers in training.

He takes a seat near the others. On screen, a roughly-printed credit suddenly appears: COMBAT DEMOLITION ENGINEERS—RESTRICTED.

NARRATION *(off-screen)* This is a beach somewhere on the west coast of Wales. It has been prepared to be an exact duplicate of the beaches of France where the invasion of Europe will take place. Every foot has been mined. A six-foot barrier blocks any approach at the low-water mark. Three years of German ingenuity have gone into making that beach impregnable. How will we get our troops, tanks and weapons across that beach?

MADISON *(to Cummings)* How did I get into this anyway?

NARRATION *(off-screen)* That's the job of the Navy Combat Demolition Engineers. Here, on this secret beach in Wales, the Navy Engineers train for their hazardous duty.

An explosion on the screen blasts through the theatre. Madison looks back to the screen. On the screen we see a squad of demolition engineers splashing through shoulder-high water.

NARRATION *(off-screen)* This is only a dry run. On D-Day, these engineers will be under heavy mortar and artillery fire.

MADISON Thanks a lot.

ELLENDER Shut up, Charlie, I'm trying to watch the picture.

MADISON You won't like it, Marv. It got lousy reviews.

Another explosion as another mine is blown up on the screen. Madison winces.

NARRATION *(off-screen)* Those pieces of tape are to mark the cleared channels.

Another explosion on screen. Madison sighs.

NARRATION   *(off-screen)*   Each squad must clear an alley fifty feet wide for our troops to advance on the beaches.

Somebody slips into the seat behind Madison. He looks to see who it is; it's the Admiral.

NARRATION *(off-screen)* These American sailors will actually be the first men to assault Hitler's European bastion.

The Admiral leans forward in the seat behind Madison.

ADMIRAL JESSUP   That fact, Charlie, is exactly what I want clearly recorded on film. I want you and your photographers to get into the water with those engineers and film their activities right up to the beaches.

MADISON   Would you like us to start the movie again from the beginning, sir?

ADMIRAL JESSUP   *(standing)* No, I've got to run. You're on the right track, Charlie.

Admiral Jessup starts up the aisle to the rear as another explosion blasts from the screen.

MADISON   *(stands)* Sir?

ADMIRAL JESSUP   *(almost to rear doors)* Yes, Charlie?

NARRATION   *(off-screen)* End Reel One, Combat Engineers, Wales, Training Film.

MADISON   Sir, I get the feeling a man could get killed making this movie.

ADMIRAL JESSUP   *(curtly)* A lot of men are going to get killed on D-Day, Commander.

MADISON I would like to be relieved of this assignment, sir. It seems like a lot of risk to take for no particular reason, sir.

The temperature in the empty theater drops about forty degrees as the Admiral examines Madison with an icy look. Ellender, who has been dozing, wakes up. Cummings, who has been sitting, now stands.

ADMIRAL JESSUP I'm ordering you to make this film, Commander. That's reason enough.

MADISON It seems to me, sir, the only thing at stake here is a matter of Naval Public Relations.

ADMIRAL JESSUP *(barks)* No, Commander! What's at stake here is the essence of the military structure, the inviolability of command! I've given you an order. You'll obey it, or I'll have you brigged! Is that clear?

MADISON Yes, sir.

There is a brisk exchange of salutes between the Admiral and the members of his team. The Admiral exits. Nobody else moves. A long silence settles over the theater.

MADISON *(perching on an arm of a seat)* Well, what do we do now?

CUMMINGS *(starting up the aisle)* Well, I don't know what Marvin's going to do, but I'm going back to my office and cut your orders, Charlie.

MADISON What orders?

CUMMINGS Orders authorizing you to transfer unattached personnel to your photographic unit.

MADISON Oh, come on, Bus. I'm not going to make any silly movie.

CUMMINGS Charlie, there aren't any unattached photographic personnel. I already checked. So report to me next week about that, and I'll cut you some new orders. I'll cut you temporary duty orders, flight orders. By the time I finish cutting you orders for this movie, the war'll be over. Now, do it my way.

MADISON I don't like it. It's devious.

CUMMINGS Well, you tried the forthright frontal assault, and you pretty near got yourself court-martialled, stripped of your commission, and sent to the Arctic Circle to do polar research. Man, you don't tell Two-star Admirals you don't approve of their orders. Now you're on the Admiral's brig list, so I'll assign you to Exeter and Portland or one of those other channel ports for the purpose of making preliminary investigations, and just stay out of the Admiral's sight. I'll assign Emily as your driver. And you just have yourself a vacation. Now do this my way, Charlie.

Madison stares sceptically at Cummings and then at Ellender, dozing off in his chair.

MADISON A nutty situation, huh, Marv?

Ellender shrugs.

MADISON *(to Cummings)* All right. I'll go to Sussex with Emily for a week. Not such a bad deal. Sussex should be lovely this time of year.

THE ROLLING DOWNS OF SUSSEX. DAY.

The LANDSCAPE of the rolling downs on a lovely June afternoon is a particularly idyllic scene, with a small herd of sheep grazing on a high ground, and a stream overhung with shady trees. A punt, poled by an indistinguishable male, drifts lazily into view. The man turns out to be Madison in his Navy trousers with the cuffs rolled and his shirt open at the collar. Emily, in a skirt and sweater and flourishing a parasol, reclines against pillows in the bow. A picnic hamper sits in the middle of the punt. An Edwardian pastoral. Emily, eyes closed, is utterly at peace.

EMILY As Sheila would say, "It's too bloody love-ly, really it is."

MADISON *(having his troubles steering the punt)* Well, she's not doing the bloody poling.

EMILY It's defiant, is it? Just give it a big push.

Madison thrusts the pole into the bank with the intention of pushing strenuously off, but the soft earth of the bank yields and the pole slips. Madison almost pitches into the river. The punt lunges out into midstream and slides softly across to a heavily-shaded little island in the river. Emily laughs.

ISLAND IN THE RIVER. DAY.

Emily, holding her parasol and followed by Madison carrying the picnic hamper, climbs a small grassy knoll, obviously for the use of picnicking lovers. Little eruptions of laughter escape her, and she has to wipe the tears from her eyes. She sinks down onto the grass, her shoulders shaking silently. Madison sets the hamper down and stands looking down at her. She bursts helplessly into an unleashed spasm of open laughter and falls back on the grass to lie staring helplessly up at the sun glinting in fragments through the overhanging foliage, laughing as if she had finally remembered the mechanics of it. Madison looks down at her, very much in love.

CLOSE-UP of Emily lying on the grass, eyes closed, as the spasm slowly subsides. Finally, a long last sigh shudders through her. Her eyes open slowly, and she stares up at Madison, as he sits beside her.

EMILY *(murmurs)* Oh, Charlie, Charlie, Charlie...

TIGHT TWO SHOT as they embrace on the grass.

MADISON I love you, Emily.

EMILY How many more weeks do we have, Charlie?

MADISON Three, maybe four. I know the Admiral has to be back in Washington by the end of June.

EMILY Oh, Lord, I hope I don't get pregnant. *(She sits up.)* I've told myself a hundred times, "Don't get earnest about this man. It's a casual
thing, a brief, passionate explosion. Don't get sticky about it, for
heaven's sake."   Well, I'm sticky, Charlie. I'm sticky as hell! I'm
insanely in love with you.

*She cries bitterly. Madison reaches over for his jacket on the ground a few
feet away.*

MADISON Have you ever given any thought to getting married?

Emily abruptly stops crying.

EMILY You really do cut to the core of things, don't you.

MADISON *(extracting some papers from his jacket)* I've got some Navy marriage applications here.

EMILY Charlie, let's be sensible about this.

MADISON Emily, we're both nuts about each other; let's get married.

EMILY But we're essentially incompatible, Charlie. Don't leer; it's got
nothing to do with that. It's our fundamental approaches to life.
We're poles apart. I have this ingrained British morality, and you're
the most immoral man I've ever met. You're a shameless coward, selfish as a child, interested only in what's in it for you, and pretty ruthless about getting it. For all your charm, you're a scoundrel, Charlie.
It seems I don't mind making love to a scoundrel, but I think it
immoral to marry one. You lack principles, Charlie. Isn't there anything you'd die for?

MADISON Sure. I'd die for you, if it ever came to that.

EMILY *(deeply touched)* I really believe you would.

MADISON There's a lot of things I'd die for, Emily—my family, my home,
my country. But that's love, not principle. Now, if I were to bring a

raging lion into the house and wrestle it just to prove I'd die for you, that would be highly principled of me. But what's a lion doing in a man's house anyway?

EMILY *(hushing him with a kiss)* Oh, shut up.

MADISON Emily, Washington's a big, international city with a large British colony. There's probably half a dozen people there you already know.

EMILY As a matter of fact, there is.

MADISON It isn't going to be purgatory.

EMILY *(smiling through the tears)* It wouldn't matter if it were. Whither thou goest, Charlie. *(She folds the applications.)* Charlie, I don't want to sign these right now. I'll take them back to London with us tonight. I don't know why, but I feel I need a few hours alone with this.

MADISON Sure.

They are both embarrassed by her reluctance. They avoid each other's eyes.

HOTEL. NIGHT.

Their car pulls up to the hotel, with Madison driving and Emily dozing off, her head against the window.

HOTEL, MAIN ENTRANCE.

The car now comes to a halt in front of the hotel, and Madison shakes Emily's shoulder.

MADISON We're back.

He slips out of the car. Emily, with a drowsy sigh, slithers across behind the wheel. Madison opens the rear door and fetches out his valise. He closes the rear door, and now the driver's door, leans on the open window, and he and

*Emily regard each other with the bemused smiles of intoxicated lovers.
Madison leans on the car window toward Emily behind the steering wheel.*

EMILY Charlie, I've been so silly. Of course I'll marry you. I'll give you
the signed documents in the morning. I love you so much.

MADISON Lord, I hope you do get pregnant.

He withdraws from the window, turns and drifts up the steps into the hotel.

HOTEL HALLWAY OUTSIDE ADMIRAL JESSUP'S SUITE.

*Madison comes ambling dreamily down to the door of the suite. He extracts
a key from his pocket, lets himself in.*

MADISON'S ROOM.

*Madison enters. He switches on the overhead light, sinks onto the soft chair
by the bed, an incorrigibly self-satisfied smile on his face. There is a white
8 x 12 paper on his bed. After a moment, it catches his eye. He turns his
head every so slightly to get a better look, and finally reaches over for it with
a weary sigh. He reads the sheet disinterestedly for a moment, but, bit by bit,
his attention is involved.*

MADISON Who? What? What? What is this?

*He stands, moving a step into better light and finishes reading the mimeo-
graphed paper. Then, turning on his heels, he strides past the crates and cartons to the door leading to the...*

HALLWAY.

*Madison strides up the corridor three doors to the door of Lt. Commander
Cummings' room. Without bothering to knock, he opens the door and enters.*

CUMMINGS' ROOM.

As Madison strides inside, a shaft of light from the hallway follows him.

Otherwise, Cummings' room is dark. Two bodies leap from the bed. They are Cummings in his pajama top and still another of his NAMELESS BROADS who is not even wearing that.

NAMELESS BROAD NO. 2 *(promptly wailing away)* I've never done this before! He got me drunk! I was dragged up here against my...

CUMMINGS Oh, shut up!

MADISON *(brandishing the paper)* What's this all about?

CUMMINGS For Pete's sake, close the door!

NAMELESS BROAD NO. 2 I'm a decent girl! They gave me knockout drops!

CUMMINGS *(closing the door)* Will you shut up!

MADISON *(turning on the light)* Now, look, Bus...

NAMELESS BROAD NO. 2 Who turned the bloody lights on?

CUMMINGS Charlie, turn off the bloody lights!

MADISON I want to read this thing to you.

CUMMINGS *(turning off the lights)* I know what it is! I drew it up!

MADISON This is an order assigning me to a demolition unit in Portland.

CUMMINGS *(raising his voice)* I know what it is!

MADISON What are you yelling about?

CUMMINGS What do you mean, what am I yelling about? Don't you ever knock?

MADISON All right. I'm sorry.

CUMMINGS For Pete's sakes. *(He snaps at the Nameless Broad, who is dart-ing around the dark room.)* Will you stop jumping around!

NAMELESS BROAD NO. 2   I'm naked, dear. I'm looking for something to put on.

CUMMINGS This is my best friend, you dotty witch, not the house detective. Now, just stand at attention while Commander Madison and I confer.

The Nameless Broad, naked as a jaybird, stands to attention in the back-ground. Cummings sits wearily down on the edge of the bed.

CUMMINGS I'll tell you, Charlie, ever since you're away all the time, I have to dig up my own girls, and I sure get some beauts. Now, Charlie, the Admiral came into my office yesterday and said, "I want Madison immediately assigned to a demolition unit." So I cut your orders. You and your camera crew will report to the Port Command-er at Portland at twenty-two hundred hours on the fourth of June...

MADISON Tomorrow is the fourth of June.

CUMMINGS I know the fourth of June is tomorrow. Just fill in the names.

MADISON What names?

CUMMINGS The names of your camera crew.

MADISON I don't have any camera crew. What's the matter with you, Bus?

CUMMINGS I know you don't have any camera crew, but by ten-hundred hours tomorrow morning, I'll have cut flight orders for this camera crew you don't have on the nineteen-hundred flight to Portland with a copy of each order for COMINCH, SHAEF, COMNAVEU, COMLANCRABEU and for the Port Commander Portland POR-LANCRABEU. It'll take me at least two hours just to rescind those orders, let alone draft you new flight orders, new requisition orders, new pay orders, new...

MADISON All right, don't get so swept up by the sheer artistry of it all. Look, these orders specifically state I'm assigned to the Sixth Naval Engineer Unit. It makes this whole silly movie official Navy business, with a copy each for COMINCH, SHAEF and PORLANCRABEU.

CUMMINGS Charlie, the balloon's going up any day now. The Admiral's been down in Southampton at Supreme Command more often than he's in town this last week. Charlie, trust me. Within a week, this whole movie thing will slowly disappear into the swamps of Navy red tape.

Madison appears reasonably mollified.

MADISON All right. Listen, can you assign Emily and me to the Lake District next week?

CUMMINGS The Lake District?

NAMELESS BROAD NO. 2 Oh, it's lovely up there.

Cummings looks wearily to the Nameless Broad, still standing at attention in the background.

CUMMINGS *(grumbling to Madison)* This one really takes the cake, Charlie. Look, we don't have anything in the Lake District. How about Cornwall? Land's End. Rocky cliffs overlooking the sea. It's very romantic. We've got an amphibious training base in Falmouth. I could assign you there.

MADISON Sounds very nice. We'll take it.

He starts for the door, then pauses, with his hand on the knob.

MADISON *(matter-of-factly)* Oh, Bus, I'm going to marry her.

Cummings, sitting on the bed, looks slowly up. In moments of stress, Cummings has a tendency to get a bit earnest, if not utterly cliché. He strides forcefully to Madison at the door, grips his friend's hand and stares searchingly into Madison's eyes.

CUMMINGS Charlie, you're getting a great girl!

MADISON Thank you, Bus.

CUMMINGS *(now thumps Madison's shoulder)* Buddy, I'm going to throw you the biggest spread this old town's ever seen. The whole works, formal Annapolis wedding, arch of sabers and everything. *(He clutches Madison's hand, all Academy earnestness again.)* Congratulations, Sailor.

MADISON *(deeply fond of Cummings, despite the latter's impulse to intense sincerity)* Thank you, mate. I'll see you tomorrow morning in the office.

He opens the door. Cummings administers one more comradely poke in the shoulder.

CUMMINGS See you tomorrow morning, buddy.

MADISON Okay, buddy.

He exits, closing the door. Cummings turns to the Nameless Broad, still at attention in the background shadows, and beams at her.

CUMMINGS You may stand at ease now, sailor.

NAVY BUILDING, CUMMINGS' OFFICE. NEXT MORNING.

Cummings is busy on the phone behind his desk, and Madison, who has pulled a chair up to the desk, is on the other phone.

MADISON ...I don't want ninety proof...

CUMMINGS Motor Pool, please...

MADISON This is for some Russians, Iggie. You know how they're always making cracks about the impotence of our American vodka...

CUMMINGS Cummings here in Admiral Jessup's office...

MADISON *(hangs up, immediately picks up the receiver again as he speaks to Cummings)* These Russians still like their women short and fat and reactionary?

CUMMINGS *(nods; on phone)* A driver to take Admiral Jessup to Southampton at o-nine-thirty...

MADISON *(to Cummings, nodding his head in the direction of the Admiral's door)* Who's in with him? Marv?

Busy, Cummings nods back, only to avoid answering.

ADMIRAL JESSUP'S OFFICE.

The Admiral is behind his desk. Captain Ellender sits in front of it, face down, intently reading from a notebook on his lap.

ELLENDER Now, Jessie, we come to your research project in the Arctic Circle. We received a second cable yesterday afternoon from Norris. Jessie, the North Pole project is going to go right down the drain unless you raise a little hell again. Jessie...

Ellender pauses in his pitch and just stares at the Admiral. An odd humming SOUND begins to suggest itself into the background.

ELLENDER *(showing concern)* Jessie...

CAMERA SLOWLY DOLLIES from behind the Admiral to BEHIND Captain Ellender until we see what the Captain is seeing. Admiral Jessup is seated behind his desk, slumped, his eyes staring vacuously at his desktop, his lower jaw hanging slackly, and the odd humming SOUND is coming from his oddly open mouth. Ellender is just a little bit frightened.

ELLENDER Jessie...

CUMMINGS' OFFICE.

Cummings is now busy over his deskful of administrative papers, but Madison is still hunched over his phone.

MADISON *(on phone)* Ah, Imogene, tracked you down. Charlie Madison here. Listen, love, you haven't lost any weight, have you?

Madison and Cummings are busily at work, when the Admiral's door opens: Ellender appears in the doorway, visibly upset.

MADISON *(on phone)* ...or sacrificed any of your Tory principles...Yes, some more Russians...

ELLENDER Hey, come here a minute.

Madison and Cummings look up.

ELLENDER *(barking)* I said, come here a minute!

MADISON *(on phone)* I'll call you back.

He hangs up. He and Cummings both rise and go around the desk to join Ellender in the doorway to the Admiral's office.

Their P.O.V.: Jessup is now squatting in a corner of the room, his knees drawn up to his chin, staring with unrelenting vacuity at the bare wall opposite him.

REACTION SHOT of his three aides: Ellender registering compassion, Cummings confusion, and Madison shock.

REVERSE TIGHT SHOT of the Admiral, squatting in his catatonic state.

MADISON'S VOICE Admiral...

REVERSE ANGLE on the three aides.

CUMMINGS Holy cow.

MADISON We better get a doctor.

ELLENDER Jessie...

The three aides step back into Cummings's office. Cummings quickly closes the Admiral's door.

CUMMINGS He's supposed to be in Southampton in an hour at a meeting of the Joint Supreme Command.

MADISON Are you out of your mind? That poor man's in a schizophrenic state. We've got to get him to a hospital.

CUMMINGS Yeah, I suppose you're right.

He goes to the door, pauses.

CUMMINGS He's really flipped, huh? Yeah, I better tell Admiral Healy about this. (*exits*)

HALLWAY OUTSIDE CUMMINGS' OFFICE.

Cummings comes out and hurries down the hallway to a corner office. Two SEAMAN-CLERKS hurry past him going the other way.

Cummings opens the door of the office and goes in.

CAPT. SPAULDING'S OFFICE.

Cummings enters, nervously closing the door after himself. Spaulding, who is Admiral Healy's administrative aide, has an office identical to Cummings'.

SPAULDING *(at his desk)* Hiya, Bus.

CUMMINGS Listen, Harry. Something serious just happened. I think Admiral Jessup has just gone mad. He's really flipped. Now would you tell Admiral Healy about this right away.

SPAULDING *(looking up from his work)* Admiral Healy's on his way to Southampton with Admiral Jessup in about five minutes.

CUMMINGS No, no no! Admiral Jessup isn't going to Southampton. Harry, now this is urgent. Admiral Jessup has cracked up.

SPAULDING What do you mean, Admiral Jessup has cracked up?

CUMMINGS I mean he's cracked up. He's sitting on the floor of his office right now in a trance.

Spaulding regards Cummings quizzically.

SPAULDING Do I read you right, Commander? Are you saying that Two-star Admiral William Jessup has cracked up?

CUMMINGS You know, Harry, you're a pompous ass.

SPAULDING *(stands)* This better not be a gag.

CUMMINGS Do you think I'd joke about a thing like this?

SPAULDING *(coming around the desk)* The Service takes a dim view of Lieutenant Commanders who go around calling the Special Assistant to the Secretary of the Navy a nut.

Cummings wrenches the door open and hurries out into the hallway, followed by Captain Spaulding, who has paused to collect the cane he affects.

HALLWAY OUTSIDE SPAULDING'S OFFICE.

Cummings and Spaulding come out and stride down to Cummings' office.

The Admiral comes out of that office and up to Spaulding's office. He is car-rying his attaché case and seems in the best of spirits.

ADMIRAL JESSUP *(as they pass each other)* Hello, Harry, Admiral Healy ready?

SPAULDING *(continuing on to Cummings' office)* He's waiting for you, sir. Admirals Hoyle and Magnuson are in his office.

Spaulding and Cummings realize Admiral Jessup has just gone by, and Spaulding does a complete turn and starts back after the Admiral. Then, he does another turn to find Madison and Ellender coming out of Cummings' office.

SPAULDING Now, what the hell is this all about?

MADISON Harry, Admiral Jessup's a very sick man, and...

SPAULDING You know, this sort of joke is tasteless enough from you two...*(He turns to Cummings who is confused.)*...but from an Academy man, it's obscene.

He follows an unhappy Cummings into...

CUMMINGS' OFFICE.

Cummings enters, followed by Spaulding, Madison and Ellender.

SPAULDING You shore sailors ought to be sent out on a tour of duty just to...

CUMMINGS *(erupting)* All right, Spaulding, I've had just about enough of your bilge! This blowhard here did four months as a mess officer in the South Pacific, and he's been spouting old sea-salt ever since. Well, I didn't ask for a desk job. I've applied for line duty seven times, and you know it! And don't start pulling Academy on me. I was a cadet four-striper; you never made more than midshipman adjutant of a lousy battalion.

SPAULDING This outburst is bad joss, Commander, bad joss.

CUMMINGS Well, don't start jacking me up like you were my senior cadet officer.

MADISON Listen, while you two schoolboys...

CUMMINGS *(wheeling on Madison)* And I don't want to hear any more cracks about us schoolboys! You civilian sailors seem to think there's something funny about a man taking pride in his service! Well, sir, permit me to inform you, sir, that I am damn proud of being an Annapolis man, sir!

He wheels back to Spaulding, throws a whacking sharp salute. Spaulding returns a whacking sharp salute, turns crisply on his heels and strides out of the office.

MADISON Look, fellows, right now the Admiral is on his way to South...

CUMMINGS *(still fuming)* I didn't ask for this lousy desk job! I've got bad eyes! Now what can I do? Do you think I want to tell my kids that on D-Day, their father was shacked up at the Westchester Hotel?

MADISON For Pete's sakes, Bus!

The door suddenly opens, and Spaulding reappears. He is quite somber now. The others turn to him, sensing something has happened.

SPAULDING Admiral Healy wants to see you, Bus.

CUMMINGS What happened?

SPAULDING I don't know. They took Admiral Jessup back to his hotel.

CUMMINGS He must have flipped again.

ELLENDER We better get over to the hotel, Charlie.

SPAULDING No, stay here. Healy may want to see you both too. They're getting a doctor for him.

He follows Cummings who is hurrying out of the office. A moment of silence. Madison sits on a chair. Ellender strolls to the window and stares out.

ELLENDER Well, that's the end of your silly movie anyway, Charlie.

MADISON *(depressed)* Yeah. Poor old guy.

ADMIRAL HEALY'S OFFICE.

Admiral Healy sits behind his desk, and Cummings stands at formal ease in front of it. Admiral Hoyle sits to the side of the desk, and a third admiral, ADMIRAL MAGNUSON, leans against a wall.

ADMIRAL HEALY *(squinting at Cummings)* A movie? A movie designed to show the first dead man on Omaha Beach was a sailor?

CUMMINGS Yes, sir.

Captain Spaulding enters from his own office with a letter for Admiral Healy.

ADMIRAL HEALY *(taking the letter)* I got an odd letter from the Under Chief of Naval Operations in today's pouch. That's what I was asking Jessup about when he went wild.

Captain Spaulding returns with a file folder which he places before Admiral Healy. The Admiral extracts a paper.

ADMIRAL HOYLE It's nearly twenty of ten, Tom.

ADMIRAL HEALY Yeah.

He reads from the letter.

ADMIRAL HEALY   Et cetera...et cetera...et cetera... The President expressed interest in some moving picture Jessup is making. Apparently, Jessup has written directly to the President about this. I wish Jessup would keep me informed, even on these little private projects of his. *(scowls and reads on)* Also, at the end of the meeting, Harry Begley, the President's assistant, made reference to a Tomb for the Unknown Sailor.

Healy puts the paper down and looks across to Cummings.

ADMIRAL HEALY   What Tomb for the Unknown Sailor, Commander?

CUMMINGS   I don't know, sir. I had no idea that Admiral Jessup was in communication with the President or Harry Begley.

ADMIRAL HEALY   *(to the other Admirals)* Do you know anything about a Tomb for an Unknown Sailor?

ADMIRAL MAGNUSON   I assume Jessup meant the first dead sailor on Omaha Beach to be the sailor in the tomb.

ADMIRAL HEALY   What tomb?

CUMMINGS   The Tomb for the Unknown Sailor, sir.

ADMIRAL HEALY   There is no Tomb for... Oh, I see. I take it this is another one of Jessie's projects. *(hands the file back to Spaulding)* This movie about the demolition engineers, Commander, is such a movie being made?

CUMMINGS   Not really, sir. We've...

ADMIRAL HEALY   Well, get it made. *(Healy stands.)* I want this incident closed, and I want it closed fast. I don't want anything that's happened to get outside of this office. We all know what some members of Congress and the newspapers could make out of this. Aside from the embarrassment caused to the Navy, I don't want the name of one of the finest men in our country stained by one unfortunate incident. I don't want even the President of the United States to know about this. Put together some kind of a movie, Commander, that I can give to Mr. Begley and that he can show to the President, who will then write Admiral Jessup a polite note, and this whole unhappy matter will be closed. *(Healy puts on his hat and goes to the door.)* Harry, I want to be informed every hour about Admiral Jessup's condition.

SPAULDING Yes, sir.

ADMIRAL HEALY *(followed out by the other Admirals)* A hell of a day for this to happen.

Cummings and Spaulding salute the departing Admirals crisply. The Admirals return the salutes laconically and exit out through Spaulding's outer office and into the hallway.

SPAULDING *(as he crosses into his own office)* Now what is so crazy about a Tomb for the Unknown Sailor? Frankly, I think there's something splendid in the idea.

CUMMINGS *(pensive)* Yeah, it does have a kind of a ring to it, doesn't it?

CUMMINGS' OFFICE.

Madison and Ellender rise as Cummings enters.

ELLENDER How's the old man, Bus?

Cummings nods but says nothing. Rapt in thought, he moves slowly around to sit behind his desk. At last, he looks up at Madison.

CUMMINGS You know, Charlie, the President has expressed an interest in Admiral Jessup's movie.

MADISON Naturally.

CUMMINGS The Navy has committed itself to this movie, and it'll be pretty damned embarrassing if it isn't made. So, Charlie...*(stands and regards Madison earnestly)*...we're going to make that movie.

MADISON That's very spunky of you, Bus.

Cummings comes around his desk, beams at Madison, and gives him a comradely poke on the shoulder.

CUMMINGS *(the old Navy grit)* You and I are going to get on that twenty-one-hundred flight to Portland this evening, and we're going to make that movie. I'm going in on this with you, buddy. I'm cutting orders for the both of us right now.

Madison exchanges a look with Ellender but says nothing.

CUMMINGS *(poking Madison again on the shoulder)* Damn it, Charlie, it's exciting, isn't it!

MADISON Will you quit giving me those comradely pokes?

CUMMINGS This is it, kid! This is the big show, and we're going to be in there for the first shot!

MADISON *(regards Cummings warily)* Just how did you and I suddenly become the Charge of the Light Brigade, Bus?

CUMMINGS Charlie... *(moves to the window, stares out, seeing a vision)* ...there's a lot more to this movie than we knew about. The Admiral had a much larger vision in mind. Apparently, the Admiral's idea is to build a Tomb for the Unknown Sailor, and to put the first dead man on Omaha Beach into it.

The idea is almost too much for Cummings. His eyes blink with tears, and his spectacles cloud with moisture. Madison and Ellender, on the other hand, find this new thought a little too much to take in one gulp. Madison looks blankly at Cummings, then turns and moves slowly to a chair.

MADISON A tomb for the what?

ELLENDER Well, that's a new one on me too.

Cummings turns stiffly on the other two.

CUMMINGS All right, sailors, that'll be all. (*yanks open a drawer, pulls out a stencil sheet, angrily rolls it into his typewriter, and types away*) The Navy wants this movie made, so it's going to be made. So you just get back to the hotel, Charlie, and pack your gear because you and I are going to be on that twenty-one-hundred flight to Portland. That's an order, Commander.

MADISON A Tomb for the Unknown Sailor! Holy Cow, Bus!

Cummings pauses in his typing to regard Madison.

CUMMINGS Charlie, you and I have had it too easy. I think we've forgotten we're officers in the United States Navy. It's not up to us to approve of our orders, even if those orders mean risking our lives. (*rips the stencil from the typewriter*) These are your orders, Charlie. You'll have a mimeographed copy in half an hour.

MADISON I'll risk my life for my country, Bus. But this movie's just an unnecessary piece of Naval public relations, and I won't risk my life for that.

CUMMINGS (*quietly*) You have your orders, Charlie.

MADISON (*just as quietly*) Well, I'm not going to do it.

CUMMINGS You will be on that twenty-one-hundred flight with me, or I'll put you on charges, Charlie.

MADISON Then you just put me on charges, Bus.

The phone RINGS. Cummings picks it up.

CUMMINGS *(on phone)* Admiral Jessup's office...Oh yes, sir...We'll be there directly, sir. *(He hangs up and stands.)* They want us at the hotel.

He puts on his hat and goes into the hallway, carrying the stencil with him. Madison and Ellender are still seated. We look through the open doorway to Cummings in the hallway.

CUMMINGS *(calling out)* Sailor! Take this down to mimeograph!

He exits the frame.

MADISON Tomb of the Unknown Sailor. Holy Cow!

ELLENDER *(standing, reaching for his hat)* He's in one of his Annapolis moods, so for heaven's sakes, Charlie, hold your temper.

Madison shouts to Cummings in the hall.

MADISON Well, I'm not going to do it, Bus! I'm not going to do it!

HOTEL, MADISON'S ROOM.

CLOSE-UP of Madison, hissing in a violent whisper.

MADISON I'm not going to do it, Bus!

WIDE ANGLE SHOT shows Madison bent over to Cummings who is perched on the window sill, staring out over Park Lane, his face frozen in fury. Ellender is slouched in the soft chair, nursing a scotch. The scene is played in whispers so as not to be overheard, but this does not diminish the intensity of the moment.

MADISON Bus, I'm in love. I'm in love like I never thought possible. Life is especially dear to me right now, and I'm not going to leave mine on some beach in France just to satisfy your grotesque sense of service loyalty. *(He storms away, then storms back to Cummings, hisses.)* You don't really think I'm going to spend two years in the brig for this? I can't believe you're serious, Bus. If it's the Navy's public image that concerns you, just think what this will look like in the newspapers. The first dead man on Omaha Beach. The Tomb of the Unknown Sailor. What a hurricane Drew Pearson could make out of that! You must remember that small off-shore squall he kicked up the time General Patton slapped that soldier.

Cummings turns slowly from looking out the window and stares at Madison, at first shocked, and then in utter contempt.

CUMMINGS *(stands)* Madison, you're despicable.

MADISON *(throws up his hands)* This is insane! How did we ever get into this? *(He turns back to Cummings.)* Now, Bus...

He is interrupted by a ringing slap across the face administered to him by Cummings, who now trembles with emotion.

CUMMINGS *(his voice quivering)* You're not fit to wear the insignia of a Naval Officer.

He reaches out and rips one of Madison's shoulder epaulettes from its mooring. Madison stares at him dumbfounded, then at Ellender.

MADISON Well, that was pretty baroque, wouldn't you say, Marv?

CUMMINGS You're a coward and a scoundrel. If you want to make anything of that, I'll be in my room.

He turns and goes to the door with as much dignity as he can manage, considering he gets his sleeve caught on a crate and he stumbles over a low carton on his way out.

MADISON *(calling after him)* I'll send my second with a choice of weapons.

Cummings exits, slamming the door. Madison sits wearily on the bed. He is actually quite hurt by Cummings's outburst.

MADISON *(after a moment)* Well, Marv, it's your turn. Would you like to break my saber over your knee and snip off my buttons?

ELLENDER You're not going to expose anything to Drew Pearson, and you know it, Charlie. You're much too fond of the Admiral, and you're much too decent to expose that old man to public ridicule.

Caught off-guard, Madison stares down at the floor.

ELLENDER You're going to have to find a better angle out of this than that.

MADISON I'm supposed to be on a plane to Portland at nine o'clock this evening. Bus and I are supposed to report to the Port Commander at Portland at eleven o'clock tonight. That's not much time to think up angles.

ELLENDER You'll think of something.

The door to the living room opens, and a NAVY DOCTOR stands in the doorway.

THE DOCTOR The Admiral would like to see you in his room, Commander.

MADISON *(stands)* Is he all right?

THE DOCTOR He's fine.

Madison follows the Doctor into the living room.

ADMIRAL JESSUP'S SUITE, LIVING ROOM.

The Doctor and Madison cross to the Admiral's room.

ADMIRAL JESSUP'S BEDROOM.

MADISON, pausing in the doorway, sees the Admiral sitting on a chair in his nightshirt. In the dimly lit curtained room, the Admiral seems suddenly a fragile old man with watery old eyes. Madison, behind him, massages the old man's neck and shoulders.

ADMIRAL JESSUP *(smiles weakly)* Well, it seems I cracked up, Charlie.

MADISON That's the price a sane man pays in this world, sir.

ADMIRAL JESSUP They say a few days in the hospital. I wouldn't mind, except that I'll have to miss the big show. Admiral Kirk asked me to observe from his flagship.

MADISON Yes, I know, sir.

ADMIRAL JESSUP It's tonight, you know. The balloon goes up tonight. I expect you've already heard that by now.

MADISON Well, we all knew it was imminent, sir, but we didn't know it was tonight.

ADMIRAL JESSUP Yes, the first boats push off at twenty-one-thirty hours.

Madison is about to shift his hands to the other shoulder when something in him snaps.

MADISON The first boats push off at twenty-one-thirty hours, sir?

ADMIRAL JESSUP Well, the Irish-based transports will start earlier, of course.

MADISON I've never licked military time, sir. Twenty-one-thirty hours—that's half-past nine in the evening, right?

ADMIRAL JESSUP Right.

Madison begins massaging the Admiral again, his mind clicking away. After a moment, a slow smile settles on his face.

MADISON Now, that's what I call an angle.

ADMIRAL JESSUP Did you say something, Charlie?

MADISON No, sir.

ADMIRAL JESSUP Watch yourself, Charlie. You'll be cracking up yourself soon.

Madison nods, continues massaging.

CUMMINGS' ROOM.

Madison enters. The room is fairly dark, the curtains drawn. Two bodies leap from the bed. Needless to say, they are Cummings and still another NAMELESS BROAD. Cummings is in his shirttails.

CUMMINGS Close the door!

Before Madison can make a move, Cummings strides to the door. Shirttails flapping, he slams it shut.

CUMMINGS And don't turn on the lights! And what do you want?

Madison looks down at the floor, scuffs his feet.

MADISON Bus, I...I don't know how to tell you, but... *(looks up slowly)* I'd like to apologize for my contemptible behavior before... I'd like another chance and...well, I've packed my gear... well, we've got a job to do, and I'm ready to do it.

The Nameless Broad, in the background, sits casually on the bed, legs crossed and studying her fingernails.

CUMMINGS *(with a proud smile)* Underneath it all, you're a pretty gutsy guy, aren't you, Charlie.

MADISON I don't know what came over me before. I showed the white feather, I suppose.

CUMMINGS *(gripping Madison's shoulders)* Oh, forget about it, Charlie.

NAMELESS BROAD NO. 3 *(lighting a cigarette)* Could you ring up for some food, love? I haven't had my lunch yet.

The two men don't hear her. They are swept up in an emotion greater than that between a man and a woman—the comradeship of brave men.

MADISON I know we don't have much time, Bus, but could I have leave to say goodby to my girl?

CUMMINGS Oh, for Pete's sake, Charlie, of course. You're making a big dramatic deal out of this. You do have a tendency to be overly sincere, you know.

MADISON Yes, I guess I do.

CUMMINGS You've got seven hours yet. Take Emily to lunch. Pick me up around eight. I'll have her assigned to drive us to the airport. Would you like that?

MADISON *(simply)* Thanks, Bus.

CUMMINGS All right, man. Don't be so dramatic about it. What is it, raining?

MADISON Yes, just started.

Now, it is Madison's turn to poke Cummings a comradely poke on the shoulder, after which he slips out into the hallway.

LONDON COUNTRYSIDE. RAINY NIGHT.

A Navy Chevrolet buckets through the sloshing rain of a June night.

GATES AT HENDON AIRPORT. RAINY NIGHT.

The car pulls up to the MP at the gates of the airport. Cummings shows the beslickered MP his credentials through the rear window of the car. The gates open, and the car drives into the area.

HENDON AIRPORT, A LANDING STRIP.

A DC-4 waits in the foreground, standing on the strip in the rain, as the Navy Chevrolet pulls up in background.

ACROSS Emily in the driver's seat to Cummings getting out of the car.

CUMMINGS   Charlie, you still have a couple of minutes to say goodby.

MADISON   Thanks, Bus.

Cummings exits the frame. Madison slithers across the seat and gets out of the car. Emily suddenly turns in her seat to Madison.

EMILY   *(cries out)*   Charlie!

MADISON   *(pulling his overnight bag out of the car)*   What?

Emily opens her door and flings herself into his arms.

EMILY   Write to me.

MADISON   What do you mean, write to you?   With any luck I'll be back in London for lunch tomorrow.

He looks across to the DC-4 where Cummings is standing in the open door of the plane, watching the lovers' farewell.

MADISON   Honey, let me make it clear again.   I couldn't make this invasion if I wanted to.   The demolition engineers will have shipped out a good two hours before Bus and I even report in. The Port Commander is going to look at us as if we're nuts.   I'll see you tomorrow.

Emily is for some reason put out.

EMILY It's like you were taking an overnight business trip.

MADISON Well, that's what it amounts to. If I can't book a flight, I'll catch an afternoon train.

EMILY Well, it's a hell of a D-Day, that's all I can say. To be honest with you, Charlie, there's something very unpleasant about this little deceit you're pulling on the Navy. You've been cackling away all afternoon, as if the Invasion, in which the fate of nations and the lives of millions of men are at stake, is nothing more to you than a private joke. I just keep thinking of all those men trooping onto all those ships tonight, wondering if they'll end up bodies on a beach.

Madison, who had taken a step to the plane, now takes a step back.

MADISON Honey, I'm not cackling because there are going to be bodies on a beach tomorrow. I'm cackling because I'm not going to be one of them.

EMILY And you've been pulling poor Bus Cummings's leg all the way out here in the car. The poor fellow really thinks he's going off on a gallant mission, and you led him on, and I think cruelly.

MADISON I didn't lead him on. I just didn't stop him.

EMILY You could have told him before there wasn't a chance of getting there on time.

MADISON If I told him before, he'd have arranged an earlier flight, and, if I tell him now, he'll never forgive me for not having told him before. Honey, we're both getting drenched.

He strides off, gets halfway to the plane when she calls him again.

EMILY Charlie, I can't marry you.

MADISON *(sighs)* I've been waiting for that. We'll talk about it when I get back.

EMILY I don't want to see you when you get back. I don't want to see you again.

MADISON Look, Emily, I will not be brushed off in a driving drizzle and with my plane about to take off.

EMILY Oh Charlie, for pity's sake. We both know it's finished. Let's break it off now, in one snap, before we say things we'll regret.

MADISON No, let's say them. There should be something we regret.

EMILY Very well! I despise cowardice. I detest selfish people, and I loathe ruthlessness. Since you are cowardly, selfish and ruthless, I cannot help but despise, detest and loathe you. That's not the way a woman should feel about the man she's going to marry.

MADISON Don't be facile, Emily.

EMILY I am not being facile. I've been up all bloody night, staring at your bloody marriage applications. Well, I've signed them. They're in my purse. I was going to give them to you this afternoon when you came prancing in with this very funny joke you're playing on Bus and the Navy and your country and the whole bloody world. Well, I suppose I'm an incorrigible romantic, but I feel the joke's on me too, for I believe in honor and service and courage, in fair play and cricket, and all those other symbols of the British character which have civilized half the world.

MADISON You British plundered half the world for your own profit. Let's not pass it off as the Age of Enlightenment.

EMILY Yes! That's the American way of looking at it, isn't it?

MADISON Emily, let's not get into one of these "the trouble with you Yanks" things. It's got nothing to do with it.

EMILY It's got everything to do with it! I'm British, and you're a bloody fool American, and I don't want to see you again!

She flounces into the car behind the wheel and slams the door shut. Madison stands dripping in the rain, regarding her.

MADISON General Kitchener aside, Emily, all that's going on here is a woman trying to shake off her lover. If you don't love me, just say so.

Emily bursts into tears, hiding her face in her hands.

MADISON Nobody gets moral unless they're trying to get something or get out of something. Well, you're trying to get out of marrying me. If you don't love me, say so. *(he waits; she turns away)* Otherwise, I figure you're just frightened.

EMILY *(wheeling on him)* Frightened of what?

MADISON Frightened of getting married.

EMILY Don't be an ass.

MADISON The weekend passion is over, and now it's down to signing applications, babies, setting up house. You have to commit yourself to life now, Emily, with its disease and desolation and its startling satisfactions. I don't want to know what's good or bad or true. I let God worry about truth. I just want to know the momentary fact of things. Life isn't good or bad or true; it's merely factual; it's sensual; it's alive. And my idea of living, sensual facts is you, a home, a country, a world, a universe in that order. I want to know what I am, not what I should be. Well, the fact is I'm a coward; I never met anyone who wasn't.

EMILY I'm not.

MADISON You're the most terrified woman I've ever met. You're even scared to get married.

EMILY I've already been married.

MADISON Sure, you married him three days before he went to Africa. Thank God he never came back. You're forever falling for men on their last nights on furlough. That's about the limit of your commitments, one night, a day, a month. You prefer lovers to husbands, hotels to homes. You'd rather grieve than live.

EMILY You're not only cowardly and selfish; you're remarkably cruel as well.

MADISON Come off it, Emily. The only immoral thing you've got against me is I'm alive.

Emily opens the car door, steps up to Madison, and regards him with actual hatred.

EMILY I'm going to slap your face, Charlie.

MADISON Go ahead. I won't hit you back. I'm a coward.

She slaps his face smartly.

MADISON On the other hand, I'm selfish and I don't easily give up what's mine. You're mine, Emily, and I'm not going to let you go.

She slaps him a second time. Madison rubs his sore cheek, his face streaked with rain.

MADISON All you have to say is "I don't love you."

Emily's face is streaked with tears.

EMILY I don't love you, Charlie.

At the open doorway of the waiting DC-4, Cummings looms into view. He has to smile at the sight of the two lovers in the rain. By George, it does look like farewell on Waterloo Bridge from here.

CUMMINGS *(calling out from the plane)* Hey Charlie, it's time to go.

MADISON Well, you're a good woman. You've done the morally right thing. God save us all from people who do the morally right thing. It's always the rest of us who get broken in half. You're a bitch.

He turns and strides off, fumbling in his pockets for something. Halfway to the plane, he turns. He seems to be chewing on something.

MADISON I want you to remember that the last time you ever saw me, I was unregenerately eating a Hershey bar.

Emily stands stiffly by her car, as Madison strides to the airplane where Cummings and the crew help him clamber up into it.

PORT OF PORTLAND, THE HARBOR. RAINY NIGHT.

The harbor is a madhouse of activity in the dark, rainy night. Out on the water, an ominous shadowy fleet. Out of the wet, shouting background of men and machines, the bulky, trench-coated figure of the Port Commander, CAPTAIN ROY FRAZER, climbs up toward the CAMERA. The CAMERA PANS him as he sloshes along to a group of quonset huts. Waiting are Lt. Commanders Cummings and Madison, an ENSIGN, a BOATSWAIN, and two SHORE PATROLMEN. They all snap to attention.

CAPTAIN FRAZER Now, what the hell is this all about?

CUMMINGS Sir...

CAPTAIN FRAZER What is this, some featherheading gag, Commander? The demolition units sailed off two hours ago! You featherheads in London, all you want to do is make movies. Who's running this featherheading war anyway, Ginger Rogers? The demolition units are halfway across the English Channel!! The Invasion started two hours ago. Great Scott! Movies! *(He wheels on the Ensign.)* Edwards! Hide these Hollywood people somewhere where they're out of my featherheading way. *(He strides out.)*

CUMMINGS *(calling nervously after him)* But sir, we didn't know.

THE ENSIGN We'll have to put you up in one of the supply depots, sir.

CUMMINGS *(staring at Madison)* It's D-Day, Charlie! Tonight's D-Day, can't you get that through your head?

MADISON *(simply couldn't be more disappointed)* It looks like the feather-heading balloon just went up without us, Bus.

THE ENSIGN *(to the Boatswain)* Take these officers to one of the depots and get some cots for them.

OUTSIDE SUPPLY DEPOT. RAINY NIGHT.

Madison stands in front of a Nissen hut, smoking a cigarette, staring out over the harbor.

HIS P.O.V.: The harbor is now utterly empty and ghostlike, not a boat to be seen.

Madison, pleased as punch, goes into the Nissen hut.

INSIDE SUPPLY DEPOT.

CAMERA DOLLIES BACK to show Madison sleeping peacefully on his cot. Cummings's cot is empty. A BOATSWAIN'S MATE enters and leaves the door ajar so that the gray morning light diffuses into the room. Madison is waking now. He gets up on one elbow, regards the Boatswain's Mate, now checking off a list.

MADISON How's the Invasion going, Bosun?

THE BOATSWAIN'S MATE *(looking up briefly)* They called it off, sir, didn't you know?

The Boatswain's Mate goes back to his list. Madison sits up, stretches, yawns.

MADISON (*agreeably*) What do you mean they called it off?

THE BOATSWAIN'S MATE The visibility never cleared up enough for the airborne troops. The whole fleet turned around in mid-channel and came back. It looks like we're going to have to do the whole thing again tonight.

MADISON (*rubbing his eyes*) I don't follow you, Bosun. What do you mean, we're going to have to try all over again tonight?

But the Boatswain's Mate has picked up a pile of blankets and is out the door. Madison remains sitting on the cot in his shorts, slowly adjusting to the new day. Suddenly it hits him.

MADISON (*shouting after the Boatswain's Mate*) What do you mean, they called it off? What are you talking about?

He stands, aching in every bone from the uncomfortable sleep. Barefooted and in his shorts, he strays across the room to the open doorway.

Madison's eyes blink against the daylight. Then a look of utter, mute astonishment spreads over his face.

MADISON'S P.O.V.: WIDE ANGLE SHOT of the harbor, clogged with all its boats bobbing at their moorings, hundreds of men moving about on the docks, on the boats, getting in and out of trucks. A hurrying SHORE PATROLMAN suddenly barges into the foreground of the frame, turns to CAMERA.

SHORE PATROLMAN Hey, Sailor, get your pants on!

The Shore Patrolman hurries on. Madison is stupefied by this incredible, nightmarish turn of events.

CUMMINGS (*off-screen voice*) Hey, Charlie! (*fully dressed, groomed and carrying an Eyemo camera, hurries up the rise in ground from the docks*) I've dug up one camera, anyway, Charlie.

He comes up to the doorway, where Madison is still trying to gather his wits.

CUMMINGS Let me in, Charlie.

Madison, not believing his eyes, steps back to let Cummings hurry into the supply room.

MADISON What happened?

Cummings puts the camera on the counter as Madison stands at the doorway, perturbed.

CUMMINGS What do you mean?

MADISON *(erupting)* What do you think I mean? I mean are you trying to tell me five thousand boats filled with one million men, tanks, trucks, airplanes, bombers, the whole incredible schmear, just turned around in the middle of the ocean and came back?!

CUMMINGS *(looking up)* The moon didn't come out.

Madison steps into the doorway, looks up to the sky, and lets out the anguished cry of a man who has lost his god.

MADISON What do you mean, the moon didn't come out?! How could you do this to me?!

In background, a jeep drives by. An M.P., riding in it, shouts at Madison.

M.P. IN JEEP Hey, Mac, get some clothes on!

DISSOLVE TO:

PORTLAND HARBOR. AFTERNOON.

It is drizzling now, but the SHOUTING and intense ACTIVITY continues. Two bedraggled SAILORS in slickers, a man in his late forties and a kid of nineteen, both fairly crocked, slosh unsteadily along to a group of Nissen huts near the docks. They peer at the lettering on the door of the first hut and then lurch on to the next hut.

PORTLAND, SQUADROOM, 6TH ENGINEERS UNIT.

Madison sits glumly at the Officer of the Day's desk. He is also pretty crocked. On the the desk, there is a fifth of scotch from which he now takes a swallow. Also on the desk is the Eyemo camera. Madison is fully dressed. The two sailors unsteadily enter.

THE OLD SAILOR *(grumbles)* Commander Madison?

MADISON *(takes another belt at the bottle)* Yeah.

THE OLD SAILOR We were told to report to you.

Madison regards the two other drunks blearily.

MADISON What for?

THE OLD SAILOR I don't know. A Lt. Commander Cummings, he comes in the galley. He says, "Hey, anybody here know anything about cameras?" I said, "I do a little home movies." So he says, "Report to Commander Madison in the squadroom of the 6th Naval Engineers."

THE YOUNG SAILOR Yeah.

MADISON Yeah, what?

THE YOUNG SAILOR Yeah, that's what happened to me.

Madison slugs away at the bottle.

THE OLD SAILOR What's this all about, Commander?

MADISON If I told you, you'd rap me in the mouth. Hey, maybe you men better have a drink of this.

THE OLD SAILOR Sure.

The two sailors unbutton their slickers, shamble over to the desk, pull up chairs and join Madison. For a moment, nothing is said. The bottle is passed from one to the other, and each takes a swig.

THE OLD SAILOR *(studying the nearly empty bottle)* We're running a little low here.

Madison silently produces another bottle from behind his desk, uncorks it with enormous concentration.

MADISON *(opening the bottle)* Well, men this is the deal. At seventeen-hundred, we get ferried out to an L.S.T to join the 6th Naval Engineers who are already on board. At twenty-hundred, we shove off. At o-five-hundred tomorrow morning, we transfer into an L.C.V.P. with the engineers. We'll be about three thousand yards off Omaha Beach. We start moving towards the beach until we get to the minefields and the barricades. Then the engineers get into the water and start clearing the mines and barricades. We get into the water with them.

THE OLD SAILOR What for?

MADISON We're going to make movies. We're going to shoot movies of those engineers clearing the mine fields and barricades all the way to the beach. Mostly, we want to shoot movies of engineers getting killed, especially the first body that washes up on Omaha Beach. That's the deal. What do you think of that, mates?

The Old Sailor, who has been listening to all this without expression, reaches for the bottle and takes another belt. Madison takes another belt.

THE OLD SAILOR Commander, I think you're out of your ever-loving mind.

MADISON You can say that again.

THE YOUNG SAILOR *(suddenly stands)* Well, men, I'm cutting out. *(He sits down again.)*

THE OLD SAILOR *(picking up the camera)* Hey, what's this?

MADISON That's a camera.

THE OLD SAILOR How do you work it?

MADISON How the hell do I know?

THE OLD SAILOR *(opening the camera)* Well, this is a pretty intricate camera. Back home I got a little old eight millimeter Bell and Howell. I never saw anything like this before.

MADISON *(suddenly standing)* Well, that's what they gave me.

He weaves aimlessly around the room, not quite sure why he stood up in the first place.

THE YOUNG SAILOR *(not even bothering to stand)* Well, men, I'm cutting out.

The Old Sailor squints at the open camera in his hand and the Young Sailor belts away at the second bottle, as Madison weaves around the room.

THE OLD SAILOR I'll tell you one thing. You got to put film in this camera.

Madison pauses in his weaving to study the Old Sailor blurrily.

MADISON Are you sure of that, Sailor?

THE OLD SAILOR Well, for the love of Mike, I mean, what's the matter with you? You have to have film if you're going to shoot a movie. Even I know that much.

MADISON No, we're going to shoot this movie without film. This movie, Sailor, can't be made, has no reason for being made, and none of us knows how to make a movie anyway, so what's the sense using film?

THE OLD SAILOR That makes sense. *(He takes another swig.)*

THE YOUNG SAILOR *(sliding slowly down from his chair onto the floor)* I'm cutting out of here.

Madison looks down at the boy on the floor, then sits on the floor himself.

THE OLD SAILOR *(lurching to Madison)* Commander, you see that kid on the floor? Well him and me have been loaded for two days. We start-ed off with three bottles of vanilla extract. Then, we got in with some submarine fellas, and we finished a Number Ten Can full of torpedo alcohol. You gotta be pretty stoned after that, right?

MADISON I would think so.

THE OLD SAILOR *(sits)* But we ain't that stoned, Commander. I mean, we ain't that stoned that we're going out on the beach and take any pictures of dead bodies without any film in the camera.

MADISON Then, what do you say we just don't make this movie?

THE OLD SAILOR Hey, I say swell.

The door to the squadroom opens, and Cummings comes staggering in under a load of supplies and equipment. He is completely armed and outfitted for the Invasion, dressed now in fleece-lined pants, wool shirt, wind-breaking jacket and helmet. He also wears a sleeveless canvas jacket which supports a ten-pound camera battery on his back. He has a Rolliflex and a Leica cam-era dangling from around his neck.

CUMMINGS All right! Up and at 'em!

He stares at the Young Sailor on the floor, at Madison and the Old Sailor sit-ting soddenly against the wall, the bottles on the desk.

CUMMINGS You're crocked! You're all crocked!

He dumps the load of things he is carrying onto the desk and begins yanking the Young Sailor up off the floor.

CUMMINGS Get up! Madison! Get that man on his feet! *(He manages to get the boy sitting on the chair.)* Now, listen to me, you sots!

Madison and the Old Sailor slowly get to their feet. Cummings throws a windbreaker at each of them.

CUMMINGS Get into these and get into them fast, or so help me God, I'll have the three of you shot! Now, how am I going to get you drunks on board that L.S.T.?

L.S.T. AT PORTLAND HARBOR. RAINY AFTERNOON.

WIDE ANGLE SHOT along the side of the L.S.T., showing Madison hoisted up into the L.S.T. by way of pulley and tackle and tugged through a davit. The gunwale of the L.S.T. is lined with soldiers and sailors all watching the event with considerable interest and much advice. ("Watch your head, Commander!"—"Watch his head, you jerk!"—"Do you get flight pay for that, Commander?"—"Is this trip necessary?" etc.)

The long-boat, from which he is being hoisted, circles and backs alongside. The L.S.T. rolls and washes in the waves.

Madison is pulled to the top of the gunwale and is helped over into the lower deck by infantrymen and sailors. In background, we see the L.S.T. is a two-deck vessel with its commander, a LIEUTENANT J.G., watching from the bridge. It has four tanks on it and two "ducks" or swimming trucks; also, some ninety men—a sixteen-man demolition unit and an infantry platoon, all of whom have been stuck on board this heaving vessel for two and a half days and are pretty damn seasick. Madison looks pretty green-eyed himself.

PORTLAND HARBOR, ABOARD THE L.S.T. AFTERNOON.

A wobbly Madison is helped along the lower deck, which is jammed with sol-

diers and sailors, sprawled, sitting, standing. In the foreground are the Old Sailor and the Young Sailor, apparently already derricked aboard, and sitting slumped against the gunwale amid a pack of similarly seasick and miserable INFANTRYMEN. Madison sinks slowly to the deck, leaning back against somebody's field pack.

FIRST INFANTRYMAN *(whose foot he sits on)* Watch it, Mac.

GROUP SHOT with Madison, the Old Sailor, the Young Sailor and several Infantrymen: A whip of spray splashes over the gunwale wetting everyone in the shot, but everybody is too wretched to care.

LIEUTENANT J.G. *(on bridge, shouting)* All right! Now hear this! Now hear this!

THE YOUNG SAILOR I'm sick, man.

SECOND INFANTRYMAN How many days we been on this bathtub?

THIRD INFANTRYMAN Three days.

LIEUTENANT J.G. I am going to read you a message from your Supreme Commander!

A VOICE FROM THE LOWER DECK We already heard it!

CUMMINGS *(squats down beside Madison)* All right, Charlie, here's your camera.

He sticks an Eyemo camera on Madison's lap. Madison doesn't bother to acknowledge receipt. His head is back against the field pack and his eyes are closed.

LIEUTENANT J.G. *(reading from a piece of paper)* "You are about to embark on a Great Crusade toward which we have striven these many months...

CUMMINGS I'll bring your camera batteries in a minute with your battery pack.

LIEUTENANT J.G. *(reading at the top of his lungs)* "...The hopes and prayers of liberty-loving people everywhere go with you!"

A VOICE Ah, can it!

LIEUTENANT J.G. *(shouting down to the lower deck)* Lieutenant, can't you keep your men quiet?

AN ARMY LIEUTENANT *(standing up from the crowded deck)* All right, you men, shut up!

A VOICE You already read us about the great crusade, Lieutenant.

AN ARMY LIEUTENANT I know! Now *he's* reading it! So shut up!

THE YOUNG SAILOR I'm sick.

An Infantryman leans across, offering a helmet to the Young Sailor.

LIEUTENANT J.G. "...The hopes and prayers of liberty-loving people everywhere go with you!..."

The Young Sailor is now retching piteously into the Infantryman's helmet. Madison, his head now lolling on his chest, is fast asleep. Lieutenant J.G.'s pronouncement continues.

LIEUTENANT J.G.'S VOICE *(off-screen)* "...In company with our brave allies and brothers-in-arms on other fronts, you are bringing about the destruction of the German war machine, the elimination of Nazi tyranny over the oppressed peoples of Europe..."

CAMERA NOW SLOWLY PULLS BACK AND UP to reveal the whole endless fleet of vessels, bobbing, pitching, tossing on the choppy waters.

LIEUTENANT J.G.'S VOICE *(off-screen)* "...and security for ourselves in a free world."

The Old Sailor puts his face in front of the misery-ridden Madison.

THE OLD SAILOR Commander Cummings wants us on the bridge, sir.

MADISON Where the hell are we?

THE OLD SAILOR About five miles off the coast of France, sir. You better get up on the bridge, sir.

Madison rises wearily, with difficulty, and follows him along the deck.

MID-CHANNEL, CABIN ON L.S.T.

Cummings, in his long-john undershirt, has just finished shaving himself. There is a Photographer's Mate, ENRIGHT, standing by the wall of the tiny cabin, wearing a field jacket, canvas battery vest, helmet, and with his pockets bulging with film-packs. There is a KNOCK on the door.

CUMMINGS Come in.

In the mirror, we see the door open, and Madison and the Old Sailor enter.

CUMMINGS Close the door, Charlie. *(putting his razor away)* We got a real break. There's a Navy camera unit assigned to this ship. This is Photographer's Mate Enright who's going to show us how these cameras work.

MADISON Swell.

CUMMINGS *(putting the razor case in his toilet kit)*   Go ahead, Sailor.

Photographer's Mate Enright looks serious. Madison sits bleakly on the bunk.

ENRIGHT Well, I don't quite understand your assignment, sir. Let me see if I can get this straight. You and your men are going to get into the water with the Engineers. As I understand it, sir, that's about four feet of water. That's pretty rough seas, and you'll be lucky to keep your feet. *(He takes Madison's camera.)* They're pretty heavy.

He now hoists the ten-pound battery from the floor and sticks it into the canvas jacket on Madison's back. Madison almost sags to the floor.

ENRIGHT *(to Cummings, now tying his tie before the mirror)* I've got a suggestion, sir, that you and your men should stay in the L.C.V.P. with my crew. It's going to be bouncy, but at least, you'll be able to hold your cameras reasonably steady.

CUMMINGS *(fixing his tie)* We want to be on that beach with the very first men, Sailor.

ENRIGHT Well, my helmet goes off to you gentlemen. I'll go down and get some gelatin and waterproof your cameras.

CUMMINGS *(slipping into his windbreaker)* We'll be down in the wardroom, getting a bite to eat, Enright.

ENRIGHT *(at the cabin door)* Yes, sir.

He exits. Cummings leans across Madison to fetch a revolver belt and holster from the bunk. He takes out the .45, checks its movement, puts it back in the holster, and buckles the belt around his waist.

CUMMINGS Men, before we go down to eat, I want to read you a message from our Supreme Commander.

He takes a piece of paper out of his pocket. Madison stretches out on the bunk with an anguished sigh. The Old Sailor stands, staring bleakly down at his feet.

CUMMINGS *(reading)* "Soldiers, sailors, armies of the Allied Expeditionary

Forces. You are about to embark on a Great Crusade toward which we have striven these many months. The hopes and prayers of liberty-loving people everywhere go with you..."

MID-CHANNEL, L.S.T. RAIN. DAWN.

HIGH WIDE-ANGLE SHOT looking down on the deck of the L.S.T., now the scene of considerable excitement and activity. The men are all on their feet, checking their equipment. Officers and non-coms move around the deck, shouting: "Sergeant, line those men up!"—"All right, get in those trucks!"—"Navy Engineers to the bow!"—"Get over there!"—A high Tennessee twang rises about the other voices: "Now, I want all you men to check your goddam equipment one more time!" The very first gray streaks of dawn lighten the sky, and the rain pours down in sheets of heavy drizzle.

CHIEF PETTY OFFICER Lower that boat, damn it!

ANGLE SHOT looking up from the water to the L.S.T. as an L.C.V.P. is being lowered over the side. Another L.C.V.P. is already in the water, along-side, bucking and tossing. All around, other L.C.V.P.'s are being lowered, and men are climbing down the nets on other L.S.T.'s. The air is filled with shouts and curses.

It is still quite dark out, and the scene is grotesque. A scream rips out of the night, and then a shout. "He fell! He fell!" A patrol boat streaks through the melange of assault boats. A loudhailer suddenly bursts out in the night air: "Keep in line! Keep in line!"

On the lower deck of the L.S.T, Cummings, Madison and the Old Sailor are surrounded by Demolition Engineers. Cummings is checking everyone's equipment.

CUMMINGS *(to Madison)* All you have to do is pull this trigger, and that starts the camera.

MADISON *(too miserable to do anything but complain)* Miserable rain.

In the background, Infantrymen are loading into the ducks. A public address system suddenly blares out.

P.A. SYSTEM   Now hear this! Okay, First Division! Get in there, and give 'em hell!

CUMMINGS *(looking widely about)* Where's the kid?

THE OLD SAILOR   He's too sick, sir.

LT. J.G. OF DEMOLITION UNIT   *(calling to his men)*   All right, men, first demolition team over the side and into the boats!

CUMMINGS *(to Madison)*   All right, Charlie, this is it!

Two L.C.V.P.'s swash and pitch alongside, smashing up against the side of the L.S.T. The climbing nets and ladders are filled with Demolition Engineers, the bottom men, trying to time their jump into the L.C.V.P. with the rise of the boat on the waves. Madison clambers over the rail. Suddenly, a scream, almost in his ear. He turns, terrified. An L.C.V.P. has suddenly washed high up against the L.S.T. and has crushed against the descending engineers. Shouts: "Move! Keep moving you stupid nut!" etc.

SHOOTING UP from the L.C.V.P. pitching wildly alongside, as Madison, clutching his camera, jumps. TIGHT SHOT looking down on Madison lying on the deck of the L.C.V.P., eyes closed and clutching his camera. A wave splashes over the boat, drenching him. Over all this, we hear the constant BOOMING of the naval artillery.

7,000 FEET FROM THE BEACHES. DAWN.

LONG WIDE ANGLE SHOT shooting out from the beaches to the Channel. The sky is still dark gray, but dawn is breaking slowly. We can see more clearly now the vast conglomeration of L.C.V.P.'s and other beaching craft chugging slowly in towards us from across the choppy sea. Behind them, the hulking L.S.T.'s and other transports, the huge rhino barges. Patrol boats scoot between the mess of slowly oncoming craft. Loudhailers BLEAT out: "Keep in line! Keep 'em moving! Keep 'em moving!" etc. Far behind it all we can see the flashes of the big naval guns as they continue their relent-less barrage.

5,000 FEET OUT, ABOARD THE L.C.V.P. DAWN.

Photographer's Mate Enright stands in the bow of the L.C.V.P., his camera braced on his shoulder, shooting back to the stern of the boat, his CARRIER behind him. Dawn is breaking more quickly.

Enright is standing, braced against the pitch and toss of the boat, his camera pressed against his face. His Carrier, Cummings and the Ensign are also in the bow. In the foreground are Madison, the Old Sailor, and six Demolition Engineers, seated wet and shivering. Madison is absolutely numb with cold and wet and just plain terror.

Cummings and the Ensign stare straight ahead to the beaches. The rain drizzles down, and nothing but white mist fills the gray skyline. The L.C.V.P. rises and shoots forward on a sudden swell of water.

CUMMINGS *(shouting)* About how far out are we?

ENSIGN *(shouting back)* Maybe five, maybe six thousand feet. We should see the low-water mark any time.

CUMMINGS *(shouting to Madison)* We're about five, six thousand feet out, Charlie!

A BOATSWAIN'S MATE of the engineers stands up midship.

BOATSWAIN'S MATE *(yelling to the engineers)* All right, let's get up front.

ENSIGN *(shouting)* There's the low-water barrier!

Now, in the gray-white mist, washed by waves of dark water, there can just be seen, some five hundred feet ahead, thick ends of iron and steel rails poking out over the sea-line.

ENSIGN *(shouts)* Stand by to lower the ramp!

Engineers crowd into the frame to look over the bow.

FIRST ENGINEER How're we going to get at the damn things?

SECOND ENGINEER We're going to have to shinny up!

Suddenly, a BURST of mortar and 88s firing from ahead.

ENSIGN They're shooting at us!

A German flare explodes high over them and bleaches the last remnants of night. Cummings cups his mouth and shouts something.

THE OLD SAILOR *(lurching up to the bow)* I can't hear you!

ENSIGN Let down the ramp!

The engineers splash out into the water which comes up to their necks. Splashing, struggling, they edge forward toward the low water barricade which now looms up in front of the L.C.V.P. It consists of a six-foot barricade of jagged iron and steel rails, wired and mined. The engineers shout instructions at each other: "Get on my back!"—"Frank, shinny up that damn pole!" etc. In the L.C.V.P., Cummings is pushing a numb, half-frozen Madison to the bow-ramp.

MADISON I'm freezing!

CUMMINGS Let's go! Let's go!

ENSIGN *(shouting at the Engineers)* Blow something up! They're zeroed in on us here!

Nothing more can be heard although everyone is shouting. The air is one continual thrum of EXPLODING shells and naval artillery. The sky flares with red, yellow, incandescent bursts. Engineers splash through the water. A barricade is blown up. Rifle and machine gun FIRE adds to the ineffable din. Suddenly, the L.C.V.P. is nearly struck by an 88 shell, and the whole boat, with its ramp open, is swept right into the air and through the newly-breached barricade towards the beach.

Madison, Cummings and the Old Sailor are pitched into the air and come swirling down, gasping for breath, thrashing about on the beach side of the barricade.

TIGHT SHOT of Madison thrashing about in the water, gasping for air, still clutching his camera. He looks desperate.

MADISON'S P.O.V.: Not more than a thousand feet directly ahead of him stretches the naked, white, unoccupied stretch of sand called Omaha Beach. Its clean white expanse is covered with steel jackstraws, wooden stakes and long fences of tubed steel, all wired, all mined, and all obviously sinister.

Madison stands knee-deep in water, staring at the beach, clutching his camera. He promptly wheels about-face and begins splashing away from the beach and back to the L.C.V.P. about five hundred feet to his seaward side.

2,000 FEET OUT, ABOARD THE L.C.V.P. DAWN.

WIDE ANGLE SHOT looking seaward through the open ramp of the L.C.V.P., singles out Enright, braced against the jamb of the ramp, filming furiously.

ENRIGHT'S P.O.V.: We see what he is filming. Madison is splashing his way seaward to the L.C.V.P., and Cummings is splashing his way beachward to Madison.

CUMMINGS You're going the wrong way. The beach is that way!

Madison splashes toward us, shouting.

MADISON I know where the beach is! They're shooting at us! What's the matter with you?

Cummings and Madison splash toward each other in belt-high water. Disaster, death and the havoc of WAR in the background. Cummings yanks his revolver from its holster.

CUMMINGS *(shouting)* You yellow rat! Head into that beach!

MADISON What's the matter with you?

They are barely ten yards apart. Cummings points the revolver at Madison.

CUMMINGS *(screaming)* Take pictures! Take pictures!

MADISON *(screaming)* What?

Cummings FIRES. The SHOT hits Madison in the thigh, spins him partly around and almost knocks him into the water.

Madison flails about in hip-deep water, staring aghast at Cummings. Then, in total terror, he wheels and starts splashing to the beach as fast as he can. Enright is taking movies of Cummings splashing after Madison, who is now splashing headlong into the shallows of Omaha Beach.

Dead bodies float in the water, pitched about by the surge and swell. The air is deafened by BOMBS, MINES, MORTARS, ARTILLERY, MACHINE GUNS.

REVERSE LONG SHOT from the beach seaward. Madison comes dashing up on the beach, the first man on the long, white empty expanse of sand by some twenty yards. He is bug-eyed with terror.

The CAMERA PANS him across the four hundred feet of beach as he dashes heedlessly past the steel jackstraws and wooden stakes on the beach, ripping his trousers on the barbed wire, stumbling against the steel obstacles. He vaults the four-foot wall about three hundred feet up the beach like Jesse Owens, flinging his camera into the air as he does so, and sprints the last hundred feet to the steep escarpment at the end of the beach, clutching his right thigh. Just as he reaches the base of the escarpment, he apparently trips the detonator of a land mine, for there is an EXPLOSION just behind him, and he is thrown, arms outflung, onto the sand.

LONG WIDE ANGLE PANORAMA SHOT showing Madison's body sprawled on the beach. For the length of this shot, Madison's body is the only body on the long white stretch of Omaha Beach.

CLOSE SHOT of Enright, hiding behind a logpile obstacle, loading his camera. He snaps his camera shut, dashes further up the beach towards the escarpment. Behind him, the beach is beginning to fill with the black forms of soldiers, tanks, trucks. The overwhelming THUNDER of artillery, mortar and machine-gun fire continues. A mine EXPLODES in the foreground. Enright dashes up to where Cummings is standing beside Madison, staring down at his best friend's body, numb with shock.

ENRIGHT   Well, he's the first dead man on Omaha Beach, if that means anything, Commander.

Cummings stares at Enright, then bursts into tears.

CUMMINGS   *(sobbing)* Now, that's funny, that's funny, oh, my God, that's funny.

A mine EXPLODES about twenty feet away, showering the screen with sand. Enright and Cummings dash off along the escarpment. We hear the WHINE of ricocheting bullets as a MEDIC, identified by his red-cross armband, crawls across the frame to Madison's body.

FADE OUT.

FADE IN:

EMILY'S HOME, HER BEDROOM.

A camera study in grief. Emily sits woodenly in the chair by her window, unaware of the sun streaming in through the white curtains, bleaching her face. She seems unaware of anything, really. She is in her bedclothes and a wrapper, her face sallow, her lips pale, almost imperceptible, her eyes swollen and dry, long past tears. She sits numbly, her external self as dead as Charlie, content apparently with the interior world she can create for herself out of fragments of memory, and supported by the rigid premise that Madison is not dead. There is a gentle knock on the door which she doesn't seem to hear. Then the door opens to admit her mother.

MRS. BARHAM Emily, Commander Cummings is here to condole again.

Emily is annoyed by the interruption of exterior life.

EMILY I can't very well be condoled with since I'm still pretending Charlie's alive.

MRS. BARHAM Well, as long as you still know it's pretending. I do think, Emily, we've had enough of this sinister withdrawal of yours. It's eight days since you went off into this medieval retreat. You know, you're doing just what I did, and you'll end up just as dotty. There's very little satisfaction in it.

Emily says nothing, already oblivious of her mother. Mrs. Barham exhibits polite disapproval, backs out of the room, and closes the door softly.

LANDING OUTSIDE HER BEDROOM.

Mrs. Barham comes out, closing the door. For a moment, in the half-darkness of the upstairs landing, she allows her face to reveal her own grief and genuine concern for her daughter, but she quickly reassumes her old potty self and goes sailing down the stairs to the living room.

EMILY'S HOME, LIVING ROOM.

Bus Cummings rises from an overstuffed chair at her entrance. He is holding a folded newspaper.

MRS. BARHAM *(cheerfully)* Absolutely wooden with grief. Sends her best, but asks to be excused.

CUMMINGS Oh, yes. Of course. I understand. I just stopped by to show her this. *(extending the newspaper)* Thought it might make her feel a little better.

INSERT CLOSE-UP of the newspaper, opened for our inspection. It is a copy of the New York Globe, *June 14, 1944, the headline being whatever it was for that date and presumably, dealing with the advances made by the Allied Armies.*

However, what is most eye-catching is a four-column photograph of Madison as he leaped over the sea-wall on Omaha Beach, his head thrown back, his arms outflung; all-in-all, a photographic masterpiece in the study of gallantry.

CUMMINGS *(off-screen)* That's yesterday's *New York Globe.*

MRS. BARHAM *(off-screen)* Yes, I'm on to that. What is it you want me to see?

CUMMINGS *(off-screen)* The photograph, ma'am. Charlie Madison, the first American on Omaha Beach. It's on the front page of the *New York Globe.*

Mrs. Barham looks at the newspaper, politely interested.

MRS. BARHAM Well, it can't be said to be a very good likeness. It's mostly his back, isn't it?

CUMMINGS Ma'am, this photograph is on the front page of almost two hundred newspapers in the United States alone. We honestly didn't think it would catch on that big. Our Press Office people just sent it out as a standard release, and first thing we knew—well, Mrs. Barham, this picture was in practically every London newspaper yesterday. I was sure you'd seen it. Charlie's a hero, ma'am! Our Public Relations office is talking now of holding some sort of ceremony over his grave, building some sort of monument.

MRS. BARHAM *(appalled)* A monument?

CUMMINGS Probably nothing more than a simple bronze plaque, but the Free French have indicated they'd be willing to declare Charlie's grave a French national shrine.

MRS. BARHAM That's depraved!

CUMMINGS We think the President of the United States will make a statement about Charlie. I didn't want to tell you about these things yet because we haven't got firm commitments, but Admiral Jessup is very close to the President. I don't know if we can get Charlie the Congressional Medal of Honor, but he's a cinch for the Navy Cross. As soon as I get an extra copy of *Life* magazine, I'll bring it to you.

MRS. BARHAM What on earth for?

CUMMINGS *(beaming)* This picture of Charlie's on the cover of *Life* magazine!

MRS. BARHAM Oh, this is shoddy! A French national shrine, indeed! One must expect, I suppose, this sort of scandal-mongering from the French. But you're supposed to be his friend. Couldn't you have done something more to keep this whole sordid business out of the press?

CUMMINGS Ma'am?

MRS. BARHAM Of course, we're very disappointed in Charlie, but he has paid his price and there's no need to rake it up.

CUMMINGS I'm not sure you have this exactly right, Mrs. Barham. Charlie's a hero.

EMILY *(off-screen)* Mother?

MRS. BARHAM Oh, dear, there she is. Now don't say a word to her about any of this. I'll tell her when I think she's well enough.

She moves out to the foot of the stairs in the foyer, leaving behind Cummings, who is beginning to feel like a hero in Kafka.

EMILY'S HOME, FOYER.

Mrs. Barham is at the foot of the stairs. Emily walks down, hair tidied, dressed in her uniform now, and buttoning her jacket.

MRS. BARHAM Going into work. That's very sensible of you.

EMILY I don't know how you put up with me this long, mother.

At the foot of the stairs, Mrs. Barham takes her daughter's arm and whispers quickly.

MRS. BARHAM Don't forget that man is still here, come to commiserate. This is his third visit, and he's going to say a lot of comforting things. So you will be polite, won't you?

EMILY Oh, he's just a bit sincere.

MRS. BARHAM I must say, I find him grotesque.

She adjusts a smile onto her face, and the pair move into the living room.

EMILY'S HOME, LIVING ROOM.

ACROSS Emily and her mother to Cummings, standing with head bowed, hat in hand. He slowly looks up to reveal an extravagantly grave face. He comes forward to Emily and merely takes her hand and looks mutely into her face.

CUMMINGS Yes. Emily, you're doing the right thing. Bury yourself in work. We've all got to keep going.

Emily's eye is caught by the New York Globe *lying on the sofa, and she crosses over to it.*

MRS. BARHAM Emily, well, I must warn you. Charlie's picture is in all the papers, and they're going to build a monument on his grave.

EMILY *(studying the* Globe*)* What on earth for? All he did was die. Dear me, we shall be celebrating cancer and automobile smash-ups next.

CUMMINGS *(erupting)* He didn't just die, Emily! He sacrificed his life!

MRS. BARHAM Well, that was very pagan of him.

CUMMINGS He was the first American to die on Omaha Beach.

EMILY Was there a contest?

CUMMINGS Emily, I don't understand you. I thought you'd be proud.

EMILY *(handing the paper to her mother)* You might as well burn this, mother—along with yesterday's *Daily Mail* which I fished out of the garden fire. *(to Cummings)* We no longer take pride in death in this house, Bus. What was admirable about Charlie was his sensation of life. His cowardly, selfish, greedy appreciation of life, unadorned and uncertain as it is. I loved him very much. I don't think I shall ever love anyone as much again. But I shall try. *(She starts out to the foyer.)* Are you going back to the Navy Building, Bus?

Cummings turns to Mrs. Barham, hoping for sanity from that quarter.

CUMMINGS No, I have to stop by the hospital to pick the Admiral up.

EMILY *(disappearing into the foyer)* Drop me at Edgeware Road. I'll take the bus there.

MRS. BARHAM *(nudging an unhappy Cummings)* You know, I thought I saw her peering at me through the window when I was burning those newspapers.

LONDON SUBURB, NAVY HOSPITAL, PRIVATE ROOM.

Admiral Jessup, dressed in his shirt and pants, puffs a cigar, his old, brisk, groomed self again. He is putting toilet articles into a small valise on the bed, which is otherwise already packed. Cummings is standing on the other side of the bed, holding the Admiral's jacket on its hanger, even more unhappy than he was in the last scene.

ADMIRAL JESSUP I was damned fond of Charlie. He was one of the few really decent human beings I've ever known aside from being the best dog-robber in the world. What the hell was Charlie ever doing on Omaha Beach in the first place?

CUMMINGS What, sir?

ADMIRAL JESSUP Exactly what was this movie Charlie was making on Omaha Beach? What was Charlie doing making a movie in the first place?

CUMMINGS He was making your movie, sir.

ADMIRAL JESSUP Yes, you keep saying my movie. What do you mean, my movie?

CUMMINGS The movie you wanted made about the Demolition Engineers, sir.

ADMIRAL JESSUP I don't remember any... *(He turns, puzzled, back to knotting his tie before the mirror. Suddenly, he understands, and he turns back in utter horror to Cummings.)* Oh my God, Bus, was this some idea I conceived when I was cracking up? I don't remember any movie. I... And you went ahead and did it? But I was unbalanced at the time, Bus! I wasn't responsible! You mean, Charlie Madison... Oh, my God! *(He sinks, aghast, onto the bed.)*

CUMMINGS Well, sir, we wanted a hero. Now we've got one.

ADMIRAL JESSUP You don't send a man to his death because you want a hero!

CUMMINGS Well, sir, the whole purpose of our coming over here, was to find something to catch the eye of the Committee on Military

Affairs, to remind them that the Navy is still an essential service.
We're trying to keep from being scrapped, sir.

The Admiral stands, still shaken.

ADMIRAL JESSUP May God forgive me; I'll never forgive myself. *(He turns
back to the mirror and his tie, still pained, but he has his work to do.)* If you
want to catch the eye of the Joint Committee on Military Affairs, Bus,
you'll have to bury Charlie in Washington, not on Omaha Beach,
preferably right in the middle of the Senate committee room and certainly no further away than Pennsylvania Avenue. I will not authorize
funds for any monument on Omaha Beach. We need something more
immediate than that. Give me my jacket. *(slips into his jacket)* Have
you got my flight orders?

CUMMINGS Yes, sir. You leave for Washington tonight with Marv
Ellender on the twenty-two-hundred flight.

ADMIRAL JESSUP *(buttoning his jacket)* The only solace any of us has
is that if Charlie were here, he'd be laughing himself silly.

PORT OF SOUTHAMPTON. DAY.

*Lt. Commander Charles E. Madison slowly descends the ramp of a hospital
ship. We know it's a hospital ship because we can see the huge red cross painted on the hull of the ship behind him. Out of the hold, an endless file of
wounded men are being carried on stretchers down to the docks. Madison is
one of the ambulatory cases. He wears a red regulation hospital robe and blue
hospital pajamas. An oaktag label dangles from his lapel. He requires a
cane.*

*His face is set in a rigid mask of bitterness. The other ambulatory patients,
hobbling and lurching along down the ramp with him, on crutches or with
bandaged arms and heads, are all in the best of spirits.*

VOICES AND SHOUTS Oh, man, I thought I'd never see this side of the
Channel again!—Hey, Nurse! Hey, Lieutenant! Where are we sup-

posed to go?—Hey! They're serving food!—Oh, man, look at that
nurse! How'd you like to have *her* stick a thermometer in your
mouth?—Louise! If we get separated, remember I'm in the 8th
Infantry, 112th Regiment, I Company!

*The good spirits of all the others contrast with the somber, coldly belligerent
set of Madison's face. ANOTHER ANGLE as Madison and the other
ambulatory patients reach the docks at the bottom of the ramp. A MEDIC
gently herds them to the dock railing.*

MEDIC Ambulatory patients over here. You're now at the Sixth Medical
Relocation Center in Southampton. You'll all be properly taken care
of in just a few minutes. Is there anyone who needs immediate attention? We're here to help you.

*Madison and the other ambulatories hobble along to join other ambulatory
patients in their tagged robes. We see now the docks are filled with rows of
stretchers and bandaged men. Uniformed NURSES and MEDICS move up
and down between the stretchers, checking the identification labels, marking
their clipboards and ministering to the wounded. Volunteer English RED
CROSS LADIES add to the crush by wheeling tea carts of coffee and magazines. Indeed, one Red Cross Lady suddenly wheels her cart into the foreground, piled high with newspapers and* Life *magazines.*

We see Madison's picture is on the cover.

RED CROSS LADY *(to Madison's group)* Newspapers? Magazines? Any of
you chaps want a copy of *Newsweek? Life* magazine? *(to Madison in
particular)* Want a copy of *Life?*

*TIGHT SHOT across the Red Cross Lady to Madison staring somberly out
over the harbor. He turns, showing us again the quiet anger on his face.*

MADISON *(coldly)* No, thank you, I've seen it already.

*He turns back to staring fixedly out over the harbor, while VOICES fly
around him.*

VOICES All I want is three days in London. I hear you have to beat them off with clubs...You know what's a great town for broads? Liverpool! You have to beat them off with clubs.

HENDON AIRPORT. NIGHT.

LONG ESTABLISHING SHOT almost duplicating the shot that began the film—a DC-4 looming vaguely on the black landing strip, three official cars lined up some yards away, a clump of uniformed people by the cars, some loading activity at the plane. In short, a high-level military mission is about to depart.

ACROSS Emily at the door of the car to the Admiral and Cummings, with Ellender and Captain Spaulding supervising the transfer of the luggage to the plane.

ELLENDER *(to one of the plane's crew)* Leave the attaché case and the little bag. The rest can go.

We get the feeling a car is approaching us in the dark night, its headlights dimmed for blackout purposes.

ADMIRAL JESSUP *(to Cummings)* You and Adams lock up the shop. I want you both in Washington by Wednesday night. And forget about that tomb.

CUMMINGS Yes, sir.

Cummings' attention, however, is to the car, which screeches to a halt fifteen yards away. The Admiral gives it a brief glance and turns to Ellender.

ADMIRAL JESSUP Admirals Koenig and Ridgeway are supposed to testify on Thursday. I don't think they'll get to us before Monday.

ELLENDER More likely Tuesday, the way Congressional hearings usually run.

Chief Petty Officer Adams, who is driving the newly-arrived car, opens the door and gets out. He is obviously in distress.

ADAMS Hey, Bus, can I see you a minute?

CUMMINGS Something the matter?

ADAMS *(as Cummings moves to him)* Yeah, I'll say something's the matter.

TWO SHOT of Adams and Cummings. In the background, the Admiral and Ellender are fishing their attaché cases out of the first of the cars. Captain Spaulding waits in attendance on them.

ADAMS *(lowers his voice to a conspiratorial mutter)* I just got a call from the Sixth Relocation Center in Southampton. That's where they bring the casualties from France. They've got a Lieutenant Commander Charles E. Madison there ready to be released. Would we arrange transportation for him and bring him a uniform? I don't know whether to laugh or cry.

During this speech, Cummings nods, purses his lips and cleans his glasses, as if he were listening to the most perfunctory of problems.

ADAMS I don't know if you heard me, Bus. I said—

CUMMINGS Yes, I heard you Paul. What's the gag?

In the background, the Admiral, Ellender and Spaulding, carrying their attaché cases and hand luggage, are crossing the landing strip to the plane.

ADAMS I spoke to him, Bus. He's alive.

CUMMINGS What do you mean, he's alive? He was practically a French national shrine. How the hell can he be alive?

As Adams and Cummings speak, Emily stands in the background by her car.

ADAMS He got on the phone, he said, "Hi, Paul," I said, "Hi, Charlie."

He said, "Do me a favor, Paul. Call Miss Barham in the Motor Pool and tell her I'm all right."

CUMMINGS I saw him with my own eyes, Paul!

ADAMS He also said, "Tell Bus, if I ever lay my hands on him again, I'm going to belt him right in his big, fat stern-sheets."

CLOSE-UP of Cummings: he's convinced but miserable about it.

CUMMINGS He's alive. The first dead man on Omaha Beach is alive. Oh boy, that's great! Two hundred newspapers in the United States alone—the front cover of *Life* magazine—every newsreel in the world—and he's alive!

ADAMS What's he mad at you for, Bus?

The expression of chagrin on Cummings' face changes to one of horror.

CUMMINGS Not only is he alive, he's a coward! We had a nice dead hero; now, we have a lousy live coward.

ADAMS What's the matter with you, Bus?

Cummings suddenly seizes the startled Adams by his jacket collar, almost throttling the poor fellow.

CUMMINGS *(screaming)* Is this a gag, Paul?!

ADAMS *(screaming)* It's no gag!

Cummings thrusts his Chief Petty Officer from him, breaks for the DC-4, shouting to Admiral Jessup, who is about to be helped into the plane.

CUMMINGS *(shouting)* Admiral, sir! He's alive, damn it!

The Admiral, Ellender and Spaulding turn to see what all the agitation is about. In the background, Emily takes a few steps forward, not quite sure what was shouted. The Admiral stares at Cummings, who now comes to a halt in front of him.

ADMIRAL JESSUP Alive? Madison?

CUMMINGS Yes, sir. The relocation center in Southampton, waiting to be released right now, sir.

ADMIRAL JESSUP Thank God!

ELLENDER Oh, that's wonderful, Bus. Wonderful.

Now Emily emerges more clearly out of the darkish background, approaching the group on the plane, utterly unconscious of what she's doing, too terrified to believe what she suspects she has heard.

ADMIRAL JESSUP *(beaming at Cummings)* Now, Bus! Now, we can bring your first man on Omaha Beach right into Room Number 610 of the Senate Office Building!

CUMMINGS Sir?

ADMIRAL JESSUP I want Madison flown to Washington on the first plane out of Southampton. We're going to give Charlie a parade right down Pennsylvania Avenue and right up to the front lawn of the White House where the President himself will decorate Charlie with the Navy Cross.

CUMMINGS *(unhappily)* I'm not so sure if we should involve the President in this, sir.

ADMIRAL JESSUP The President's an old Navy man. He's sympathetic to our position throughout.

CUMMINGS Yes, sir, but I just don't think we should go that big.

ADMIRAL JESSUP *(positively elated)* We're going to make a big, brass-band hero out of Charlie, using every coarse theatricality the Public

Relations Office is overpaid to think up. And when I walk into that hearing on Monday or Tuesday, I'll smile my crisp military smile at all those Senators; and then, in a perfunctory way, I'll introduce my two aides, "Captain Ellender here, my technical adviser, and Lieutenant Commander Charles E. Madison, gentlemen, the first American on Omaha Beach. A sailor." Bus, that's what's known as letting them have it in spades, doubled, redoubled and vulnerable. *(He positively guffaws.)* Charlie will then modestly answer a few of the Senators' questions.

CUMMINGS *(beginning to feel genuinely ill)* Oh, he'll be modest all right. Sir, I better tell you what really happened on D-Day, sir.

The Admiral, however, has turned his attention to Emily, who has been advancing on the group, one dazed step after another.

EMILY *(almost too terrified to ask)* Is he alive? Is he alive? Is that what you're saying? That he's alive?

ADMIRAL JESSUP Yes, Miss Barham, we think he is.

EMILY Oh, dear...oh, dear...

It's all she can get out. She stares helplessly at all of them, her eyes blinking, and then, raises her face, tears slipping in individual beads out from beneath her lashes, nevertheless exhilarated by a faint, mute smile of ineffable joy.

ADMIRAL JESSUP Miss Barham, we're almost as happy about this as you are.

EMILY Thank you, sir.

ADMIRAL JESSUP Hey, Bus, I want you to drive this young lady down to Southampton just as fast as you can make it. Get going. *(shakes Spaulding's hand)* Goodby, Harry.

SPAULDING Good trip, sir.

He turns, seizes the hands being offered to him from the open doorway of the DC-4 and clambers up into the plane. The Admiral suddenly reappears in the doorway of the plane, and calls to Cummings.

ADMIRAL JESSUP   Oh, Bus...

CUMMINGS   Yes, sir.

ADMIRAL JESSUP   You were going to tell me something before about Charlie on D-Day.

Cummings hesitates briefly, then calls back to the Admiral.

CUMMINGS   Oh, nothing, sir. Have a good flight.

ADMIRAL JESSUP   *(to Cummings)* Well, don't forget. I want him in Washington tomorrow. I don't care what brass you have to throw off the plane.

CUMMINGS   Yes, don't worry, sir. I'll have him on the first flight out of Southampton.

A GROUND CREWMAN   *(moving into the background)* You better move back there, sir.

Cummings nods brusquely, turns on his heel and strides off in the direction of Chief Petty Officer Adams, waiting apprehensively by his car. Emily, still enchanted, trots along behind him. Spaulding swerves off to where the official cars and the other drivers are waiting.

In the background, propellers of the DC-4 suddenly whir into activity. About halfway to Adams, Cummings whirls on Emily and shouts something at her. The DC-4 slowly taxies off in the background.

CUMMINGS   *(shouting to be heard over the motors)* What I didn't tell the Admiral back there was that Charlie Madison became the first man on Omaha Beach because I chased him up there with a Colt 45! He was, in fact, running the other way!—bolting under fire, an errant act of cowardice in the face of the enemy! Our big brass-band hero is a big brass-band coward! But I didn't tell the Admiral that because the Navy needs a hero, even a miserable, lousy yellow cowardly hero like Charlie Madison! It's a hoax, Emily, a hoax! The whole thing's a hoax!

EMILY *(couldn't be prouder)* Ah, that's my Charlie! Craven to the end!

Behind them, the DC-4 suddenly fills the night with the ROAR of its motors. Cummings strides off again to Adams at the car, Emily happily behind him.

CUMMINGS *(shouts to Spaulding)* Harry, clear me a space for Madison on the next flight out of Southampton! I'll call you from the hospital there!

HOSPITAL ADMINISTRATION OFFICE.

A typical, improvised military office in another, smaller, quonset hut. One enters from the street through a plain wooden door. A second one in the opposite wall leads outside to the interior area of the hospital. This door bears a placard: NO ADMITTANCE EXCEPT AUTHORIZED PERSONNEL. A NURSE CAPTAIN sits behind the principal desk; several ARMY CLERKS sit behind other desks rattling away on their typewriters or filing in the many cabinets. Cummings is standing by the desk on the phone, as we cut in.

CUMMINGS *(on phone)* Harry, I'm in the Administrative Office right now—

Chief Petty Officer Adams is studying the bulletin board which has a splendid large poster on it advising G.I.s to watch out for V.D. Emily is pacing restlessly around the crowded, clattery room.

CUMMINGS *(on phone)* I can have Madison at the airport by one o'clock. Now don't worry about it. You just clear a place on the plane for him, that's all.

Emily, in a feverish state of impatience, goes to the door marked No Admittance, opens it halfway, and looks out. The Nurse Captain notes this sympathetically.

CUMMINGS *(on phone)* You told Grissom? When? You told the Public Relations Office? Harry, what the hell's the matter with you. We'll have every correspondent in London down here —

THE NURSE CAPTAIN *(solicitously, to Emily at the door)* Honey, why don't you go on through and wait for him outside.

EMILY Thank you.

She steps out of the office.

HOSPITAL, OUTSIDE OFFICE. NIGHT.

A very long paved footpath and arcaded passageway are lit just enough for camera purposes. The rest of the hospital sleeps silently in the dark night. Emily smokes anxiously. Now, a NURSE trundles a small medical cart across the roofed passageway at the extreme background of the frame, and Emily whirls to it. Disappointed, she turns full-face to to the camera and lights another cigarette. How silent it all is now. Suddenly, she senses Madison through the small of her back, and she slowly turns so that we see ACROSS her down the long length of dimly-lit footpath. There, at the far end, turning in from the roofed passageway, is Charlie. He is dressed, walking with a noticeable limp, using a cane. She starts involuntarily a few paces up the path, then stops.

Madison, who had been rapt in his brown study, looks up, stops.

MADISON'S P.O.V.: Looking down the footpath to Emily, half-shadowed but lit enough to see she is smiling. Behind her, the Administration Office hut, black-out shades drawn, with cracks of light here and there.

EMILY You're limping, Commander. The old wound acting up?

Madison limps a few slow steps down toward her. He stops, regards her warily. Emily now ambles slowly up the path to him.

EMILY Well, where have you been? We expected you back a week ago yesterday.

MADISON I'm sorry, I had to go to France for a few days. It's out of season this time of year.

EMILY No one worth knowing was there, I'm sure.

MADISON Very rough element going to France these days.

The two of them regard each other on the footpath. Then suddenly, she whirls over the few yards separating them and into his arms. They embrace.

EMILY Oh, Charlie. Oh, Charlie, Charlie—

MADISON Hey, careful of my leg.

EMILY Oh, shut up. Let me hold you.

HOSPITAL, ADMINISTRATION OFFICE.

The office is jammed with NEWSPAPERMEN, perhaps twenty of them, both uniformed and civilian, with and without cameras. Cummings, Adams and a Clerk are trying to get them back outside.

CUMMINGS *(shouting)* All right! All right! I haven't seen him myself yet!

A camera-flash explodes almost in his face.

NURSE CAPTAIN *(shouting)* You'll have to wait outside! I'm terribly sorry! You'll have to wait outside!

SHOUTS and VOICES from the reporters: "When was he brought here?!"

—"*Is he seriously wounded?!*"—"*Is he coming out? What's going on?*"—
"*What's this about de Gaulle?*"

CUMMINGS (*to Adams*) I better get him.

Cummings crosses quickly to the door marked No Admittance, reaches for the knob.

Madison and Emily are still embracing as Cummings comes out. He quickly shuts the door and hurries up the path to the lovers.

FULL SHOT of Madison and Emily in embrace. Madison looks up over her shoulder and Emily turns her head to see what the flare of noise was.

CUMMINGS Hey Charlie!

MADISON Don't you come within cane's distance of me, you fink. You tried to kill me.

Madison releases himself from Emily's arms.

CUMMINGS Oh go on, Charlie. Don't make such a big dramatic deal out of this. Right now, I've got a plane waiting to take you back to Washington. Now we have to be at the airport in half an hour, and there are about twenty reporters in that office and more piling in by the minute. We have five minutes for pictures and a few questions, so let me brief you quickly on what you're to say.

MADISON I'm going to say the truth, Bus.

CUMMINGS I don't know how much of my little hoax you know, Charlie...

MADISON Enough.

CUMMINGS Well, your last words as you led the charge up the beach were, "Okay, men, let's show 'em whose beach this is!"

MADISON   Not quite the epic stature of "We've just begun to fight," Bus.

CUMMINGS   Yeah, well...you know...

MADISON   I'm going to tell them the truth, Bus. I'm going to tell anyone who wants to know the plain, unattractive and not very epic truth.

CUMMINGS   Charlie, we don't have much time—

MADISON   I'm going to tell them that a deranged Admiral had a demented idea for a lunatic movie whose only purpose was to juice up the Navy's bid for military appropriations; that my gallant wounds were inflicted on me by my brother officer, the fink...

CUMMINGS   (beginning to suspect Madison is serious) Charlie, you've got a legitimate beef against me, okay...

MADISON   ...and that my last inspirational words as I led the charge away from the beach were, "Let's get the hell out of here."

Cummings and Emily look quizzically at Madison.

MADISON   I've had a bad week, Bus. I've been in battle and I've seen the howl and heard the horror of it again. I will not contribute to your wretched little hoax. I will not help you preserve the wonder of war. I want people to know I was a coward. I want people to know the whole shabby story about my heroism.

Emily doesn't quite trust her ears.

CUMMINGS   Charlie, I don't understand you. Do you know what'll happen if...

MADISON   Oh, I know what'll happen. I'll embarrass my country, dishonor my service, disgrace my admiral, humiliate my family, and probably get myself thrown in the brig for a couple of years.

EMILY Then why do it?

MADISON Because it's the right thing to do.

CLOSE-UP of Emily, stunned, open-mouthed with disbelief.

EMILY I can't believe it! Is this the Charlie Madison who once said: "God save us all from people who do the right thing! It's the rest of us who always get our backs broken!?" Are you seriously going to destroy everything that means anything to you, Charlie, in a futile gesture of virtue? And you're going to put yourself in jail, are you?

MADISON I don't care what happens to me.

EMILY How bloody brave of you. But you do care what happens to me. At least you said you did. What am I supposed to do while you sit about in your prison cell for five or six years, admiring the glisten of your own martyrdom?

MADISON Emily, I want the world to know what a fraud war is.

EMILY But war isn't a fraud, Charlie; it's very real. At least, that's what you've always tried to tell me, isn't it? That we shall never get rid of war by pretending it's unreal? It's the virtue of war that's the fraud, not itself. It's the valor and the self-sacrifice and the goodness of war that needs the exposing. Here you are, being brave, self-sacrificing and positively clanking with moral fervor, perpetuating the very things you detest, merely to do the right thing. Honestly, your conversion to morality is actually funny, Charlie. All this while, I've been terrified of becoming Americanized, and you, you silly ass, have turned into a bloody sentimental Englishman.

MADISON Emily, there's a matter of principle involved here.

EMILY A matter of *what*? Oh, Charlie, didn't you once say, "What's a lion doing in a man's house anyway?"

MADISON Emily, if a man knows the truth, he has to say it.

Madison and Emily regard each other, shamelessly in love.

EMILY *(meaning: "I love you")* Is this the Charlie Madison who once said: "I'm not equipped to deal with the truth. I let God worry about the truth. I just want to know the momentary fact of things." Your idea of facts, you said...

MADISON *(meaning "I love you too")* ...were you, a home, a country, a world, and a universe in that order.

EMILY Well, I'm quite prepared to supply all that as my end of the deal.

MADISON What do you get out of it?

EMILY I'll settle for a Hershey bar.

They embrace. The door of the Administration Office opens, and Chief Petty Officer Adams comes hurrying out. Behind, the Nurse Captain fills the rectangle of light made by the open doorway.

ADAMS *(hurrying up)* Hey, Bus! There must be a hundred of them! There's correspondents all over the place. *(in passing)* Hi, Charlie!

THE NURSE CAPTAIN *(calling from the door)* Commander, would you please come? We can't have all these people here!

Madison, who has been locked in a mutually-obsessed trance with Emily during all this, now smiles and turns to Cummings, who hasn't understood a word that was said during the previous dialogue.

MADISON *(wrapping one arm around Emily and the other around Cummings, He jovially says to Cummings)* All right, fink, how do you want me to play it? Modest and self-effacing?

CUMMINGS *(as they move down the path to the Administration Office)* Thanks, Charlie. I'll make this up to you. I'll do anything you say.

MADISON *(beaming at his friend)* Oh, I've got something in mind for you, buddy.

By now, the rectangle of light made by the open Administration Office door is filling up with correspondents, and, in a moment, the whole screen is a constant flare of flashbulbs.

THE NORTH POLE. DAY.

Actually, we dissolve in on a photograph of a parade on Pennsylvania Avenue in Washington, D.C. Madison stands in the back of the main limousine, waving at the crowds who are flinging ticker-tape at him.

DOLLY SLOWLY BACK to show, first, that it is a photograph on the front page of the New York Globe. *Then, we see that the man looking at the* Globe *is Lieutenant Commander Cummings, swathed in furs and parka with just enough of his frozen face sticking out to identify him.*

CONTINUE TO DOLLY EVEN FURTHER BACK until all that can be seen of poor Cummings is a small black figure on an endless desolation of snow and ice.

On screen the following legend:

VIRTUE IS ITS OWN REWARD

and

FADE OUT.

THE END

The Collected Works of Paddy Chayefsky

The Stage Plays

WITH AN INTRODUCTION BY ARTHUR SCHLESINGER, JR.

MIDDLE OF THE NIGHT

"The town has a new hit! Chayefsky inaugurates something new in the modern theater...**ARRESTING AND BRILLIANT.**"
— John McClain, NY JOURNAL AMERICAN

THE TENTH MAN

"**A MASTER OF THE THEATER WITH A FIRST-RATE IMAGINATION.**" — Gore Vidal, THE REPORTER

GIDEON

"**AN HYPNOTIC DRAMA** of simple distinction and artistry. **AN ENTHRALLING WORK!**"   — John Chapman, NEW YORK DAILY NEWS

THE PASSION OF JOSEF D.

"Scenes of enormous compulsion....**INCISIVE AND ARRESTING.**"— NEW YORK JOURNAL-AMERICAN

THE LATENT HETEROSEXUAL

"**FUNNY...HILARIOUS...PROFOUND**...Mr. Chayefsky attacks with the vigor the new materialism, with its almost religious rites of financial sanctity...Undoubtedly, Mr. Chayefsky's most serious work." — Clive Barnes, THE NEW YORK TIMES

ISBN: 1-55783-192-0 $12.95 Trade Paper

The Collected Works of Paddy Chayefsky

The Television Plays

HOLIDAY SONG

PRINTER'S MEASURE

THE BIG DEAL

MARTY

THE MOTHER

THE BACHELOR PARTY

"Paddy Chayefsky makes it a habit of writing for television as if he had invented the medium....**A SINGULARLY ENDOWED CRAFTSMAN!**"

— VARIETY

"TELEVISION'S FINEST DRAMATIC WRITER."

— THE NEW YORK TIMES

ISBN: 1-55783-191-2 $12.95 Trade Paper